GAY HOLLYWOOD
Film & Video Guide

OVER 75 YEARS
OF MALE HOMOSEXUALITY
IN THE MOVIES

STEVE STEWART

COMPANION
PUBLICATIONS

Laguna Hills, Californi

Companion Publications
PO Box 2575
Laguna Hills, California 92654

Printed in the United States of America

Library of Congress Catalog Card Number: 93-71831

ISBN: 0-9625277-3-4

ACKNOWLEDGEMENTS

In 1983 I met and photographed the late film historian, Vito Russo at his home in New York City, for my first book, *Positive Image: A Portrait Of Gay America*. His pioneering book, *The Celluloid Closet*, is still considered by most to be the seminal work on homosexuality in the movies.

Vito and *The Celluloid Closet* were the inspiration for this guide. As films with gay themes and characters are flourishing in the 1990s, and older films are becoming available on video, a comprehensive, easy-to-use guide to this growing genre seemed essential. *Gay Hollywood* is meant as a companion book to other books that tackle this topic from a historical, social, political or psychological perspective.

Other reference works and authors that provided helpful resource material include: *A Pictoral History of Sex In Films* by Parker Tyler, *Sex In The Movies* by Sam Frank, *Sex On The Screen* by Gerard Lenne and *The Lavender Screen* by Boze Hadleigh.

In addition, I would like to thank the Los Angeles, New York and San Francisco Lesbian and Gay Film Fesitvals for providing a helpful source of information. And finally I must thank Jim Fredrickson and Peggy Stuart for their helpful suggestions and critical eyes for detail.

PHOTO CREDITS:

CONTENTS

RATING SYSTEM

Poll any two moviegoers after seeing a film, and you'll just as often find that one viewer loved the film while the other loathed it. For this reason, I advise readers to use the following subjective star ratings merely as a guide.

Ratings reflect a single *gay perspective* and are intended only as a personal recommendation or warning. Your personal rating may differ, so don't let a low rating stop you from viewing any of the films in this book— they each have something to offer.

★★★★★ Excellent

★★★★ Very Good

★★★ Good

★★ Fair

★ Poor

INTRODUCTION

"Movies are such garbage, who can take them seriously? However, thanks to the silver screen your neurosis has got style."
—Frederick Combs, *The Boys In The Band*

As this first edition of *Gay Hollywood* goes to press, nearly every major film studio seems to have a gay-themed film either in production or about to be released. This is a first in movie history—and it only took an AIDS epidemic and 100 years to get here!

Randy Shilts's long-awaited AIDS drama, *And The Band Played On*, is scheduled to be released by HBO in the fall. 1991 Oscar-winning director Jonathan Demme's AIDS film *Philadelphia*, starring Oscar-winning Denzel Washington and Tom Hanks, is also slated for fall release. Francis Ford Coppola is reportedly in preproduction on *The Cure*, also about AIDS, while Barbra Streisand is working on Larry Kramer's *The Normal Heart*. And the list goes on.

FROM INVISIBLE MAN TO SUPERMAN

For the first 50 years of film, homosexuality either was submerged and had to be read between the lines, or it appeared in the form of a person who was a sissy. Spotting a gay character in a major motion picture before the 1960s required a keen eye and an *unnatural* interest. Most of the early gay characters described in this book were camouflaged as sissies or drag queens. But it was obvious to gay viewers that these stereotyped characters were simply a subterfuge.

By the 1960s and 1970s, gay characters had come out of the cinema closet, but for the most part, they were portrayed either as demented murderers or as murder victims, made to pay for their new visibility.

In the 1980s, in large part a result of the AIDS epidemic, it was not entirely unusual to spot a positive gay character every now and then, or one who just happened to be gay.

Today, gay characters are occassionally even the heroes, or the most well-adjusted people in the film. And it's difficult to see a movie today that doesn't have at least one character or a few gay jokes tossed in. Even bone-crunching he-man Steven Seagal found himself exchanging catty, gay one-liners in *Under Siege*, a 1992 box-office smash. No genre is safe. In film, these are truly the "Gay '90s."

But old Hollywood habits die hard. While three of the five films nominated in 1991 for Best Picture Academy Awards included prominent gay characters, only one was treated as a realistic human being.

In *The Prince Of Tides*, the gay character is a

nonstereotypical, well-adjusted friend of the central character. Oliver Stone's *JFK*, however, portrays a group of gay men as vicious, murdering drag queens. Finally, the Best Picture Oscar that year went to *The Silence Of The Lambs*. The central character of this film is a psychopathic, transvestite killer who skins his victims. Well, that's one out of three.

FROM *ONLY YESTERDAY* TO *PARTING GLANCES*— WHAT'S INCLUDED

It may surprise you to discover how many Hollywood classics, Oscar winners and box-office hits are featured in this guide. On the other hand, there are many obscure films included here that you won't find mentioned in other guidebooks.

The title *Gay Hollywood* was chosen to distinguish it from gay porno film guides. While many of the films in this guide include nudity and sexuality, and a few even border on soft porn, these are not gay porno films, but films with gay themes, gay characters and/or related characters.

Mainstream, independent, foreign and documentary features covering every genre are represented. All films are feature-length, with the exception of silent-era films, which were often shorts. (Most shorts, however, have been repackaged on video as feature-length collections). Contemporary shorts, often shown at film festivals, aren't included here.

The 400-plus films featured in this guide range from those produced in the silent era to films made this year. They cover all genres, include many of Hollywood's finest actors, both past and present, and taken together, paint a moving political, sociological and historical picture. They also can be enjoyed simply as pure entertainment.

As to the types of gay characters featured in this guide—if you're searching for asexuals, bisexuals, closet cases, drag queens, hustlers, sissies, transvestites or transexuals, you'll find them here. My definition of *gay* is broad enough to include the full spectrum of sexuality related to gay-male identity.

Lesbian characters and films, however, haven't been included. With the number of such films proliferating, I believe the subject deserves a guide of its own, and I look forward to seeing one in the near future.

THE PURPOSE OF A GAY-VIDEO GUIDE

The reason for compiling this gay-video guide is simple. There are no other guides like it on the market. There are over a dozen popular mainstream film and video guides being sold today, but even if you consulted them all, you wouldn't find all of the films listed here. Nor would you find them rated critically from a gay perspective. If you did find them reviewed, chances are the reviews wouldn't even mention the gay characters, no matter how prominent they might be. There are also a number of books that discuss the political or social perspective of gays in film, but there have not been complete film and video guides on the subject—until now.

So whether you're viewing them for the first time or revisiting favorites, I hope that you enjoy watching them as much as I have enjoyed writing about them.

Steve Stewart
Laguna Hills, California

NOTES TO READER

Types of films that are included.

What is a gay film? Or for that matter, what is a gay character? For the purpose of this book I have chosen to define *gay* very broadly. Included are not only films depicting male homosexuality, but also those films exploring male androgyny, asexuality, bisexuality, transvestitism and transsexuality either in theme or in character.

The 400-plus films listed in this guide represent nearly every major film studio as well as the independents. In addition, every genre category is represented: action, adventure, animation, comedy, documentary, drama, fantasy, foreign, horror, musical, science fiction and thriller.

Types of films that are not included.

While a few films border on soft pornography, hardcore gay pornographic films are not included—numerous video guides are already devoted exclusively to this genre.

Some viewers may find it surprising that lesbian-themed films are not included. Often appropriately grouped together with gay males in political and historical contexts, I felt it would be a disservice to lump these two very different genres together in this book. I believe the growing lesbian sensibility in film deserves a guide exclusively devoted to the topic—written by a woman.

Also, with the exception of short features from the silent era (often repackaged into full-length video collections), gay shorts are not included, since few are available, either theatrically or on video.

Finding a film.

The listings of films is divided into two sections. The first section, "Films From A To Z," includes a complete description of each film. These are films that contain gay themes or gay characters who play a central role. Section two, "Additional Films," includes only brief descriptions. The films in this section contain gay themes or gay characters who are considered minor or secondary.

The films in these two sections are arranged alphabetically. All articles, such as "A," "An," or "The," that begin a film title follow the rest of the title for alphabetizing purposes. For instance, *The Boys In The Band* would appear in the "B" section as *Boys In The Band, The*. Charlie Chaplin's film *A Woman* would appear alphabetically under "W" as *Woman, A*.

Finally, this book contains five different indexes: alphabetical, genre, star-rating, companion films (films with similar themes) and a general index.

Finding an actor or a director.

All of the "Films From A To Z" include the

director and principal actors/actresses within each listing. The "Additional Films" section includes the director and actors/actresses who portray a central gay character or characters, where appropriate. A complete Index is provided for easy reference as well.

Finding films with similar themes.

Following each film entry in the "Films From A To Z" section is a "Companion Films" subheading. Similarly-themed films are listed by heading. Headings include such categories as "AIDS," "Boys Schools," "Coming Out," "Drag Queens," "Fascists and Nazis," etc. These headings can be found in the "Companion Films Index" on page XXX.

A five-star rating system.

At best, a rating system is highly subjective. Therefore, I recommend that viewers decide for themselves. All of the films in this guide are worth viewing. No matter how few stars they have received, each has something to offer. Stars are intended simply as a personal recommendation or warning—depending on the film—from a single "gay perspective."

The ratings are as follows: ★★★★★ Excellent (possibly even a classic), ★★★★ Very Good, ★★★ Good, ★★ Fair and ★ Poor.

Ratings for nudity, sexuality and violence

Each film in the "Films From A To Z" section includes the rating assigned by the Motion Picture Association of America (MPAA). Many foreign, independent and older films have not been rated. In these cases, whenever possible, I have included what would probably be an equivalent rating.

Male and female nudity and sexuality are also briefly described, but it should be noted that there are often different versions of the same film in circulation.

It is becoming quite common for studios to edit out nudity and sexuality for theatrical release to avoid receiving an NC-17 rating (considered the equivalent of an X rating). When the film is later released on video, the *objectionable* scenes are often added back, and the video is considered "unrated."

On the other hand, films that once appeared in theaters with nudity and sexuality are often later edited so as not to offend family video buyers. Whenever possible, I have indicated if a film is available in more than one version.

Film and video availability.

While many of the films in this guide are rare or difficult to find, most are available on video—although not necessarily at your local video store. Those films that are not on video are periodically shown on television and occasionally at film festivals, film retrospectives and revival-house theaters. Half the fun of viewing many of these films is to be had simply in locating them.

For the film buff willing to make the effort, a section titled "Mail-order Video Sources" has been included. A list of national video sources that rent and sell videos by mail will give you access to hundreds of gay-themed films on video.

Another source for the serious viewer is film festivals. Hundreds of new gay films are shown each year at gay and mainstream festivals nationally and internationally. Many of these films never get picked up by a distributor. Others often take years to make it to theaters or video, so this is an excellent showcase for those impatient viewers.

FILM QUOTES

The following quotes and one-liners are predominantly taken from the films featured in this guidebook. For additional quotes, see film listings for the most memorable lines from each film.

MEN

**"You don't understand,
I'm a man."
" Well, nobody's perfect."**
—Jack Lemmon and Joe E. Brown,
Some Like It Hot

"John Wayne? You're gonna tell me he's a fag!"
—Jon Voight, *Midnight Cowboy*

"Goddamn it, you're the nellie, not me. I'm the pitcher, not a catcher and don't you ever forget that, you hear?"
—Tom Berenger,
Looking For Mr. Goodbar

"What do I look like, a midnight cowboy?"
—Robert Beltran,
*Scenes From The Class Struggle
In Beverly Hills*

"I'm twice the man you are."
"So is she, and it's driving me crazy."
—John Savident and John Turturro,
Brain Donors

"I ain't a for-real cowboy, but I am one helluva stud."   —Jon Voight, *Midnight Cowboy*

"But Arthur's the most normal man I've ever known."
"What better disguise?"
—Anna Massey and Rupert Everett,
Another Country

"Honey, I'm more man than you'll ever be and more woman than you'll ever get."
—Antonio Fargas, *Car Wash*

"I think all men are dogs. All men start barking sooner or later."
—Octavia Saint Laurent, *Paris Is Burning*

"You know the difference between straight guys and gay guys?"
"I forget."
"There isn't any. Straight guys are jerks. Gay guys are jerks."
—Steve Buscemi and Richard Ganoung,
Parting Glances

"When you were a young cock, you crowed too."   —Il Moro, *Fellini Satyricon*

"Can I make you a drink?"
"Make him a man first."
—Neil Cunningham and Saeed Jaffrey,
My Beautiful Laundrette

"Bulls are bulls, and roosters don't try to lay eggs."

—Charles Durning, *Tootsie*

"Back in the old days, there were 'Johnsons' as far as the eye could see."
"And what a lovely site it was."

—George Robertson and George Gaynes,
Police Academy

"Try to fix him up with a nice girl. I'm not sure his penis is in full working order."

—Roshan Seth, *My Beautiful Laundrette*

"If we ever get out of this, things are going to be different, I promise you. I'm going to be the man I was when we first met."
"You weren't blonde then, and you wore a lot less makeup."

—Pam Dawber and John Ritter,
Stay Tuned

"I'm fighting my prejudices, but it's clear that you're acting—well I hate to put it this way—like a man."
"You watch your language."

—Katharine Hepburn and David Wayne,
Adam's Rib

"Let's step outside and settle this like men."
"We are outside."
"Then why don't we step inside and settle this like women."

—John Turturro and John Savident,
Brain Donors

"God made man in his own image, and he blew it!"

—Anne Heywood, *I Want What I Want*

"I'm old-fashioned. I like two sexes."

—Spencer Tracy, *Adam's Rib*

"I'm gonna make a man of you yet."
"If being a man means being what you are, I'd rather be queer!"

—An alcoholic father and
Wayne Maunder, *Porky's*

"Do some push-ups. It'll straighten you out."

—David Alan Grier, *Streamers*

"Pretending to be a man has its disadvantages."

—Robert Preston, *Victor/Victoria*

"You've got me so convinced, I may even go out and become a woman."
"And you wouldn't have far to go either."

—David Wayne and Spencer Tracy,
Adam's Rib

"Who taught you to sew like that?"
"My father."

—Meg Foster and Perry King,
A Different Story

"Who the hell are you?"
"Luther Quigly, but I'll be anyone you want me to be."

—Tim McIntire and a gay man,
The Choirboys

"No perfume on guard duty."

—John Cleese, *Privates On Parade*

"Now remember, it's BYOL—bring your own leather."

—Jean Smart, *Protocol*

"They say the Navy makes men. Well, I'm living proof. They made me."

—George Hamilton, *Zorro, The Gay Blade*

"Try to walk like John Wayne. No, that's John Wayne's sister, Fay."

—Ugo Tognazzi, *La Cage Aux Folles*

"Why do you think I'm a homosexual?"
I guess it's because you never talk about girls."
"I never talk about dogs either. Does that make me a cocker spaniel?"
—Corey Parker and Matthew Broderick,
Biloxi Blues

"What happened to you? You used to be normal."
"I grew out of it."
—Kenneth McMillan and Aidan Quinn,
Reckless

"There are no men anymore ... facsimiles, that's all, facsimiles."
—Angela Lansbury,
Something For Everyone

WOMEN

"I'm a one-woman man and I've had mine, thank God."
—Alan Bates, *Butley*

"I've got this thing about girls—they just sort of leave me cold."
—Tony Curtis, *Some Like It Hot*

"For years my dad's been telling me teenage boys want just one thing. I always thought he meant girls."
—Michelle Meyrink, *The Joy Of Sex*

"Statistics show there are more women in the world than anything else—except insects."
—Glenn Ford, *Gilda*

"They almost didn't hire me because they thought I was too feminine."
—Dustin Hoffman, *Tootsie*

"You've got to listen to me Michael. There are no other women like you. You're a man."
"Yes, I realize that of course, but I'm also an actress."
—Sydney Pollack and Dustin Hoffman,
Tootsie

WHAT A DRAG

"What's more boring than a queen doing a Judy Garland imitation?"
"A queen doing a Bette Davis imitation."
—Kenneth Nelson and Frederick Combs,
The Boys In The Band

"I'm telling you, if I didn't have a dress on, I'd kick his arrogant ass in."
—Dustin Hoffman, *Tootsie*

"What better cover for someone like me than total indiscretion?"
—Rupert Everett, *Another Country*

"The wedding was gorgeous. The best man gave the groom away, my father gave the bride away, and the fact that I wanted to be flower girl gave me away."
—Michael Greer, *The Gay Deceivers*

"Why don't you take your dress off and fight like a man."
—Larry Casey, *The Gay Deceivers*

"Why do you want to be a cop?"
"I like to dress like a man."
"So do I."
—Steve Guttenberg and Kim Cattrall,
Police Academy

"It works, but don't play hard to get."
—Sydney Pollack, *Tootsie*

"I was a better man with you, as a woman, than I ever was with a woman, as a man. Know what I mean? I just gotta learn to do it without the dress."
—Dustin Hoffman, *Tootsie*

"Remember, my people, there is no shame in being poor ... only [in] dressing poorly."
—George Hamilton, *Zorro, The Gay Blade*

"My tits! Where are my tits?"
—Rex Reed, *Myra Breckinridge*

"I'm suppose to be the grand duchess Anastasia, but I think I look more like Tugboat Annie."
—Christopher Hewett, *The Producers*

"It's gorgeous. Let's face it Roger, that dress is you."
—Zero Mostel, *The Producers*

"I don't want to go on, night after night, painting my face."
—Albert Finney, *The Dresser*

"I can waltz in like Ozzie or I can waltz in like Harriet, but I can't waltz in like Ozzie and Harriet. It's just too taxing."
—Wallace Shawn,
*Scenes From The Class Struggle
In Beverly Hills*

"How come he dresses like a woman?"
"I do that sometimes."
—Two peasants, *Stay Tuned*

"Roy, you have boobs!"
"They're not mine."
—Pam Dawber and John Ritter, *Stay Tuned*

"I just told him I had the teeniest touch of syphilis. Wait till he gets a load of what little old Elke's got."
—Liza Minnelli, *Cabaret*

"Pull in your reel, Mr. Fielding, you're barking up the wrong fish."
—Jack Lemmon, *Some Like It Hot*

"How many Zsa Zsa Gabors can there be in a room at one time?"
—Richard Easley, *Outrageous!*

"Are you unhappy because you didn't get to wear my dress?"
"If I had worn your dress it would have hung properly."
—Maggie Smith and Michael Caine,
California Suite

"How were you supposed to know they were all cops in drag?"
—Sasha Mitchell, *Spike Of Bensonhurst*

"There's nothing more inconvenient than an old queen with a head cold."
—Robert Preston, *Victor/Victoria*

"If that is a mask please take it off now, or keep it on forever."
—Colin Firth, *Apartment Zero*

"Holy shit! Your hair has a hard on."
—Bette Midler, *The Rose*

"Underneath that pose is just more pose."
—Lenny Baker,
Next Stop, Greenwich Village

"Since when has it been a crime to play charades?"
—Glenda Jackson, *Salome's Last Dance*

SEX

"Normal sex is still a novelty
to most people"
—An editor, *Prick Up Your Ears*

"If you haven't gotten a blow job from a superior officer, well, you're just letting the best in life pass you by."
—Jack Nicholson, *A Few Good Men*

"Gertrude Stein was right. A mouth is a mouth is a mouth"   —Ray Sharkey,
*Scenes From The Class Struggle
In Beverly Hills*

"Can I buy you a drink?"
"Confidentially, with me one's too many and a million's not enough."
"I've got the same problem with men."
—Eddie Garrett and Diane Keaton,
Looking For Mr. Goodbar

"Eighteen. Is there any word in the English language as sexy as that?"
—Robin Williams
The World According To Garp

"Sex happens to be the one subject I can speak about with absolutely no authority whatsoever."
—Justin Ross, *A Chorus Line*

"I'll sleep with you for a meatball."
—Julie Andrews, *Victor/Victoria*

"I can never get a zipper to close. Maybe that stands for something. What do you think?"
—Rita Hayworth, *Gilda*

"Did you hear about me? If I'd have been a ranch they would have named me the Bar Nothing."
—Rita Hayworth, *Gilda*

"I don't sell my fantasies."
—Corey Parker, *Biloxi Blues*

"I was more familiar with Africa than I was with my own body, until I was 15."
—Beryl Reid, *Entertaining Mr. Sloane*

"Sex changes everything. I've had relationships before where I know a guy and then have sex with him, and then I bump into him someplace, and he acts like I owe him money!"
—Teri Garr, *Tootsie*

"Who wants to be felt up by faggots?"
"I can think of two people in this room who would love it."
—Gerry Salzberg and Craig Russell,
Outrageous!

"Don't be so British. You'll feel terrific afterwards. You know you want to."
—Liza Minnelli, *Cabaret*

"Screw Maximillian."
"I do."
"So do I."
—Michael York and Liza Minnelli, *Cabaret*

"I was naughty all day yesterday."
"Not with me you weren't."
"You'll just have to learn to show up on time."
—Michael Caine and Maggie Smith,
California Suite

"Hey, your fly's open."
"Of course. I gotta go to work too."
—Diane Keaton and Richard Gere,
Looking For Mr. Goodbar

"Housework is like bad sex. Everytime I do it I swear I'll never do it again, until company comes by."
—Party guest, *Can't Stop The Music*

"I have something to tell you. I'm not a monk."
—Aidan Quinn, *An Early Frost*

"Do you want to perform sex with me?"
"Perform sex? I don't think I'm up to a performance, but I'll rehearse with you, if you like."
—Diane Keaton and Woody Allen, *Sleeper*

"It's hard to believe that you haven't had sex for 200 years."
"Two hundred and four if you count my marriage."
—Diane Keaton and Woody Allen, *Sleeper*

"I've got a Ph.D. in oral sex."
"Did they make you take any Spanish with that?"
—Diane Keaton and Woody Allen, *Sleeper*

"What do you believe in?"
"Sex and death—two things that come once in a lifetime, but at least after death you're not nauseous."
—Diane Keaton and Woody Allen, *Sleeper*

"Why is it only my *ass* that ever gets invited places?"
—Vicki Frederick, *A Chorus Line*

"I can resist anything but temptation."
—Nicholas Grace, *Salome's Last Dance*

"You took advantage of my position."
"And I might be tempted to do so again if you don't close your mouth."
—Douglas Hodge and Nicholas Grace,
Salome's Last Dance

"I hear you have a taste for little boys."
"No Caesar, big boys"
—Peter O'Toole and Malcolm McDowell,
Caligula

"Sounds like an Agatha Christie novel—*Sodomy on the Orient Express*."
—Corey Parker, *Biloxi Blues*

"Have a wank? It would be easier to raise the Titanic!"
—Alfred Molina, *Prick Up Your Ears*

"They used me—like a woman!"
—Sal Mineo, *Exodus*

"I suppose you find promiscuity admirable?"
"I couldn't care less. I was brought up on the farm, and the lesson of the rooster was not entirely lost on me."
—Cliff Robertson and Lee Tracy,
The Best Man

"You cocksucker."
"Not me chief. I'm not the one on my knees."
—Police chief and Charles Durning,
The Choirboys

"Who do you have to fuck to get a drink around here?"
—Cliff Gorman, *The Boys In The Band*

"I'm hooorny!"
—Leslie Ann Warren, *Victor/Victoria*

"You can't do much in a stuffed shirt."
"Very well then. Let's strip and do it properly"
—Alan Bates and Oliver Reed,
Women In Love

**ALL MEN ARE NOT
CREATED EQUAL**

**"Man is not known by
inches alone."**
—Dan Monahan, *Porky's*

18

"Do you think it's easy to run when you're holding a banana the size of a canoe?"
—Woody Allen, *Sleeper*

"You know, I've dreamt a lot about your prick lately."
"Was it nicer in your dreams?"
—Jeanne Moreau and Brad Davis, *Querelle*

"I never saw one so small."
—Ray Sharkey,
*Scenes From A Class Struggle
In Beverly Hills*

"Say, why did the guy give a name to his penis? He didn't want a stranger making all his decisions."
—Phil Hartman,
National Lampoon's Loaded Weapon 1

"Who are you?"
"I'm your worst nightmare."
"No, waking up without my penis is my worst nightmare."
—Emilio Estevez and Tim Curry,
National Lampoon's Loaded Weapon 1

"The penis astonishes me. It can give pain and pleasure, it can give life and now it can give death."
"Pesky little devils aren't they."
—Party guest and Kathy Kinney,
Parting Glances

"I need a rubber—It's too big."
"We don't have any training rubbers."
—Dan Monahan and student, *Porky's*

"Can we call it tallywacker? 'Penis' is so personal."
—School principal, *Porky's*

"My brain? It's my second-favorite organ."
—Woody Allen, *Sleeper*

"I'd recognize that penis anywhere."
—Nancy Parsons, *Porky's*

"What ya got there?"
"What's it look like?"
"A prick, only smaller."
—A girl in a car and Paul Sorvino,
Bloodbrothers

"I'm afraid you've caught me with more than my hands up."
—Sean Connery, *Diamonds Are Forever*

"I had mine removed surgically under general anesthesia, but to have it bitten off in a Buick—it's a nightmare."
—John Lithgow
The World According To Garp

BORN THAT WAY

"It's just a phase you're going through. Last year it was miniature golf."
—Kay Ballard, *The Ritz*

"Get this Mr. Munson. I was born last night when you met me in that alley."
—Glenn Ford, *Gilda*

"You're kidding. You really are queer? But you're so attractive."
—Leslie Ann Warren, *Victor/Victoria*

"You know what I think? I think we're all in our private traps. I was born in mine."
—Anthony Perkins, *Psycho*

"Nature played me a dirty trick."
—Charles Lloyd Pack, *Victim*

"You've got to let me be who I am."
—Barry Tubb, *Consenting Adult*

"What are you for Christ's sake? How long has this been going on?"
"All my life."
—Harry Andrews and Anne Heywood,
I Want What I Want

LIFE'S A BITCH

"I figured, as long as I had to suffer I might as well get a tan."
—Harry Hamlin, *Making Love*

"What a nasty streak you have when you drink. Also when you eat and sit and walk."
—Michael Caine, *California Suite*

"Growing up is harder than learning to fly. One requires truth, the other only fairy dust."
—Joanne Woodward,
Summer Wishes, Winter Dreams

"When the going gets tough, the tough get gorgeous!"
—Craig Russell, *Too Outrageous!*

"I've been poor all my life."
"You've got it all wrong honey, you've been cheap all your life."
—Divine and Lanie Kazan,
Lust In The Dust

"You could eat off this floor, and you probably will."
—Divine, *Lust In The Dust*

"Six dollars and ninety-five cents? Would it be possible to just rent a couple of drinks?"
—Jane Fonda, *California Suite*

"You make me sick. When you can't have what you want, you make certain that everyone around is equally as miserable."
"I haven't noticed any equals around me."
—Michael Caine and Maggie Smith,
California Suite

"You wouldn't know reality if it was stuck up your ass."
—Raul Julia, *Kiss Of The Spider Woman*

"The nicest thing about feeling happy is that you think you'll never feel unhappy again."
—William Hurt, *Kiss Of The Spider Woman*

"The world is full of whores. What it really needs is a good bookkeeper."
—Shelley Winters, *The Balcony*

"What's it feel like to be dead for 200 years?"
"Like spending a weekend in Beverly Hills."
—Diane Keaton and Woody Allen, *Sleeper*

"I told her you spoke two languages. She said yes, English and Gucci."
—Ron Silver, *Garbo Talks*

"My recipes—better burn them lest they fall into the wrong hands."
—John Glover, *An Early Frost*

"I ask for nothing."
"And you shall receive it in abundance."
—Patricia Quinn and Tim Curry,
The Rocky Horror Picture Show

"Writing is one-tenth perspiration and nine-tenths masturbation."
—Gary Oldman, *Prick Up Your Ears*

IN GOOD TASTE

**"You lack the imagination
to be a homosexual."**
—An interviewee, *Improper Conduct*

"Oh, I have the napkins that match your hat."
—Goldie Hawn, *Protocol*

"Not too much culture please. I'm on my holiday."
—George De La Pena, *Nijinsky*

"My taste is impeccable, even when it's bad."
—Alan Bates, *Nijinsky*

"Is that pornography or art?"
"If it's in focus, it's pornography. If it's out-of-focus, it's art."
—Paul Sonkkila and Linda Hunt,
The Year Of Living Dangerously

"Is that his name? Sounds like a flavor in a gay ice cream parlor. Strawberry Swirl, Chocolate Mocha Madness, Michael Milton."
—Robin Williams,
The World According To Garp

BISEXUALITY

**"You prefer nymphs to satyrs?"
"I like both lord."**
—Malcolm McDowell and a Roman,
Caligula

"If there's anything I hate, it's a bisexual homosexual—or is it the other way around?"
"It works either way."
—Maggie Smith and Michael Caine,
California Suite

"You can't have two kinds of love. You can't have it because it's impossible."
—Jennie Linden, *Women In Love*

"I played the bride, now I get to play the groom."
—Perry King, *A Different Story*

A BOY'S BEST FRIEND

**"A boy's best friend is
his mother."**
—Anthony Perkins, *Psycho*

"I can be butch when I have to—I get it from my mother."
—Peter Friedman, *Single White Female*

"It's not like losing a son—it's like gaining another son."
—Eric Idle, *Too Much Sun*

"I promised my mother on her death bed that I would not go out with any girls."
—Arthur Storch, *The Strange One*

GAY PRIDE

**"Anyone who can swallow two
Snowballs and a Ding Dong
shouldn't have any problem
with pride."**
—Steve Guttenberg, *Can't Stop The Music*

"How can sleeping with a woman make you proud of yourself if you know you'd rather be with a man?"
—Harvey Fierstein, *Torch Song Trilogy*

"You show me a happy homosexual, and I'll show you a gay corpse."

—Kenneth Nelson,
The Boys In The Band

"Listen, I wasn't thrilled about it either, thinking I was one of them, but you know it is the only fraternity I ever rushed that let me in."

—John Glover,
An Early Frost

"Pity we couldn't have done it with the curtains open."

—John Dall, *Rope*

"There's nothing I need from anyone except love and respect, and anyone who can't give me those two things has no place in my life."

—Harvey Fierstein,
Torch Song Trilogy

"You make respectability seem disrespectful."

—Janet Leigh,
Psycho

"You have to take sides, make a contribution to the fight."
"What fight?"
"Any fight. The one you believe in."

—Corey Parker and Matthew Broderick,
Biloxi Blues

"Do you intend to spend your entire life admiring yourself?"

—Quentin Crisp's father,
The Naked Civil Servant

"I have been called 'Negro' and 'queer,' but I've never been called 'French.'"

—Benny Luke,
La Cage Aux Folles

HOMOPHOBIA

"Oh my god, I knew it! We enjoyed it! We're homos. We're rump rangers."
—Thomas Ballatore, *Once Bitten*

"It's not possible to enjoy being hated so much."
—Shirley Anne Field,
My Beautiful Laundrette

"Why can't he stick with his own sort."
—Dawn Beret, *Victim*

"You'll never forgive me, will you?"
"It's not your fault you haven't got enough brains to understand."
—Dawn Beret and Alan Howard,
Victim

"They disgust me. I felt physically ill. They're everywhere. The police do nothing. Someone's got to make them pay for their filthy blasphemy."

—Margaret Diamond, *Victim*

LOVE

"The next time you have the need to say 'I love you' to someone, say it to yourself— and see if *you* believe it."
—Harvey Fierstein, *Torch Song Trilogy*

"You strangled the life out of a human being that could live and love like you never could."
—Jimmy Stewart, *Rope*

"He should have loved me. I offered it."
—Alan Bates, *Women In Love*

"Which do you prefer, young boys or mature men?"

"I think that when you really love somebody, age shouldn't matter at all!"

—Mike Kopscha and Kevin Coughlin,
The Gay Deceivers

"Why should you love him, when all the world hates him?"

"Because he loves me more than all the world."

—Executioner and Steven Waddington,
Edward II

"Goddamn it, I think I'm falling in love with her."

"Oh, I'm so sorry."

—Fritz Wepper and Michael York,
Cabaret

"Have you ever been in love?"

"Yes, for as long as I can remember—with myself."

—Laurence Harvey and Julie Christie,
Darling

PERVERSIONS

"What the hell is this place? Must be one of those gay, Arab, biker sushi bars."
—Bar patron, *Protocol*

"Are you calling me a freak?"

"I'm calling you special."

—Colin Firth and Hart Bochner,
Apartment Zero

"Do you think a homosexual elephant has a terrible time of it?"

—John Hurt,, *The Naked Civil Servant*

"I've never known anyone worth knowing who wasn't a positive fruitcake."

—Craig Russell, *Outrageous!*

"Have you ever slept with a dwarf?"

"Once, but it wasn't a lasting relationship."

—Liza Minnelli and Michael York,
Cabaret

"I love kids. I didn't know I loved them so much until I became a woman. If I'd known, I would have had some when I was a man."

—John Lithgow,
The World According To Garp

"You really are a bit odd, aren't you? Oh, I don't know, a cross between an avenging angel and a peeping Tom."

—Derren Nesbitt, *Victim*

RELATIONSHIPS

"Why would a guy want to marry a guy?"
"Security."
—Tony Curtis and Jack Lemmon,
Some Like It Hot

"I wonder if Socrates and Plato took a house on Crete during the summer?"

—Woody Allen, *Love And Death*

"Aren't we still friends?"

"No, we are not friends. I don't take this shit from friends—only from lovers."

—Dustin Hoffman and Teri Garr, *Tootsie*

"Your idea of fidelity is not having more than one man in the bed at the same time."

—Dirk Bogarde, *Darling*

"I don't talk about sex with them. They don't talk about sex with me."
"Who's talking about sex? I'm talking about us."
—Aidan Quinn and D.W. Moffett,
An Early Frost

"You'll have to find another canoe to paddle. Ours has holes."
—Tom Courtenay, *The Dresser*

"This arrangement is un-Italian, unreligious, nonsectarian and definitely anti-nature."
—Sasha Mitchell, *Spike Of Bensonhurst*

"The whole school thinks we're gay. We might as well move in together and get his and his matching towels."
—Thomas Ballatore, *Once Bitten*

"I just reached the conclusion that nothing matters in the world except the right person to take the edge off."
"Meaning a woman of course?"
"Failing that, an amusing man."
—Oliver Reed and Alan Bates,
Women In Love

RELIGION AND THE LAW

"I don't know what's worse— church or jail."
—Mary Stuart Masterson,
Fried Green Tomatoes

"That country's been sodomized by religion."
—Saeed Jaffrey, *My Beautiful Laundrette*

"I'm praying to you, look in your heart."
—John Turturro, *Miller's Crossing*

"Your soul may belong to God but your ass is mine."
—A convict, *Short Eyes*

"Catholics don't have a patent on guilt."
"No, they're just the number-one manufacturers of it."
—Zeljko Ivanek and Talia Balsam,
Mass Appeal

"Confession may be good for the soul, but it's bad for sex."
—Alan Feinstein,
Looking For Mr. Goodbar

"Do you ever wonder about a law that makes us all victims of any cheap thug that finds out about our natural instincts?"
—Paul Mandrake, *Victim*

"My god, it's enough to drive a girl into a convent. Do they have Jewish nuns?"
—Liza Minnelli, *Cabaret*

"Anita Bryant sent me down here to beat some sense into you frozen fruits."
—Craig Russell, *Outrageous!*

"Father, I'm gay. You can pray the house down, but I am what I am."
—Toon Agtenberg, *Spetters*

"Well, it used to be witches. At least they don't burn you anymore."
—Alan Howard, *Victim*

"If the law punished every abnormality we'd be kept very busy."
—John Barrie, *Victim*

"Is that how you feel about it?"
"I'm a policeman, sir. I don't have feelings."
—Dirk Bogarde and John Barrie, *Victim*

"You're too stupid to even be a good bigot."
—Scott Colomby, *Porky's*

"Loving you is a crime, but I'll pay for it."
—Antonio Banderas, *Law Of Desire*

"You're shaking the law by the tail, and I don't like it."
—Spencer Tracy, *Adam's Rib*

"I don't make the rules."
"Sure you do. We all do."
—Spencer Tracy and Katharine Hepburn, *Adam's Rib*

"If there's one thing I hate, it's a pushy priest."
—Geoffrey Lewis, *Lust In The Dust*

"Until the Reagan administration realizes that the government's responsibility is saving lives and not saving souls, we will continue to see the virus spread through our society."
—Neil Shram, *Common Threads: Stories From The Quilt*

"What's his taste in music?"
"Catholic."
—Nigel Terry and Bobbie Coltrane, *Caravaggio*

IN THE CLOSET

"Straight! He's about as straight as the Yellow Brick Road."
—Laurence Luckinbill, *The Boys In The Band*

"Can I see your closet?"
—Perry King, *A Different Story*

"If a caterpillar was afraid of wings, it would never become a butterfly, and people would say, 'Hey look. It's a worm in a tree.'"
—Hollis McLaren, *Outrageous!*

"Believe it or not, there was a time in my life when I didn't go around announcing I was a faggot."
"Well, that must have been before speech replaced sign language."
—Kenneth Nelson and Frederick Combs, *The Boys In The Band*

"You always think you can force the flowers to come out."
—Jennie Linden, *Women In Love*

"You're hiding. You'll be caught. You've got a guilty secret, but you'll be caught."
—Dirk Bogarde, *The Servant*

"I have never hidden behind closet doors, but I am discreet."
"Discreet! You did everything but lick his artichoke."
—Michael Caine and Maggie Smith, *California Suite*

"I just want to stay under the covers."
—Antonio Fargas, *Next Stop, Greenwich Village*

"He lives with another guy, and they both have great bodies. You tell me."
—Mary Louise Parker, *Longtime Companion*

"It's not as if I'm gay. I'm just curious."
—Michael Ontkean, *Making Love*

"You're not gay? What are you—a social work-
er or something?"
—Bathhouse attendant,
The Ritz

"Okay Sebastian, out of the closet."
"I came out of the closet centuries ago."
—Lauren Hutton and Cleavon Little,
Once Bitten

YOUTH AND BEAUTY

"He has unnatural, natural beauty."
—Leonard Frey, *The Boys In The Band*

"Physical beauty isn't everything."
"Thank you, Quasimodo."
—Leonard Frey and Kenneth Nelson,
The Boys In The Band

"I think that's good business—to surround your-
self with ugly women and beautiful men."
—Rita Hayworth,
Gilda

"People who are very beautiful make their own
laws."
—Vivien Leigh,
The Roman Spring Of Mrs. Stone

"What do I want to be when I grow up? Young."
—Vicki Frederick,
A Chorus Line

"I'm not knocking Urno. He's great, if you
happen to like a tall, blond, crushing, Nordic,
Aryan, Nazi type."
—Woody Allen,
Sleeper

"I am a servant of beauty."
—Hugo Netsers, *Dear Boys*

"Sidney, was I hit by a bus? I look as though I
were hit by a fully loaded, guided-tour bus."
—Maggie Smith,
California Suite

"I've aged, Sidney. I'm getting lines in my face.
I look like a brand-new steel-belted-radial tire."
—Maggie Smith,
California Suite

"Age is only a state of mind. What age do you
want me to be?"
—Michelle Johnston, *A Chorus Line*

"Are you happy?"
"For the most part."
"What about the other part?"
—Harry Hamlin and Michael Ontkean,
Making Love

DEATH

"They're doing beautifully this year. I only hope an early frost doesn't come along and nip them in the bud."
—Sylvia Sidney, *An Early Frost*

"What do you think happens when we die?"
"We get to have sex again."
—Stephen Caffrey and Campbell Scott,
Longtime Companion

"What are you going to do when he's gone?"
"Miss him."
—Kathy Kinney and Richard Ganoung,
Parting Glances

ADAM'S RIB ★★★★

(1949)

US/B&W/101 minutes

Director: George Cukor

Cast: Katharine Hepburn *(Amanda)*, Spencer Tracy *(Adam)*, David Wayne *(Kip Lurie)*, Judy Holliday *(Doris)*, Tom Ewell *(Warren)*, Jean Hagen *(Beryl Caighn)*.

Genre: Comedy—In this sophisticated comedy about the age-old double standard between men and women, all *men* are not created equal—and neither are all women.

Plot: Katharine Hepburn and Spencer Tracy play Amanda and Adam, lovers, and lawyers on the opposite sides of the same case. The case boils down to women's rights. Amanda keeps the courtroom sparks flying, while her close friend and neighbor, Kip (Wayne), provides the entertainment at home. Adam, the typical, insensitive, bewildered male, is caught in the middle.

The film, directed by George Cukor, is laced with double entendres, such as this exchange between Jean Hagen and Katharine Hepburn—"We used to shake hands quite a lot." "Did you enjoy it?" Or sarcasm, such as when Spencer Tracy exclaims, "I'm old-fashioned. I like two sexes." But it's Kip, the closeted gay man or bisexual, who provides the witty, bitchy, repartee. This is as explicit as it got in the 1940s.

"You've got me so convinced, I may even go out and become a woman," says Kip to Amanda.

"And you wouldn't have far to go either," chides Adam out of earshot as Kip leaves the room.

While Kip is obviously gay, the issue is never dealt with and his character is used simply as a sensitive-male contrast to Adam's all-American maleness. After Amanda and Adam temporarily split up, Kip attempts to woo Amanda. She, however, dismisses it with a witty line, "I'm fighting my prejudices, but it's clear that you're acting—well, I hate to put it this way—like a man."

In the end, Amanda wins her case in the courtroom, but Adam wins his case in the bedroom. Amanda concedes that maybe there is a little difference between men and women. Adam responds, "Viva la differance!"

Quotes:

"You're shaking the law by the tail, and I don't like it."

—*Tracy*

"I don't make the rules."

"Sure you do. We all do."

—*Tracy and Hepburn*

MPAA Rating: Not rated.

Companion Films: See "Neighbors, Roommates and Best Friends" in the "Companion Films Index."

ADVISE AND CONSENT ★★★

(1962)

US/B&W/142 minutes

Director: Otto Preminger

Cast: Don Murray *(Brigham Anderson)*, John Granger *(Ray Shaff)*, Charles Laughton *(Sebright Cooley)*, Henry Fonda *(Robert Leffingwell)*, George Grizzard *(Fred Van Ackerman)*, Burgess Meredith *(Herbert Gelman)*, Walter Pidgeon *(Bob Munson)*, Inga Swenson *(Ellen)*, Sid Gould *(Bartender)*, Larry Tucker *(Manuel)*.

Don Murray plays Brigham Anderson, a politician being blackmailed for a homosexual experience in his past in *Advise And Consent* (1962).

Murray enters a gay bar in *Advise And Consent* and is disgusted by what he sees. This was the first depiction of a gay bar in a mainstream American movie.

Genre: Drama—Political drama about a politician who is blackmailed when his secret past is uncovered. Based on the best-selling book of the same name, by Allen Drury.

Plot: In this story about secrets and lies, Don Murray plays U.S. Senator Brig Anderson, a happily married young man with a skeleton in the closet that comes back to haunt him.

When the ailing president nominates Robert Leffingwell (Fonda), a controversial figure with a secret past of his own, Brig presides over the confirmation hearing. When he learns that Leffingwell has lied under oath, this honest and fair-minded politician asks the president to withdraw Leffingwell's name. When the president refuses, Brig threatens to expose Leffingwell.

Before Brig can act, however, he begins receiving anonymous calls threatening to expose him as a homosexual who was once involved with a man while in the navy. The blackmailer (Grizzard) is a senator with his own axe to grind.

Instead of bending under the pressure, Brig takes a plane to New York to confront his former lover, Ray Shaff (Granger). When he finds Ray in a gay bar he is so repulsed at what he sees that he panics and flees. Ray follows and tries to explain that he went along with the blackmail scheme because he needed the money, but Brig is disgusted and pushes him into the gutter, as he drives away. The terror he experiences is so dramatic that it seems likely it is a result of long repressed feelings and memories that have resurfaced.

When Brig returns to Washington, D.C., he locks himself in his senatorial chambers and slits his throat. Everyone in this film has a secret, but the secret of homosexuality is the only one so terrible that it results in suicide.

In the end, Brig's blackmailer is confronted but not exposed. To expose him would give a bad name to the Senate, and the members agree to continue with business as usual.

Quotes:
"Son, this is a Washington, D.C. kind of lie. It's when the other person knows you're lying and also knows you know he knows."
  —*Fonda*
"It's about a woman isn't it?"
  —*Swenson*
"Of course, I am what I am and feel as I feel."
  —*Laughton*
"What I did was for the good of the country."
"Fortunately our country always manages to survive patriots like you."
  —*Grizzard and Pidgeon*

MPAA Rating: Not rated.

Trivia: This was the first time a gay bar was depicted in an American film, and considering the depictions that were to follow, it was quite *normal* in appearance, as were its patrons.

Companion Films: See "Blackmail" and "Closet Cases" in the "Companion Films Index."

AFTER HOURS ★★

(1985)
US/Color/94 minutes

Director: Martin Scorsese

Cast: Griffin Dunne (*Paul*), Rosanna Arquette (*Marcy*), Teri Garr (*Julie*), Robert Plunkett (*Street pickup*), Joel Jason (*Biker #1*), Rand Carr (*Biker #2*), John Heard (*Tom*).

Genre: Comedy—An off-beat, black comedy.

Plot: Martin Scorsese's black comedy is essentially a night in the life of an innocent

Manhattan word processor, whose world is turned upside down by a series of bizarre coincidences.

Much like Dorothy in *The Wizard Of Oz*, all Paul (Dunne) wants to do is get home. While trying to get there, he meets a series of unusual characters who have other things in mind.

His trouble begins when he meets Marcy (Arquette). Over coffee she explains to him, "My husband was a movie freak. Actually, he was particularly obsessed with *The Wizard Of Oz*. He talked about it constantly on our wedding night. When wc made love, whenever he came he'd scream out, 'Surrender Dorothy!' It was pretty creepy."

Later in the film Paul asks a man on the street to take him home so that he can use the man's phone. The lonely young man (Plunkett) believes that he is being picked up and happily agrees, saying, "I have never done this with a man before and I'm a little bit nervous." Paul is left mystified once again.

Other gay characters and oddballs pop up from time to time in this modern-day Oz, and it doesn't take long before Paul's version of Kansas and normalcy begin to look appealing by comparison.

MPAA Rating: R—Contains profanity.

Companion Films: See "Only the Lonely" in the "Companion Films Index."

AMERICAN FABULOUS ★★★

(1992)
US/Color/105 minutes
Director: Reno Dakota
Cast: Jeffrey Strouth
Genre: Documentary

Plot: Gay comedian and commentator Jeffrey Strouth plays himself in this humorous, risqué and campy series of colorful personal tales that are told from the back seat of his car while driving around America's heartland.

Like self-styled homosexual Quentin Crisp, Strouth is proud of his camp queen, non-conformist status and his ability to survive. He pronounces in one scene, "My very existence is a crime in most people's eyes." His tales are largely about surviving, having survived the wrath of an alcoholic father, life as a teenage prostitute and finally heroin addiction.

Strouth had the courage and tenacity to beat all the odds but one—he died of AIDS in 1991.

MPAA Rating: Not rated.

Companion Films: See "Documentaries" in the "Companion Films Index."

AMERICAN GIGOLO ★★★

(1980)
US/Color/117 minutes
Director: Paul Schrader
Cast: Richard Gere (*Julian Kay*), Lauren Hutton (*Michelle*), Bill Duke (*Leon*), Gordon Haight (*Blonde boy*), Barry Satterfield (*Street hustler*), Hector Elizondo (*Sgt. Sunday*), Nina Van Pallandt (*Ann*).

Genre: Drama

Plot: "Look mister. Someone's made a mistake here. I don't do fags," says Richard Gere in an early scene—unless he's forced to, that is. He doesn't mind doing a limp-wristed imitation of an affected interior decorator, however, when the need arises.

Gere plays Julian, a high-priced Beverly

Hills escort, who prefers to sleep with wealthy older women but will trick with "fags" if he doesn't have a choice. And wouldn't you know it, this homophobe's closest friend in the business is Leon (Duke), a vicious, black, gay pimp with a stable of male hustlers.

When Leon is unable to lure Julian away from his *manager* he does the next-best thing—he frames him for murder. No wonder Julian is a bit homophobic. All the gay men in this film are evil, treacherous types who only surface at night for kinky sex. Who wouldn't be afraid.

Julian goes to prison but that's preferable to where he sends Leon. In the end, the love of a good woman (Hutton) saves him from a whole new career behind bars.

Critics were not kind when the film premiered, but despite its obvious flaws it manages to be quite watchable.

MPAA Rating: R—Contains male nudity, profanity and violence.

Companion Films: See "Hustlers" and "Murderers" in the "Companion Films Index."

ANOTHER COUNTRY ★★★★

(1984)
UK/Color/90 minutes
Director: Marek Kanievska
Cast: Rupert Everett *(Guy Bennett)*, Colin Firth *(Tommy Judd)*, Cary Elwes *(James Harcourt)*, Adrian Ross-Magenty *(Wharton)*, Philip Dupuy *(Martineau)*, Tristan Oliver *(Fowler)*, Frederick Alexander *(Jim Menzies)*, Michael Jenn *(Barclay)*, Robert Addie *(Delahay)*, Rupert Wainwright *(Devenish)*, Anna Massey *(Imogen Bennett)*.

Genre: Drama—Adapted from the Guy Burgess stage play about Julien Mitchell, an Englishman who becomes a traitor and a spy for Russia in the 1930s.

Plot: This stunningly beautiful film opens in Moscow in 1983, where elderly expatriate Guy Bennett (Everett) recounts his life story for an interviewer, beginning with his youthful school days in England. The film then flashes back to the 1930s.

In the opening scene, two school boys are discovered masturbating one another in the gymnasium changing room. Facing expulsion, one of the boys, Martineau (Dupuy), hangs himself. Following the suicide, the school is determined to crack down on homosexual behavior. Bennett is a privileged, upper-class student at this prep school for boys, and a homosexual.

In an environment in which homosexuality is accepted, or at least tolerated in the closet, Bennett's flaunting of his sexuality makes him an outcast. All the boys know the system is hypocritical but fear losing their privilege and class if they try to change it, so it continues unchallenged. Bennett is the only one willing to take on the system. But when he makes a mockery of a military inspection he incurs the wrath of Fowler (Oliver), a stern, religiously devout disciplinarian who brings him up on charges. When Guy is threatened with a beating, he blackmails the committee of boys making the charge by threatening to go to the headmaster with the names of everyone he's had sex with— starting at the top. He's quickly dismissed, since he has slept with everyone on the committee.

The next time he is brought up on charges by Fowler he isn't as lucky. Intercepting a love note from Bennett to his boyfriend, James Harcourt (Elwes), Bennett not only receives a

31

Rupert Everett and Cary Elwes play gay students at an English boarding school who fall in love in *Another Country* (1984).

public beating but is denied the class position he has worked for. He believes that his future and career have been ruined. His bitterness at the system and desire for revenge (we are led to believe), lead to his rejection of his homeland and his status as a traitor. For Bennett, it isn't a very big leap, having been viewed as a traitor all his life.

This is a poignant story with impressive and memorable performances all around.

Quotes:

"I shall lay my heart at his feet."
——*Everett*

"What's wrong with being different?"
——*Everett*

"God, if our parents only knew what really went on here."
"They do know. The fathers anyway."
——*Everett and Firth*

"But Arthur's the most normal man I've ever known."
"What better disguise?"
——*Massey and Everett*

"You can't have things both ways Bennett."
"Why not?"
——*Firth and Everett*

"I'm sick of pretending. You think it's all a joke but it's not. I'm never going to love a woman."
"Don't be ridiculous."
—*Everett and Firth*

"In your heart of hearts you still believe some people are better than others because of the way they make love."
—*Everett*

"What better cover for someone like me than total indiscretion?"
—*Everett*

MPAA Rating: PG—Contains suggested sex between two young boys and brief male nudity from behind in the shower room.

Companion Films: See "Boys Schools" in the "Companion Films Index."

APARTMENT ZERO ★★★★

(1989)
UK/Color/124 minutes
Director: Martin Donovan
Cast: Colin Firth *(Adrian LeDuc)*, Hart Bochner *(Jack Carney)*, James Telfer *(Vanessa)*, Francesca d'Aloja *(Claudia)*, Cipe Lincovsky *(Mrs. Treniev)*.

Genre: Thriller—A moody, suspenseful psychological piece, centering on the relationship between two apparently very different men, with very different split personalities. In the end, however, they turn out to have more than a few things in common.

Plot: Set in Buenos Aires in 1988, Firth plays Adrian—a very repressed, lonely and desperate homosexual. An avid cinephile, he runs an arthouse theater in a town where there isn't much demand for art films. After committing his mother to a mental institution, he's forced to rent out a room in his spacious flat to make ends meet. He takes in an attractive and mysterious young man named Jack (Bochner). Adrian is immediately infatuated and becomes subservient to his new boarder.

Jack is an outgoing, flirtatious, bisexual American who immediately begins to toy with and use his vulnerable roommate. When Jack becomes friendly with the neighbors, Adrian becomes possessive and jealous.

As Adrian becomes more jealous he also becomes more suspicious and soon discovers that Jack isn't who he says he is. His fears that Jack may be the serial killer who is terrorizing the city are soon realized. When Jack kills a victim in their apartment, Adrian is forced either to help him get rid of the body or to turn him in. Out of his love for Jack and his insecurity, he helps him. Having second thoughts, however, their relationship turns tragic for them both. The surprise ending is a bit over the top and not in keeping with the setup, but is without a doubt a shocker.

This is a rich film that works on many levels. There are references to classic horror films and gay films throughout. In one scene the two men discuss Hitchcock's *Rope*, a film that this film mirrors in many ways. David Lynch's *Blue Velvet* is also discussed. In another scene, Adrian reluctantly helps Jack stuff a body into a traveling trunk, as the two gay lovers did in *Rope*.

While the technical credits are first-rate, it's the fine performances of the two leads that make this a standout from other films of this genre.

Quotes:
"If that is a mask please take it off now, or keep it on forever."
—*Firth*

"Who are you?"
"Who do you want me to be?"
   —*Firth and Bochner*
"It's going to be awhile before you find two or three other people like you."
   —*Bochner*
"You'll like him, mother. He has a certain James Dean *je ne sais quoi*."
   —*Firth*
"Are you calling me a freak?"
"I'm calling you special."
   —*Firth and Bochner*
"I haven't the heart to tell her she sounds like Erich von Stroheim."
   —*Firth*

MPAA Rating: Not rated—Contains graphic violence.

Companion Films: See "Murderers" in the "Companion Films Index."

ARABIAN NIGHTS ★★★★
(1974)
Italy/Color/130 minutes
Director: Pier Paolo Pasolini
Cast: Ninetto Davoli, Franco Merli, Ines

Hart Bochner and Colin Firth play roommates with more than a few secrets in *Apartment Zero* (1989).

Pellegrini, Franco Citti, Tessa Bouche, Luigi Rocchi, Francesco Paolo Governale.

Genre: Drama—A beautifully mounted, bawdy Pasolini fantasy of lost love. Based on the classic Arabian tales.

Plot: Pasolini imaginatively weaves together this classic series of tales—involving superstition, supernatural powers and predestination—to tell a simple story of lost love. It also provides the perfect setting for a tremendous amount of male and female nudity, and sexuality.

The entire tale revolves around Nur ed Din, a beautiful young boy, whom all desire. Nur ed Din, however, desires only one— Zumarrud, the young slave girl he has fallen in love with. When she's kidnapped, he goes in search of his true love. At the same time, other tales are told, simultaneously involving wealthy older men who pay for the favors of younger men, unrequited love, love slaves, torture and murder. Sex is a dangerous and frightening activity in these ancient times—much as it is today.

In the end, Nur ed Din finds his true love but doesn't recognize her. She has been mistaken for a man and crowned king of the land. When she orders her men to bring Nur ed Din to her bedroom, the guards joke that "He must prefer melons to plums," not realizing that the joke is on them.

Quotes:

"The less-beautiful always love the more beautiful."

—*A princess*

"Watch out—he prefers the banana to the fig."

—*A street vendor*

MPAA Rating: Not rated—Contains graphic violence, simulated sex and full-frontal male and female nudity.

Companion Films: *Arabian Nights* is the final and best film in a trilogy by this director, which includes *The Decameron* (1970) and *The Canterbury Tales* (1972).

AS IS ★★★

(1986)

US/Color/86 minutes

Director: Michael Lindsay-Hogg

Cast: Robert Carradine *(Rich)*, Jonathan Hadary *(Saul)*, Colleen Dewhurst *(Hospice worker)*, Joanna Miles *(Actress friend)*, Alan Scarfe *(Brother)*, Doug Annear *(Chet)*.

Genre: Drama

Plot: An AIDS drama adapted from the William M. Hoffman play. Rather than an inspired re-creation of the play, the film looks very staged, and suffers as a result. Nonetheless, this modern-day tragic tale has its warm and memorable moments.

Robert Carradine plays Rich, a gay writer living in New York City with his long-time lover Saul (Hadary). He leaves Saul for Chet (Annear), a younger, more attractive man, but soon learns that he has contracted the AIDS virus. His new lover Chet quickly abandons him upon learning the news. His friends and family are also put to the test. Saul is the only one who's completely there for him, and together they deal with the disease and the reactions of loved ones. In one touching scene Saul says to Rich, "I'll take you, as is. No matter what happens."

MPAA Rating: Considering its subject matter, the film is surprisingly free of much offensive language. No nudity or sexual situations.

Companion Films: See "AIDS" in the "Companion Films Index."

BEFORE STONEWALL ★★★★

(1985)

US/Color/87 minutes

Director: Greta Schiller, Andrea Weiss, John Scagliotti.

Genre: Documentary—Narrated by Rita Mae Brown.

Plot: The filmmakers document gay life in America and the growing movement that led to the 1969 Stonewall riots in Greenwich Village, New York.

Using home movies, archival footage and interviews, a portrait of a modern movement toward liberation is explored. Discrimination in the armed forces, in politics, in the media and in everyday life, from the early 1920s to the 1960s, is retraced and put into a historical context that's both horrifying and inspiring.

MPAA Rating: Not rated.

Companion Films: See "Documentaries" in the "Companion Films Index."

BEST MAN, THE ★★★

(1964)

US/B&W/103 minutes

Director: Franklin Schaffner

Cast: Henry Fonda *(William Russell)*, Cliff Robertson *(Joe Cantwell)*, Edie Adams *(Mable)*, Margaret Leighton *(Alice)*, Shelley Berman *(Sheldon Baskim)*, Lee Tracy *(President Hocksteader)*, Kevin McCarthy *(Dick Jensen)*, Ann Sothern *(Mrs. Gammidge)*.

Genre: Drama—The stakes are high when a candidate for president of the United States is unjustly accused of homosexuality in this behind-the-scenes political drama. Based on the 1960 hit stage play and adapted by the author, Gore Vidal.

Plot: Cliff Robertson plays Joe Cantwell, a ruthless, opportunistic candidate who will do anything to get elected president, but a "dirty secret" in his past proves to be his undoing.

Henry Fonda plays his fair-minded, thoughtful and leading opponent William Russell. When Cantwell threatens to destroy Russell by exposing his past psychological history, Russell's party digs up dirt of their own on Cantwell.

When Russell is given damaging evidence that he can use to counter Cantwell's dirt, he refuses to destroy a man on moral grounds, even though it means he will lose the race. "I don't believe it," claims Fonda when told that his opponent is a closet homosexual. "No man with that awful wife and those ugly children could be anything other than normal," he responds.

Russell is right; the entire incident is a lie. As it turns out, not only is Cantwell not a homosexual, he was the man who turned in the officers who were, and proudly admits, "I even got promoted on the strength of having cleared that kind out of the command." At this point the cocky Cantwell knows that his fair-minded opponent will not knowingly slander an innocent man, and prepares to win the race.

Russell, however, has one last card up his sleeve, and uses it to keep Cantwell out of the White House.

Quotes:

"I suppose you find promiscuity admirable?"

"I couldn't care less. I was brought up on the farm, and the lesson of the rooster was not entirely lost on me."

—Robertson and Tracy

"It's not that I object to your being a bastard. Don't get me wrong there. It's your being such a *stupid* bastard that I object to."

—Tracy

MPAA Rating: Not rated.

Awards: Lee Tracy received an Academy Award nomination for *Best Supporting Actor.*

Companion Films: See "Blackmail" in the "Companion Films Index."

BEST WAY ★★★
(1976)

France/Color/85 minutes

Director: Claude Miller

Cast: Patrick Deware *(Marc)*, Patrick Bouchitey *(Philippe)*, Christine Pascal *(Chantal)*, Claude Pieplu *(Camp director).*

Genre: Drama—In French with English subtitles.

Plot: Set in 1960 at a summer camp for boys, Patrick Deware plays Marc, the athletics coach. When Marc walks in on Philippe (Bouchitey), the drama coach, in his room one night, he finds him dressed in women's clothes and wearing makeup.

Marc keeps this secret to himself, but when Philippe accuses him of having secrets of his own, he becomes enraged. Unable to deal with his repressed feelings, he takes out his anger on Philippe.

To prove his manhood, Philippe invites his girlfriend, Chantal (Pascal), for a weekend visit, but he's left impotent when they attempt to have sex. Despite the constant brooding of Philippe, the story does have a number of humorous moments. In one scene the camp director reads suggestions the students have made for a farewell party. One young boy has suggested a "cock contest," which delights the counselors. Philippe, however, suggests a costume party claiming, "Everyone likes to dress up."

Chantal arrives at the party dressed as a man, complete with mustache. Marc is appropriately dressed as a matador. The last to arrive is Philippe—in full makeup and women's clothing. He asks Marc to dance. "Tonight is our night," he says to Marc in a defiant and confrontational tone. Marc enjoys the game, but when Philippe kisses him in public, he pulls back. Philippe persists and they begin to fight. Marc ends up stabbed in the leg by Philippe.

In the next scene, the film fast-forwards to a few years later in Paris. Philippe and Chantal are considering the purchase of a flat. Marc is the real estate agent. He's now married, and the relationship shared between Philippe and Chantal is left to the imagination.

While the ending is left open-ended, the film's message—that in a society and time when one way is considered the only way, sexual repression is often the path of least resistance—poignantly hits the mark.

Quotes:

"The best way to walk is our way to walk."

—Song lyrics sung by the students

"I want to know all your secrets."

—Pascal

MPAA Rating: Not rated—Contains full-frontal nudity of Deware and Bouchitey. Also includes female nudity.

Companion Films: See "Boys Schools" and "Closet Cases" in the "Companion Films Index."

BIGGER SPLASH, A ★★★

(1974)

UK/Color/90 minutes

Director: Jack Hazan

Cast: David Hockney, Peter Schlessinger, Joe McDonald, Ossie Clark, Mo McDermott, Celia Birtwell, Patrick Procktor, Henry Geldzahler.

Genre: Drama—An autobiographical fantasy about British painter David Hockney. All the characters in the film play themselves.

Plot: This semi-documentary, filmed over a period of three years, centers on painter David Hockney and his break-up with his male lover, Peter Schlessinger. David is left distraught and lonely following the split. He spends his time painting pictures of Peter from old snapshots. He also spends a great deal of time fantasizing about Peter in sexual situations with other young men. By the end of the film Hockney has worked through his pain and is ready to move on.

A Bigger Splash is an original film about an original artist. It's a portrait of an artist stripped bare and made real. Art fans will appreciate this rare portrait of the painter. The title of the film comes from a Hockney painting of a California pool.

MPAA Rating: R—Contains numerous scenes of male nudity and sexuality. Hockney appears nude in a shower scene, while Schlessinger is featured in extended full-frontal nude scenes.

Trivia: In a 1975 *After Dark* interview, the director talked about the film's reviews. "The reviews for the film were mixed in New York, and it did seem to infuriate critics there. I've thought a lot about it, and I think the reason is that they think of it as a gay movie … But what happens here is that what they think of as a gay movie is playing for a straight, middle-class audience in a straight, middle-class movie house—and that infuriates them. It does get to them because, for the first time, gayness is not made a negative quality."

Awards: Received 1974 Golden Plaque at the Chicago Film Festival for "originality of concept."

Companion Films: See "Biographies" and "Men and Boys" in the "Companion Films Index."

BILOXI BLUES ★★★★

(1988)

US/Color/106 minutes

Director: Mike Nichols

Cast: Matthew Broderick *(Eugene Jerome)*, Christopher Walken *(Sgt. Toomey)*, Corey Parker *(Arnold Epstein)*, Michael Dolan *(Hennessey)*, Matt Mulhern *(Wykowski)*, Casey Siemaszko *(Carney)*.

Genre: Comedy—Neil Simon's poignant auto-biographical look at a group of young GIs coming of age at boot camp in 1945.

Plot: Matthew Broderick plays Eugene Jerome, an aspiring young writer, doing his patriotic duty like every other red-blooded American male during World War II. A sensitive New York Jew with a sarcastic sense of humor, Jerome is singled out by a sadistic sergeant (Walken), who does his best to turn the other soldiers against him.

More than a story about the hostilities of war, this is a story about fitting in and the hostilities to be faced when one doesn't fit in. It's a story about how painful it is to be different—culturally, socially, physically and sexually.

Arnold (Parker), an effeminate, sickly, intellectual Jew from New York refuses to fit in and is quite content to suffer the consequences. Jerome is able to fit in by staying neutral, but suffers from guilt at not standing up for his friend Arnold, the only other Jew in the platoon. The most dire consequences for not fitting in, however, are reserved for Hennessey (Dolan), a homosexual who tries to pass by hiding his true identity. It's not by accident that he's the most caring, most decent of the group. When his private sex life with a young man from a nearby barracks is discovered, he's court-martialed, publicly humiliated and sent to Leavenworth prison.

At the same time, the self-appointed leader of the group is an obnoxious, insensitive, racist bully, who fits in perfectly with the establishment. As much as anything else, this is a poignant look at a twisted and perverted system that not only allows but promotes this type of behavior. Unfortunately little has changed in the Army—or society for that matter—in the past 50 years.

The film's strength is in its ability to tell this dramatic, tragic story with warmth, humor and charm.

Quotes:
"I don't sell my fantasies."
   —*Parker*
"Why do you think I'm a homosexual?"
"I guess it's because you never talk about girls."
"I never talk about dogs either. Does that make me a cocker spaniel?"
   —*Parker and Broderick*
"You would need three promotions to be an asshole."
   —*Walken*
"I never had men do push ups in bed before but I could start tonight."
   —*Walken*
"You have to take sides, make a contribution to the fight."

"What fight?"
"Any fight. The one you believe in."
   —*Parker and Broderick*
"Sounds like an Agatha Christie novel—*Sodomy On The Orient Express.*"
   —*Parker*
"One should never underestimate the stimulation of eccentricity."
   —*Broderick*
MPAA Rating: PG—For language.
Companion Films: See "Military Men" in the "Companion Films Index."

BLAZING SADDLES ★★★★★
(1974)
US/Color/93 minutes
Director: Mel Brooks
Cast: Cleavon Little *(Sheriff Bart)*, Gene Wilder *(Jim aka "Waco Kid")*, Harvey Korman *(Hedley Lamarr)*, Madeline Kahn *(Lili)*, Mel Brooks *(Gov. Le Petomane)*, Slim Pickens *(Taggart)*, Alex Karras *(Mongo)*, Dom DeLuise *(Buddy Bizarre)*, Burton Gilliam *(Lyle)*.
Genre: Comedy—A classic Mel Brooks spoof of cowboys and the Old West.
Plot: No one escapes ridicule in this hilarious, outrageous send-up. Gays, lesbians, Indians, African-American's, the elderly, the mentally impaired, the Ku Klux Klan and Nazis, for starters, are all reduced to rude, crude puns, sight-gags and one-liners. But it's all in good fun, and it's all quite entertaining and enjoyable.

In this blatant homage to manhood and the all-American male, Cleavon Little plays Bart, the sheriff of a small town who rides on a Gucci saddle. Harvey Korman plays a villain named Hedley Lamarr, but all his friends just call him

Heddy. Dom DeLuise plays Buddy Bizarre (with abandon), a swishy gay choreographer with a vicious streak.

When Buddy's all-male Busby Berkeley-style stage is overrun by cowboys from the *Blazing Saddles* set, it becomes clear that this is a film within a film. At the sight of the visiting cowboys, the men in top hats and tails swoon and fall into their arms. Gay jokes and sight-gags race through this film like a runaway train.

In the end, good triumphs over evil, the myth of the American male has been exposed for its shortcomings and the black sheriff rides off into the sunset in a Cadillac.

Now we know how the West was won!

Quotes:
"You will be risking your lives, whilst I will be risking an almost-certain Academy Award nomination for *Best Supporting Actor*."
—*Korman*
"Another twenty-five years and you'll be able to shake their hands in broad daylight."
—*Wilder*
"Gol darnit Mr. Lamarr, you use your tongue prettier than a twenty-dollar whore."
—*Pickens*
"I hired you people to try to get a little track laid, not to jump around like a bunch of Kansas City faggots."
—*Pickens*
"Unfortunately there is one thing standing between me and that property—the rightful owners."
—*Korman*
"I must have killed more men than Cecil B. DeMille."
—*Wilder*

MPAA Rating: R—For sexual situations and vulgarity.

Awards: Madeline Kahn received an Academy Award nomination for *Best Supporting Actress* for her outrageous and sexy Marlene Dietrich and Mae West send-up.

Companion Films: See "Sissies" in the "Companion Films Index."

BLOODBROTHERS ★★★
(1978)
US/Color/117 minutes
Director: Robert Mulligan
Cast: Richard Gere *(Stoney De Coco)*, Paul Sorvino *(Chubby)*, Tony LoBianco *(Tommy)*, Bruce French *(Paulie)*, J.P. Finnegan *(Bartender)*, Robert Englund *(Mott)*, Marilu Henner *(Annette)*.
Genre: Drama
Plot: This is a story about a group of macho, working-class men who have become emotionally crippled, trying to live up to society's expectations of what a real man should be.

Richard Gere stars as Stoney De Coco, a confused kid torn between his true desire to teach children—a profession considered unmanly—and his father's expectations that his son will follow in his footsteps as a construction worker.

In a brief, but poignant scene, a bartender (J.P. Finnegan), who is also a friend, explains to Stoney's uncle, Chubby (Sorvino), that he kicked his son Paulie (Bruce French) out of the house three years earlier because he was a fag. Chubby realizes that his friend regrets what he has done and tries to reconcile the two, but pride and hurt get in the way. Paulie, still angry from his father's rejection, refuses to return for a surprise party. Paulie has escaped the oppression of his father's mentality and has no intention of returning.

Though a bit dated, this is a moving portrait of traditional families with good intentions that nevertheless hurt the ones they love most.

Quotes:
"What ya got there?"
"What's it look like?"
"A prick, only smaller."
—*A girl in a car and Sorvino*
"Once you're hurt it really makes you feel for all those other people hurtin.'"
—*Henner*

MPAA Rating: R

Companion Films: See "Unhappy Homosexuals" in the "Companion Films Index."

BLUE VELVET ★★★★
(1986)
US/Color/120 minutes
Director: David Lynch
Cast: Kyle MacLachlan (*Jeffrey Beaumont*), Isabella Rossellini (*Dorothy Valiens*), Dennis Hopper (*Frank Booth*), Laura Dern (*Sandy Williams*), Dean Stockwell (*Gar*), Hope Lange (*Mrs. Williams*), George Dickerson (*Detective Williams*).

Genre: Horror

Plot: Many critics consider this film a masterpiece; critic Roger Ebert of the *Chicago Sun-Times* wasn't one of them. He refers to this film in particular when he writes, "American movies have been using satire for years to take the edge off sex and violence. Occasionally, perhaps sex and violence should be treated with the seriousness they deserve."

Though Stockwell's character is not openly gay, his character has often been cited by reviewers as a 1950s closet case. Add to this the sadomasochistic exploits and perverted behavior throughout the film and you have the standard Hollywood recipe for homosexuality.

In typical David Lynch fashion, an idyllic small town on the surface turns out to be a hotbed of bizarre perversity upon closer inspection. MacLachlan plays a college student who becomes involved in a mystery that leads him to a nightclub singer (Rossellini). She is involved in a sadomasochistic relationship and in turn involves him. These two characters represent the film's double-edged fascination with innocence and depravity.

MPAA Rating: R—For violence, nudity and profanity. Kyle MacLachlan is seen very briefly in full-frontal nudity and from behind.

Companion Films: See "Closet Cases" in the "Companion Films Index."

BOYS IN THE BAND, THE ★★★★★
(1970)
US/Color/117 minutes
Director: William Friedkin
Cast: Kenneth Nelson (*Michael*), Frederick Combs (*Donald*), Leonard Frey (*Harold*), Cliff Gorman (*Emery*), Alan McCarthy (*Peter White*), Laurence Luckinbill (*Hank*), Reuben Greene (*Bernard*), Robert La Tourneaux (*Cowboy*), Keith Prentice (*Larry*).

Genre: Drama—The advertisements for this camp classic comedy-drama read, "*The Boys In The Band ... is not a musical.*"—what an understatement. The film was based on Mart Crowley's successful Off-Broadway play, and retained the original cast.

Plot: In one of the film's most telling quotes, Michael (Nelson) the central character ex-

Frederick Combs getting ready for the big night in *The Boys In The Band* (1970).

claims, "You show me a happy homosexual and I'll show you a gay corpse." Michael is not a happy homosexual. Neither are any of the other characters in this film about the effects of self-hatred and growing up in a society that denies you even exist. Michael's only role models have been the vamps and vixens of the movies.

When the film premiered in 1970, "Gay Pride" was still an infant concept. The film had the dubious distinction of being the first mainstream film to deal openly, if not completely honestly, with homosexuality. It marked a turning point in films about gays, and today

symbolizes the pre-liberation, self-hating, neurotic, hysterically unhappy queens of the past.

Set in a spacious New York City apartment, the film centers on a group of gay men attending a birthday party. The upbeat hit song "Anything Goes" by Harpers Bazarre opens the film on a deceivingly lighthearted note. Before long the party degenerates into a long night of vicious attacks and mean-spirited party games. Following dinner, Michael announces to all that they have just eaten Sebastian Venable (Venable was the gay man cannibalized in *Suddenly, Last*

Summer). Little do they realize that he's about to do the same to them—eat them alive that is.

When Alan, a former college friend of Michael's, shows up at the party uninvited, he becomes the catalyst for the violence, anger and rage that surface throughout the evening. The only straight man, and possibly a closet case at that, he's repelled by this group of flamboyant homosexuals. When he discovers that Hank and Larry, the only straight acting men in the group, are not only homosexuals but also lovers, he's even more threatened. That they are the only well-adjusted men in the film is too frightening for Alan to comprehend.

In the end, Alan flees this freak show and runs back to the arms of his wife. A drunk, vicious, melodramatic Michael meanwhile has succeeded in trashing all the guests, including himself, and in the end is reduced to tears and self-pity.

Although the film turns out to be more a tragedy than a comedy, it succeeds in being very entertaining and enjoyable, partly as a nostalgic piece of gay history, but just as much for its sharp dialogue and fine acting. It has also aged remarkably well.

By the end of the night Kenneth Nelson (left) has insulted all of his party guests and is reduced to tears himself in *The Boys In The Band* (1970).

Quotes:
With its witty and biting one-liners, this was the film that set the standard for camp quotes in the early '70s. Few films since have managed to equal its arch charm and bitchy humor.

"It's called butch assurance."
"It's still hair spray, no matter if they call it balls."
    —*Combs and Nelson*
"What is he—a psychiatrist or a hairdresser?"
"Actually he's both. He shrinks my head and then combs me out."
    —*Nelson and Combs*
"Are you calling me a screaming queen or a tired fairy?"
    —*Combs*
"What you see before you is a masterpiece of deception."
    —*Nelson*
"What's more boring than a queen doing a Judy Garland imitation?"
"A queen doing a Bette Davis imitation."
    —*Nelson and Combs*
"Thanks to the silver screen your neurosis has got style."
    —*Combs*
"Believe it or not, there was a time in my life when I didn't go around announcing I was a faggot."
"Well, that must have been before speech replaced sign language."
    —*Nelson and Combs*
"Straight! He's about as straight as the Yellow Brick Road."
    —*Luckinbill*
"You shouldn't wear heels when you do chin-ups."
    —*Gorman*

"Bang-bang, you're alive, but roll over and play dead."
    —*Gorman*
"Who is she? Who was she? Who does she want to be?"
    —*Frey*
"He has unnatural, natural beauty."
    —*Frey*
"Well, that's the pot calling the kettle beige."
    —*Frey*
"Physical beauty isn't everything."
"Thank you, Quasimodo."
    —*Frey and Nelson*
"Who do you have to fuck to get a drink around here?"
    —*Gorman*
"You show me a happy homosexual, and I'll show you a corpse."
    —*Nelson*

MPAA Rating: R—The film received an R rating because of its "homosexual dialogue." Contains one nude scene of Frederick Combs from behind as he gets into a shower.

Companion Films: See "Closet Cases," "Sissies" and "Unhappy Homosexuals" in the "Companion Films Index."

BOYS NEXT DOOR, THE ★
(1984)
US/Color/90 minutes
Director: Penelope Spheeris
Cast: Maxwell Caufield *(Roy)*, Charlie Sheen *(Bo)*, Kenneth Cortland *(Dwayne)*, Paul C. Dancer *(Chris)*, Patti D'Arbanville *(Angie)*.
Genre: Thriller—A low-budget, B-movie splatter film.
Plot: Maxwell Caufield plays Roy, a repressed

homosexual about to embark on a killing spree. His best buddy and fellow delinquent Bo (Charlie Sheen) is just along for the ride.

On graduation night they head for Hollywood. By chance they meet a gay man named Chris (Dancer) who offers to get the under-age boys into a bar. When Roy realizes that they are in a gay bar he snaps.

When Chris suggests that they return to his apartment Roy agrees. Once there, Roy and Bo proceed to beat the surprised young man. Roy discovers Chris's gun and kills him with it.

Later, Roy uses the gun to murder a young woman Bo is having sex with. Roy's murderous rage is out of control and only ends in a violent confrontation with the police, once he's trapped.

There's little to recommend about this violent, insensitive and poorly acted gore-fest.

Quotes:

"Jesus Christ, we were beat up by a couple of girls."

—*Sheen*

"I don't want to sound like a fag or nothing, but you are my best friend."

—*Sheen*

MPAA Rating:

R—Contains graphic violence and profanity.

Companion Films:

See "Closet Cases" and "Murderers" in the "Companion Films Index."

BUTLEY ★★★

(1974)

UK/Color/94 minutes

Director: Harold Pinter

Cast: Alan Bates *(Ben Butley)*, Jessica Tandy *(Edna)*, Richard O'Callaghan *(Joey)*, Michael Byrne *(Reg)*, Simon Rouse *(Mr. Gardner)*.

Genre: Drama—Based on the Simon Gray play.

Plot: Alan Bates plays Ben Butley, a charming but sarcastic, domineering and dissatisfied middle-aged man.

A professor, Butley is a married man with a live-in male lover (O'Callaghan). Competitive and jealous, he becomes his own worst enemy. Though charming and attractive, his personality eventually alienates and pushes away his colleagues, his wife and his lover.

His lover, Joey, a former student, leaves him for Reg (Byrne), a respectable publisher who's no match for the wit and charm of Butley, but offers stability and a more equal relationship.

Fine performances and intelligent dialogue make up for an otherwise tediously long film.

Quotes: "I'm a one-woman man, and I've had mine, thank God."

—*Bates*

MPAA Rating: Not rated.

Companion Films: See "Men and Boys" and "Unhappy Homosexuals" in the "Companion Films Index."

CABARET ★★★★★
(1972)
US/Color/119 minutes
Director: Bob Fosse
Cast: Liza Minnelli *(Sally Bowles)*, Michael York *(Brian Roberts)*, Joel Grey *(Master of Ceremonies)*, Helmut Griem *(Maximillian von Heune)*, Fritz Wepper *(Fritz Wendell)*, Marisa Berenson *(Natalia)*, Ricky Renee *(Elke)*.
Genre: Musical—Based on the book *I Am A Camera,* by the late gay writer Christopher Isherwood.
Plot: Set in Berlin in 1931, the story revolves around the personal lives of a group of performers and patrons of a risqué and decadent nightclub called the "Kit Kat." Juxtaposing the rise to power of the Nazi's, with these carefree, self-centered friends and acquaintances, Fosse has succeeded in creating a modern classic.

Michael York plays Brian, a student from Cambridge working on his Ph.D. He moves to Berlin to earn money teaching English to Germans. While renting a room in a boarding house, he becomes friends with Sally Bowles (Minnelli), a flamboyant, femme fatale wannabe and singer at the Kit Kat club.

In one of many memorable scenes, Brian is startled, while standing at a urinal in the club when he is joined by Elke (Renee), a transvestite standing at the urinal next to him. Brian learns right away that this in no ordinary club.

Even the master of ceremonies (Grey) occassionally dresses in lingerie and joins the girls on stage in a dance routine poking fun at the Gestapo.

Before long, Sally makes a move on Brian, only to discover that he doesn't sleep with women. He admits, "I've gone through the motions sleeping with girls exactly three times." She's a liberated woman and understands. Sometime later, Sally is stood up by her father, who barely knows she's alive. Brian comforts her and, as often happens, one thing leads to another, and before they know it, they're making love.

Later, Sally—being the free spirit she is—picks up Maximillian (Griem), a wealthy baron, in a local laundry and brings him home to meet Brian. Max is a married man but explains to Brian, "We have quite a special understanding." Brian replies, "That must be useful at times." Sally and Brian enjoy Max's gifts, trips and attention, and before long, Max is having sex with both of them.

During an argument, Brian shouts, "Screw Maximillian," at Sally.

She responds in anger, "I do."

"So do I," offers Brian. Both are angry, but make up just in time to learn that she's pregnant and doesn't know which man is the father. Brian offers to marry her but in the end, she realizes that it wouldn't be long before he was sleeping with men again, and she has an abortion.

All the while there's an ongoing parallel subplot about a gigolo who falls in love with a Jewish girl. The problem is she won't marry him because he's not Jewish. The dilemma is he's a Jew trying to pass for a Christian and must eventually come out of his own closet.

In the end, Brian leaves Berlin just the way he came in at the beginning. But everything has

Ricky Renee plays Elke, the local transvestite in Bob Fosse's *Cabaret* (1972).

changed. The Nazis are now in power and everyone's innocence has been trampled—on a personal scale and on a grand scale. A powerful film that contains strong, memorable performances by all.

Quotes:

"Divine decadence."
   —Minnelli
"Have you ever slept with a dwarf?"
"Once, but it wasn't a lasting relationship."
   —Minnelli and York
"Don't be so British. You'll feel terrific afterwards. You know you want to."
   —Minnelli

"Maybe you just don't sleep with girls. Well, do you sleep with girls or don't you?"
   —Minnelli
"Sex always screws up a friendship anyway."
   —Minnelli
"Goddamn it. I think I'm falling in love with her."
"Oh, I'm so sorry."
   —Wepper and York
"My god, it's enough to drive a girl into a convent. Do they have Jewish nuns?"
   —Minnelli
"I feel just like Kate Francis."
   —Minnelli

"I just told him I had the teeniest touch of syphilis. Wait till he gets a load of what little old Elke's got."

—*Minnelli*

"You're about as fatale as an after dinner mint."

—*York*

"I guess it's just about the most significant baby the world's ever known—since Jesus."

—*Minnelli*

"I have this infantile fantasy that one day I'll amount to something as an actress."

—*Minnelli*

MPAA Rating: PG

Awards: *Cabaret* was nominated for a *Best Picture* Academy Award but lost out to *The Godfather*. Bob Fosse won for *Best Director*, while Liza Minnelli won the *Best Actress* Oscar and Joel Grey picked up the award for *Best Supporting Actor*. The film was also nominated for *Best Screenplay (Based on material from another medium)*, *Best Cinematography*, *Best Art Direction*, *Best Sound* and *Best Scoring*.

Companion Films: See "Bisexuals" and "Fascists and Nazis" in the "Companion Films Index."

CALIFORNIA SUITE ★★★★

(1978)

US/Color/103 minutes

Director: Herbert Ross

Cast: Michael Caine *(Sidney)*, Maggie Smith *(Diana)*, Jane Fonda *(Hannah)*, Alan Alda *(Billy)*, Walter Matthau *(Marvin)*, Elaine May *(Millie)*, Richard Pryor *(Chauncey)*, Bill Cosby *(Willis)*.

Genre: Comedy—A very successful adaptation of the Neil Simon play.

Plot: An all-star cast carries this delightful comedy—loaded with biting wit and bitchy repartee—along at a brisk pace.

This is a story about five separate couples all staying at the Beverly Hills Hotel. Their reasons for visiting Los Angeles vary, but the humor, adventure and misadventure are shared by all of them.

One of the couples is played by Maggie Smith and Michael Caine. Smith plays Diana, an English actress who's in town to attend the Academy Awards. Caine plays her husband, Sidney. Sidney is a bisexual antique dealer, and their relationship is one of convenience for them both.

Of the five couples, Smith and Caine get the lion's share of witty one-liners. A loser at the Oscars, Diana gets drunk. Bitter and angry, she confronts Sidney with her disappointments about their marriage and arrangement—it seems it's only convenient for him. She longs for what he can never fully give her—his complete affection. In a tender moment he asks, "We keep up a front for everyone else, why can't we do it for ourselves?"

Inbetween the barbs and zingers, a touching portrait of love and affection emerges. Smith's is truly an award-winning performance in an intelligently written and equally entertaining film.

Quotes:

"Six dollars and ninety-five cents? Would it be possible to just rent a couple of drinks?"

—*Fonda*

"I never liked San Francisco—I was always afraid I'd fall out of bed and roll down one of those hills."

"Not you Hannah, you roll up hills."

—*Fonda and Alda*

"I love your California clothes."

"They're Bloomingdales of New York."

"It's the best place for California clothes."

—*Fonda and Alda*

"When you were younger, you were the healthiest girl I knew. What happened?"

"With Nixon in the White House good health seemed to be in bad taste."

—*Alda and Fonda*

"I suppose if Ginny stays she'll grow up to look like that: blonde hair, blonde teeth, blonde life."

—*Fonda*

"You're worse than a hapless romantic—you're a hopeful one."

—*Fonda*

"I haven't seen your newest film. I'm told it did very well in backward areas."

—*Fonda*

"I was naughty all day yesterday."

"Not with me you weren't"

"You'll just have to learn to show up on time."

—*Caine and Smith*

"What color is this? I ask for a simple rinse, and that ditzy queen's given me crayon."

—*Smith*

"You have the most bizarre sense of humor."

"Bizarre people often do."

—*Smith and Caine*

"I lead a very gay life. Let's be honest, pet, how many antique dealers get to go to the Academy Awards?"

—*Caine*

"Sidney, I have just thrown up on some of the best people in Hollywood. Now is no time to be sensitive."

—*Smith*

"I'd like to throw up but the room's too small."

—*Pryor*

"Sidney, was I hit by a bus? I look as though I was hit by a fully loaded, guided-tour bus."

—*Smith*

"I've aged Sidney, I'm getting lines in my face. I look like a brand-new steel-belted-radial tire."

—*Smith*

"What a nasty streak you have when you drink. Also when you eat and sit and walk."

—*Caine*

"Are you unhappy because you didn't get to wear my dress?"

"If I had worn your dress it would have hung properly."

—*Smith and Caine*

"You make me sick. When you can't have what you want, you make certain that everyone around is equally as miserable."

"I haven't noticed any equals around me."

—*Caine and Smith*

"I have never hidden behind closet doors, but I am discreet."

"Discreet? You did everything but lick his artichoke!"

— *Caine and Smith*

"Screw the Oscars. Screw the Academy Awards. Screw me Sidney, please. Please."

—*Smith*

"If there's anything I hate it's a bisexual homosexual—or is it the other way around?"

"It works either way."

—*Smith and Caine*

MPAA Rating: PG

Awards: Maggie Smith won the *Best Supporting Actress* Oscar for her role as an actress who loses on Oscar night. The film also received nominations for *Best Screenplay (Based on material from another medium)* and *Best Art Direction.*

Companion Films: See "Bisexuals" in the "Companion Films Index."

CALIGULA ★★★

(1979)

US-Italy/Color/150 minutes

Director: Tinto Brass

Cast: Malcolm McDowell *(Caligula)*, Teresa Ann Savoy *(Drucilla)*, Peter O'Toole *(Tiberius)*, John Gielgud *(Nirva)*, Helen Mirren.

Genre: Drama—A soft-porn film featuring top Hollywood actors. Based on a story by Gore Vidal, the film was produced by *Penthouse* publisher Bob Guccione.

Plot: Set in pagan Rome between 37 AD and 41 AD, the film follows the rise and fall of Emperor Caligula Caesar. McDowell plays prince Caligula, a depraved, egomaniacal, narcissistic, ruthless and paranoid young man who kills his stepfather, Tiberius, his half brother and the man who brought him to power, all so he can assume the title of Emperor Caligula Caesar.

Though he prefers sex with his sister, Caligula is persuaded to marry another woman in order to have a child. He chooses a prostitute over a virgin, who would be most boring.

This is the age of decadence and insatiable appetites. Very little clothing is worn in this film, and sexual freedom is exhibited throughout. Public orgies are the entertainment of the day under Caligula's rule, and homosexuality is just another sexual pleasure. When Caligula has gone too far—has mocked the gods, insulted the Senate and incurred the wrath of the people—he's murdered by his own men. His effeminate uncle Claudius assumes his throne.

Quotes:

"I hear you have a taste for little boys."

"No, Caesar, big boys."

—*O'Toole and McDowell*

"Give him enough rope and he'll hang us all."

—*A Roman*

"You prefer nymphs to satyrs?"

"I like both lord."

—*McDowell and a Roman*

MPAA Rating: R and X—There are two versions of the film. The X-rated version includes full-frontal male and female nudity throughout, including McDowell. McDowell holds the record for most male nudity in the movies. The edited version contains only female nudity and male nudity briefly from behind.

Companion Films: See "Biographies" and "Romans" in the "Companion Films Index."

CAN'T STOP THE MUSIC ★★

(1980)

US/Color/118 minutes

Director: Nancy Walker

Cast: Valerie Perrine *(Samantha)*, Steve Guttenberg *(Jack)*, Barbara Rush *(Jack's mother)*, Bruce Jenner *(Ron)*, Tammy Grimes *(Sydnie)*, Paul Sand *(Steve)*, Jack Weston *(Bernie)*, Leigh Taylor-Young *(Reporter)* and The Village People.

Genre: Musical—An Allan-Carr-produced camp, musical-comedy showcase for The Village People, a popular disco group of the '70s. This is a dated but nonetheless nostalgically entertaining cross between a *Love Boat* rerun and a Mickey Rooney-Judy Garland *Andy Hardy* musical extravaganza. Unlike *Andy Hardy*, it was a flop at the box office.

Plot: Steve Guttenberg plays Jack, a very energetic, roller-skating songwriter, who's sworn off sex until he makes it big in the music business—which sex he's sworn off, we're never quite sure. Jack is a long-term house sitter for his pal Sam (Perrine). Sam is a former model who now spends all her free time trying to help Jack make it in the business, presumably so he once again can have sex.

Sam rounds up a few of her neighbors in the Village: Felipe, an American Indian in full drag; David, a construction worker; Randy, a cowboy; Ray, a black cop; Alexander, a GI; and Glenn, a leatherman (just your typical neighbors), and they put on a show to spotlight Jack's music. These fun, lively tunes are an instant success, and before you know it, with the help of a few good friends, the band, now called The Village People, becomes a hit sensation.

The film's most memorable moments center on a Busby Berkeley musical sendup set in the YMCA. All the while, the group is singing, "It's fun to stay at the YMCA," as sparsely clad young athletic men jump, swim, flip and frolic through the gymnasium. This scene alone is worth the price of admission.

Quotes:

"Anyone who can swallow two Snow Balls and a Ding Dong shouldn't have any problem with pride."

—*Guttenberg*

It's fun to stay at the YMCA, in Nancy Walker's *Can't Stop The Music* (1980).

"You may have given up your glamorous career, but mine is just beginning."
—*Guttenberg*
"We are going to make milk more glamorous than champagne."
—*Grimes*
"Housework is like bad sex. Everytime I do it I swear I'll never do it again, until company comes by."
—*Party guest*
"About the only relationship I can sustain is with a plant."
—*Perrine*

MPAA Rating: PG—Features another nude-young-men-in-the-shower scene. This one is staged at the New York YMCA.

Companion Films: See "Neighbors, Roommates and Best Friends" and "Sissies" in the "Companion Films Index."

CAR WASH ★★★

(1976)
US/Color/97 minutes
Director: Michael Schultz
Cast: Antonio Fargas *(Lindy)*, Richard Pryor *(Daddy Rich)*, Bill Duke *(Abdula)*, Sully Boyar *(The boss)*, Melanie Mayron *(Cashier)*, Richard Brestoff *(Irwin)*, The Pointer Sisters.
Genre: Comedy—A humorous day in the life of a group of men and a few women who struggle to get by while working at a Los Angeles car wash.
Plot: The sign on the wall—"We give the best hand job in town"—says it all. Sex is what keeps this film moving at a brisk pace. Whether it's poking fun at hookers, homosexuals or horny young hunks, the comedy and one-liners

never stray far from this familiar territory.

In a mostly African-American ensemble cast, Antonio Fargas stands out as Lindy, the flamboyant homosexual of the group. Lindy is just one of the many eccentric characters who earn their living and have a few laughs while working at the Dee Luxe car wash. It's to the film's credit that he also is one of the most likable and self-confident characters.

In the end, the teasing, pranks and superficial humor give way to real people with real feelings, who are just trying to get through life with a little help from their friends.

Quotes:
"Honey, baseball's not my game."
—*Fargas*
"Irwin, you're not a homosexual are you?"
"Not yet."
—*Boyar and Brestoff*
"Would you please get out of my face you sorry-lookin' faggot."
"Who you callin' sorry-lookin?"
—*Duke and Fargas*
"Honey, I'm more man than you'll ever be and more woman than you'll ever get."
—*Fargas*

MPAA Rating: PG
Companion Films: See "Sissies" in the "Companion Films Index."

CARAVAGGIO ★★

(1986)
UK/Color/97 minutes
Director: Derek Jarman
Cast: Nigel Terry *(Caravaggio)*, Tilda Swinton *(Lena)*, Jonathan Hyde *(Baglione)*, Michael Gough *(Cardinal Del Monte)*, Dexter Fletcher

(Young Caravaggio), Noam Almaz *(Boy Caravaggio)*, Nigel Davenport *(Guistiniani)*, Garry Cooper *(Davide)*, Bobbie Coltrane *(Scipione Borghese)*, Jack Birkett *(Pope)*, Sean Bean *(Ranuccio)*.

Genre: Drama—A quirky, stylized biography of the notorious and controversial Renaissance painter (1571-1610) Michelangelo Caravaggio.

Plot: Intellectual, poetic, austere and visually stylish, Jarman's erotic biography is equally obscure and difficult to follow unless you know the story and all the characters beforehand.

Using English actors who speak in modern-day slang to play Italian Renaissance painters and priests may be the director's trademark, but it adds to the overall disjointed quality of the film.

Caravaggio appears to be about tortured lives, love for money, murder for love, and most of all, the eroticism of love, money and death. This exercise in sensuality will appeal to the visually-oriented.

Quotes:

"God, all these quotes, I could build a Tower of Babel with them."

—Fletcher

"What's his taste in music?"
"Catholic."

—Terry and Coltrane

"You're in love with him!"
"With his money!"

—Swinton and Coltrane

"I adore strawberries. One feels so wicked eating them out of season."

—Gough

MPAA Rating: Not rated—Contains references and scenes of homoerotic sexuality.

Companion Films: Has similarities in theme and tone to Robert Altman's tortured artist biopic *Vincent And Theo* (1990) about the life of Vincent Van Gogh.

Also see "Biographies" in the "Companion Films Index."

CHAIN OF DESIRE ★★★

(1992)

US/Color/105 minutes

Director: Temistocles Lopez

Cast: Linda Fiorentino *(Alma D'Angeli)*, Elias Koteas *(Jesus)*, Tim Guinee *(Ken)*, Grace Zabriskie *(Linda Bailey)*, Assumpta Serna *(Cleo)*, Patrick Bauchau *(Jerald Buckley)*, Seymour Cassel *(Mel)*, Malcolm McDowell *(Hubert Bailey)*, Angel Aviles *(Isa)*, Jamie Harrold *(Keith)*, Dewey Weber *(David Bango)*, Holly Marie Combs *(Diana)*, Kevin Conroy *(Joe)*.

Genre: Drama—An independent, low-budget, modern day, melodramatic *La Ronde*. The tag line read, "Just when you thought you'd seen it all."

Plot: Set in New York City, the film follows a group of jaded strangers who are only connected—like a chain—through sexual encounters. Among the group are voyeurs, bisexuals, asexuals, nymphomaniacs, swingers, exhibitionists, and pedophiles—for starters. One of the more memorable roles goes to Malcolm McDowell as a married man who prefers young boys to his wife.

Before the end of the film most of the characters in this large and talented ensemble cast have slept with one another. In the end the message is clear: Serial sex in this time of AIDS can be devastating.

This new interpretation of the Arthur

Schnitzler classic play is at times uneven, but nevertheless compelling.

MPAA Rating: R

Companion Films: See "AIDS" in the "Companion Films Index."

CHANGING OUR MINDS: THE STORY OF DR. EVELYN HOOKER ★★★★

(1992)

US/Color/75 minutes

Director: Richard Schmiechen

Genre: Documentary

Plot: A powerful and moving film, the director uses interviews, photos and archival footage to piece together not only a compelling portrait of renowned psychologist Evelyn Hooker, but manages to illuminate a harrowing history of sexual repression in this country.

Hooker's pioneering research of over two decades led the American Psychiatric Association to remove homosexuality from its official list of mental disorders in 1974. Before this, the film reminds us, homosexual acts were illegal and homosexuality was considered a perversion and an illness. Psychologists routinely "treated" this so-called illness with electroshock therapy, lobotomies and castration.

A moving tribute to a remarkable woman and the often-overlooked impact she had on the entire gay movement. This is a must-see film for gay and nongay audiences alike.

MPAA Rating: Not rated.

Awards: Nominated for a 1992 Academy Award for *Best Documentary*, the film lost to *The Panama Deception*. Schmiechen was also the producer of the Academy Award-winning

The Times Of Harvey Milk.

Companion Films: See "Documentaries" in the "Companion Films Index."

CHOIRBOYS, THE ★

(1977)

US/Color/119 minutes

Director: Robert Aldrich

Cast: Charles Durning *(Whalen)*, Perry King *(Baxter)*, James Woods *(Harold Bloomguard)*, Tim McIntire *(Roscoe Rules)*, Don Stroud *(Sam)*, Burt Young *(Dominic Scuzzi)*, Louis Gossett, Jr. *(Motts)*, Clyde Kusatsu *(Francis)*, Randy Quaid *(Dean)*, Stephen Macht *(Spencer)*, Chuck Sacci *(Sartino)*, Michael Wills *(Alexander)*.

Genre: Comedy—*Porky's* collides with *Police Academy*, and *Choirboys* is the wreckage. This is a raunchy, offensive, sophomoric comedy that deserves a look, just to admire how homophobic, racist, sexist and insulting a movie can be.

Plot: This is ostensibly a film about the lives of eight cops on the Los Angeles police department. Essentially, however, it is a film about eight men and their fear of sex, based on the best-selling novel by Joseph Wambaugh.

"Choir practice" for these men is ritual, after-hours get-togethers in which they play poker, get drunk, and chase any sexual object that crosses their paths.

On one of their outings they wind up late at night in MacArthur Park. Pulling a practical joke on Roscoe (McIntire), the most obnoxious officer of the group, they strip off his pants, handcuff him to a tree and leave him. All alone, he is accosted by a flaming queen walking a hot-pink poodle. The homosexual squeals in

Cameron English (second from the right) plays Paul, one of the gay dancers in *A Chorus Line* (1985).

delight when he comes upon his naked prey, "I can't believe it, a naked man chained to a tree. It's a crazy, mad, salacious fantasy."

In the very next scene Roscoe is harassed by an undercover vice cop pretending to be gay in a men's room. It seems that "fruits" are everywhere just waiting for an opportunity to pounce on innocent and defenseless straight men. It also seems that the LAPD is determined to leave no stone unturned until they've arrested every "pervert" in the city. But when they pick up Alexander, an 18-year-old gay kid, the commander becomes compassionate. He asks the kid, "How long have you had this problem?"

When he replies, "I don't know why I'm gay, I just am," he lets the crying lad go home to his parents. This is the film's one-and-only sensitive moment. From beginning to end, this is a film that can't decide whether it's a comedy or a drama. It's a film with a very split personality.

Suffice it to say that each man has his moment of humor at someone else's expense, until in the end, the same young gay man arrested earlier is accidentally shot to death by one of the cops in the park. The murder is covered up, of course, and "choir practice" is resumed in no time.

Quotes:

"What is this, the bigot of the month club?"
   —A bystander
"Who the hell are you?"
"Luther Quigly, but I'll be anyone you want me to be."
   —McIntire and a gay man in the park
"You cocksucker."
"Not me chief. I'm not the one on my knees."
   —Police chief and Durning

MPAA Rating: R—For profanity and male nudity (McIntire) from behind.

Companion Films: See "Cops," "Murderers" and "Sissies" in the "Companion Films Index."

CHORUS LINE, A ★★★
(1985)
US/Color/118 minutes
Director: Richard Attenborough
Cast: Michael Douglas *(Zach)*, Terrance Mann *(Larry)*, Alyson Reed *(Cassie)*, Cameron English *(Paul)*, Justin Ross *(Gregory)*, Vicki Frederick, Michelle Johnston.

Genre: Musical—Based on Broadway's longest-running stage play at the time, from the book by James Kirkwood.

Plot: For those few viewers who were visiting another planet in the '80s and missed the stage version of *A Chorus Line*, the story is a simple one—it's about dreams, fantasies and talent. It's also about the anxieties, struggles and hardship of auditioning and competing for a role in a Broadway musical—and getting the part. During one long audition, all of life's failures and triumphs are masterfully displayed by a group of young hopefuls in captivating words, song and dance.

Two of the dancers who make the finalists are gay. Gregory (Ross) is a gay man who has sublimated his sexuality by devoting his life to dancing. Paul (English) is one of the youngest dancers and describes to Zach (Douglas), the choreographer, the moment when he realized he wanted to be a dancer. In one of the film's most touching moments he explains how he always knew he was gay and always knew he wanted to be a dancer. At age 15 the only dancing job he could get was in a drag show at the Jewel Box Review. "I auditioned," he tells Zach, "but they weren't interested in my dancing." Paul later twists his leg during a routine and is taken to the hospital, losing out on this job as well. The stories of both men are moving, but then so is each of the dancer's stories, which is what makes this such an inspired story.

The film itself falls short of inspiring, but manages to retain the spirit of the original. Though it contains some of Broadway's most dramatic and memorable songs, the film, for the most part, seems static and lacks the energy of the live performance. It's nevertheless an entertaining and worthwhile way of spending 118 minutes.

Quotes:
"Age is only a state of mind. What age do you want me to be?"
   —Johnston
"I don't mind being treated like puppets, but worms?"
   —A dancer
"If I could think of anything I was ashamed of I'd have tried it years ago."
   —A dancer
"He was so humiliated he didn't know what to tell his friends, so he told them all I had polio."
   —English
"Sex happens to be the one subject I can speak

about with absolutely no authority whatsoever."
—*Ross*

"What do I want to be when I grow up? Young."
—*Frederick*

"Why is it only my *ass* that ever gets invited places?"
—*Frederick*

"There I was in show business. The asshole of show business, but a job."
—*English*

"I auditioned, but they weren't interested in my dancing."
—*English*

MPAA Rating: PG-13
Awards: Nominated for three Academy Awards including *Best Sound, Best Film Editing* and *Best Song* for "Surprise, Surprise!"
Companion Films: See "Unhappy Homosexuals" in the "Companion Films Index."

CITIZEN COHN ★★★★
(1992)
US/Color/112 minutes
Director: Frank Pierson
Cast: James Woods *(Roy Cohn)*, Joe Don Baker *(Joseph McCarthy)*, Joseph Bologna *(Walter Winchell)*, Pat Hingle *(J. Edgar Hoover)*, David Marshall Grant *(Robert F. Kennedy)*, Jeffrey Nordling *(G. David Schine)*, Joe Salter *(Peter)*, Frederic Forrest *(Dashiell Hammett)*, Lee Grant *(Dora Cohn)*.
Genre: Drama—An HBO made-for-cable TV movie based on the 1988 Nicholas von Hoffman book of the same title.
Plot: Like *Citizen Kane*, *Citizen Cohn* is told in a serious of deathbed flashbacks. The film begins and ends with James Woods, who plays the unrepentant Cohn dying from AIDS in 1986. In a drug-induced dementia he's visited by ghosts of his past.

A ruthless, ambitious, scheming, paranoid, self-centered momma's boy, Cohn was notorious for persecuting Jews and crucifying homosexuals. He was both, and presumably acted out his bigotry and self-hate as a cover.

Gaining fame in the early 1950s as chief counsel to anti-Communist crusader Sen. Joseph McCarthy (Baker), he became a national household name.

When he later tries to intimidate the Army in order to obtain special privileges for his lover, G. David Schine (Nordling), he and McCarthy are humiliated during a public hearing. Later, Cohn's arrogant behavior threatens to expose J. Edgar Hoover (Hingle) and his lover as well. Cohn's egomaniacal personality would eventually destroy his career and his life, as he had destroyed the lives of so many who knew him.

A well-known homosexual with a series of lovers, Cohn continued to deny his sexuality even as he lay dying of AIDS with his lover Peter (Salter) looking after him.

While Woods' performance is inspired and engrossing, the film itself is a one-sided vilification of its protagonist that offers little insight into what attracted so many people to this monster of a man—as he is portrayed here.

Quotes:
"I hope you don't have any skeletons in your closet because boy do they have a way of coming out."
—*Woods*

"Everybody starts out straight. I've never heard of anyone being born homosexual, have you?"
—*Woods*

"Michelangelo was a great artist ... and yet, he was a pervert."

—*Woods*

"Why do I feel like Caligula?"

"Because I treat you like an emperor."

    —*Woods and Salter*

MPAA Rating: R—Contains brief male nudity from behind and profanity.

Awards: Woods received nominations for a Golden Globe and an Emmy.

Trivia: Director Frank Pierson received a 1975 Oscar for writing *Dog Day Afternoon*, another film with a central gay character.

Companion Films: See "AIDS," "Biographies" and "Closet Cases" in the "Companion Films Index."

COMMON THREADS: STORIES FROM THE QUILT ★★★★

(1989)

US/Color/79 minutes

Director and Editor: Robert Epstein and Jeffrey Friedman

Narrator: Dustin Hoffman

Genre: Documentary—Chronicles the AIDS epidemic in America, from the first reported case in 1981 to 1989 when over 100,000 people had been infected. The filmmakers personalize this tragedy in a moving, dramatic film.

Plot: Focusing on a handful of early victims of the disease, lovers, friends and family tell their stories.

David was a young hemophiliac. Rob was a black drug addict. Jeffrey was the lover of writer and gay activist Vito Russo. Tom was a world-class, Olympic medalist. David was an entertainer. These five individuals symbolize the human side of this tragedy and provide a moving tribute to all the men, women and children who have contracted the deadly virus.

Juxtaposed throughout are television news clips, newspaper and magazine headlines and sound bites of Americans as they respond to the disease. "There is no reason for panic among the general public," claimed one newscaster. It was a common belief in the early 1980s, and to some extent even today, that this was a disease that the general, straight community could ignore without any repercussions. Gay bashing increased. President Reagan refused even to mention the disease and the Moral Majority took advantage of an opportunity to spread hate and fear across America.

As a result, the gay community came together—first, to march in the streets, and demand attention and money to battle the disease and second, to create a memorial. In 1987, San Francisco gay activist Cleve Jones conceived of what would become the *Names Project* AIDS memorial quilt, in response to the death of his friend Marvin Feldman.

While difficult to watch, this is a moving portrait of a decade, a disease and thousands of courageous Americans.

Quotes:

"Until the Reagan administration realizes that the government's responsibility is saving lives and not saving souls, we will continue to see the virus spread through our society."

    —*Shram*

MPAA Rating: Not rated.

Awards: Winner of the 1989 Academy Award for *Best Documentary*.

Companion Films: For other films of interest by director Epstein see *The Times Of Harvey Milk* (1985).

Also see "AIDS" in the "Companion Films Index."

Also see "Doomed Lovers" and "Murderers" in the "Companion Films Index."

COMPULSION ★★★
(1959)
US/B&W/103 minutes
Director: Richard Fleischer
Cast: Orson Welles, Dean Stockwell, Bradford Dillman, Diane Varsi, E.G. Marshall, Martin Milner.
Genre: Drama—Based on the Meyer Levin novel which was a case study of the infamous 1924 Leopold-Loeb murder case in Chicago.
Plot: In this 1950s version, Bradford Dillman plays Artie Judd, a neurotically self-centered and arrogant young man from a wealthy family. Dean Stockwell plays Judd Steiner, a vulnerable, passive young man who reluctantly submits to his more forceful lover. Their homosexual relationship is as apparent as it can be for a film of its time.

To prove his superiority to others, Artie plots the murder of a local boy for the thrill of it. Judd feels helpless to stop it and becomes an accomplice. When the two young men are brought to trial they are represented by Orson Welles. In real life, Leopold and Loeb were represented by Clarence Darrow. Welles argues against capital punishment in the case. Performances all around are winning.
MPAA Rating: Not rated.
Awards: The Cannes Film Festival award for *Best Actor* was awarded that year jointly to Welles, Dillman and Stockwell.
Companion Films: See *Rope* (1948) and *Swoon* (1992)—both dramatize the real-life story in completely different ways.

CONFORMIST, THE ★★★
(1970)
Italy/Color/108 minutes
Director: Bernardo Bertolucci
Cast: Jean-Louis Trintignant, Stefania Sandrelli, Dominique Sanda.
Genre: Drama—Dubbed in English.
Plot: The film is set in Italy and Paris in 1938 before the fall of Mussolini. "Cowards, homosexuals and Jews—they're all the same thing. If it were up to me I'd stand them all up against the wall," complains an angry fascist in one scene. This was the prevailing attitude of the time. Come to think of it, things haven't changed all that much in many corners of the world.

Having a strong survival instinct, and a bit of a cowardly streak, Marcello Clerici, the lead character, played by Jean-Louis Trintignant, becomes a fascist to fit in and hide his homosexuality. Molested at the age of 13 by an older man (seen in flashback), Marcello is left traumatized for life by the incident—presumably because he enjoyed it. However, in the end, when the fascist regime tumbles, Marcello is left with little more than an identity crisis.
MPAA Rating: PG
Companion Films: See "Fascists and Nazis" in the "Companion Films Index."

CONSENTING ADULT ★★★★
(1985)
US/Color/100 minutes
Director: Gilbert Cates

They were the perfect family.
Happy. Loving. Together.

But sometimes the truth
can tear a family apart.

For the Lynds, it began when
their only son told them:
"I am a homosexual."

MARLO THOMAS · MARTIN SHEEN
CONSENTING ADULT
Also starring BARRY TUBB

Teleplay by John McGreevey   Based on the novel by Laura Z. Hobson
Directed by Gilbert Cates

abc An ABC Theater Presentation 9:00 PM ⑦

An ad for the 1985 critically acclaimed ABC television movie *Consenting Adult.*

Cast: Barry Tubb *(Jeff)*, Marlo Thomas *(Tess)*, Martin Sheen *(Ken)*, Talia Balsam *(Margie)*, Ben Piazza *(Nate)*, Mathew Lawrence *(Stuart)*, John Terlesky *(Pete)*.

Genre: Drama—A made-for-television, melodramatic tear-jerker based on the best-selling novel by Laura Z. Hobson. At the time, this sensitive portrayal of a son's coming out and a family's coming apart, was received positively by the gay and nongay community alike. The film is just as timely today.

Plot: Barry Tubb plays Jeff, an all-American, boy-next-door college student who can't keep his secret locked inside any longer. When he confides to his mom, Tess (Marlo Thomas), that he is a homosexual, she insists that he go for therapy to be cured. When his father discovers the secret he disowns him.

Though Tess tries to understand and accept her son, in one scene she blurts out, "I can't even say that word. I choke on it," referring to the word "homosexual." When Jeff has had enough of therapy and accepts that he isn't going to change, he angrily replies, "I'm not sick; I don't have a disease," and, "You've got to let me be who I am." The film is filled not only with fine acting and a believable story, but many memorable lines. When Tess reveals to her best friend that, "Something's got him tied up in knots," her friend replies, "At this age 'something' is usually a girl."

To its credit, the film depicts a realistic—if a bit too squeaky-clean—family coming to terms with their own prejudice and accepting it in the end. Though melancholy, the film has a very happy ending—something of a rarity among gay-themed films.

MPAA Rating: Not rated—Strictly PG. The only sex is suggested and not seen. The only scene of physical intimacy is when Jeff's lover, Stuart, puts his arms around him.

Companion Films: Martin Sheen, who plays a homophobic father here, appeared in *That Certain Summer*, one of the first gay television dramas, in 1973. His character was also a gay man.

For films of interest with Barry Tubb, see *Valentino Returns* (1988), and *Warm Summer Rain* (1989) both featuring the actor in brief full-frontal nudity.

Also see "Coming Out" and "Men and Their Mothers" in the "Companion Films Index."

CONSEQUENCE, THE ★★★

(1977)
Germany/Color/95 minutes
Director: Wolfgang Petersen
Cast: Jurgen Prochnow *(Martin)*, Ernst Hannawald *(Thomas)*.
Genre: Drama—In German with English subtitles.
Plot: In this contemporary love story, two men attempt to share a life but are thwarted by gay and straight society at every turn.

Because the central characters of this love story, Martin (Prochnow) and Thomas (Hannawald), just happen to be gay, it's no surprise that they become victims of society's intolerance and that their love is doomed.

The fine acting and credible story raise this film above mere melodrama. Critics found much to praise when the film was released in the late 1970s.

Trivia: Petersen directed the highly acclaimed international success *Das Boot* in 1981;

Al Pacino cruises New York City parks for tricks in *Cruising* (1980).

Prochnow starred as the captain.
MPAA Rating: Not rated.
Companion Films: See "Murderers" in the "Companion Films Index."

CRUISING ★★
(1980)
US/Color/106 minutes
Director: William Friedkin
Cast: Al Pacino, Paul Sorvino, Karen Allen, Richard Cox, Don Scardino.

Genre: Thriller—When this film premiered it was met with vocal opposition, protests and rioting by the gay community for its negative depiction of the gay community and of its central gay character who happens to be a psychopathic killer. In 10 long years Friedkin seems to have become less-enlightened than he was when he directed the equally controversial *The Boys In The Band,* in 1970.
Plot: In the opening scene a severed arm is found floating in New York Harbor. This sets the scene for this story, based on an actual series

of brutal and grisly murders that took place in New York City between 1962 and 1979.

Al Pacino plays Steve, a young cop who accepts a dangerous assignment to go undercover in the sadomasochistic gay underground of New York City, to capture a killer. The killer's past victims have all been dark-haired, dark-eyed, gay men that match Steve's description. All have been stabbed to death. Steve accepts the assignment ostensibly to advance in his job.

Setting himself up as bait, he lives in the gay community, frequents the S&M bars and dresses accordingly. Before long, he begins to lose himself in his role, and the film begins to look at the psychological effects and toll this double life is having on him. As he begins to fit into the community, a lead eventually helps him target the killer. After the killer is caught, however, another gay man is murdered, and we're left with the impression that a new killer has been born—in Steve.

MPAA Rating: R—For graphic violence and strong sexuality. Contains a number of nude scenes from behind, as well as gay and straight sexual scenes. This is an uneven film that most critics panned. It does, however, have its moments—if the viewer is able to get past the grisly setup.

Companion Films: See "Murderers," "S&M" and "Sissies" in the "Companion Films Index."

CRYING GAME, THE ★★★★

(1992)
UK/Color/112 minutes
Director: Neil Jordan
Cast: Stephen Rea *(Fergus)*, Jaye Davidson *(Dil)*, Forest Whitaker *(Jody)*, Miranda Richardson *(Jude)*, Adrian Dunbar *(Maguire)*, Breffini McKenna *(Tinker)*, Joe Savino *(Eddie)*, Birdie Sweeney *(Tommy)*.

Genre: Thriller—Critically acclaimed as one of the best films of 1992, Neil Jordan's "shocking" romantic-thriller is also surprisingly funny, touching and refreshingly unpredictable. There was never more truth in advertising than in the film's tag line that read, "Nothing is what it seems to be."

Plot: The rules of this intricate game of love and romance are made up and periodically changed along the way. As soon as you come to know the characters in this film, their disguises are stripped away and their "true natures" are revealed—often in tearful and touching moments.

When Percy Sledge sings "When a Man Loves a Woman" as the credits open, we don't realize it but the lyrics offer us our first clues to what will follow. It isn't until the end of the film when we listen to Tammy Wynette's theme song "Stand by Your Man," however, that it becomes apparent that even the songs aren't what they seem to be in this delightfully twisted film.

On the surface, the story appears to be a political thriller. Rea plays Fergus, an IRA terrorist who holds an English soldier named Jody (Whitaker) hostage. A kind, caring man, Fergus makes the mistake of becoming friends with his captive.

In one very humorous and powerful scene, Jody, with hands bound behind him requests permission to relieve himself. Unable to unzip his own pants, he persuades Fergus to assist him in pulling his penis out of his pants. Realizing he has no choice he manages the task—then, in a humorous moment he realizes he must put it back in when Jody has finished his business.

Jody insists, "it's just a piece of meat." The two men are forever bonded after this exchange. Later in the movie this scene takes on even greater significance in retrospect.

A short time later, Fergus is on the lam from English authorities following Jody's death. Arriving in London he makes good on his promise to Jody to look up his beautiful girlfriend and explain what had happened.

Jody's girlfriend Dil (Davidson) works in a beauty salon by day and sings in a club called the "Metro" at night. The night they meet, she sings "The Crying Game," hence the film's title. Quite unexpectedly, they fall in love. Fergus keeps it a secret that he knew Jody and was responsible for his death. Dil has an even bigger secret.

When the unsuspecting Fergus discovers her secret, he isn't half as shocked as the audience was when the film played to suburban audiences full of straight men who didn't know whether to laugh or cry—most just gasped audibly. Fergus, however, spends the next few minutes vomiting. Readers who haven't seen the film may want to stop reading at this point, or forever spoil the surprise.

Until this point Dil has been a strong, confident woman. As a rejected transvestite, however, Dil becomes a desperately tragic, whimpering, alcoholic cliché. In spite of his love for Dil, Fergus rejects him sexually. Yet out of love or perhaps guilt, he continues to protect Dil and eventually even goes to jail for him.

In the end, this is a story about the powerful forces of human nature and about the difficulties and sometimes impossibility of love between men and women or men and men.

Quotes:
"Even when you were throwing up I knew you cared."

—Davidson

MPAA Rating: Not rated—Contains brief full-frontal male nudity.

Trivia: Twenty-five-year-old Jaye Davidson was was an out-of-work fashion design assistant with no previous acting experience when he was discovered by the director at a party.

Awards:

The Crying Game appeared on nearly every critic's list of Top-10 films of 1992. In addition, the National Board of Review's D.W. Griffith awards created an entirely new category, the *Auspicious Debut Award*, which went to Jaye Davidson.

By the time Academy-Award nominations were announced on February 17, 1993, keeping *The Crying Game*'s surprise a secret had become something of a national obsession. Even more of a surprise were the six nominations it received. They included *Best Picture, Best Actor* (Stephen Rea), *Best Supporting Actor* (Jaye Davidson), *Best Director* (Neil Jordan), *Best Original Screenplay* (Neil Jordan) and *Best Film Editing*. Jordan won the Oscar for *Best Original Screenplay*.

Companion Films:

In *I Want What I Want*, Anne Heywood plays a transvestite with a male suitor who also discovers her "little" secret. Like Fergus, the man reacts with violence and rage.

Also see "Drag Queens" in the "Companion Films Index."

"S&M" in the "Companion Films Index."

DADDY AND THE MUSCLE ACADEMY
★★★
(1992)
Finland/Color/60 minutes
Director: Ilppo Pohjola
Cast: Tom of Finland, Bob Mizer, Nayland Blake, Durk Dehner, Etienne, Isaac Julien.
Genre: Documentary—A tribute to the life and work of gay icon and artist Tom of Finland. In Finnish and English with subtitles
Plot: The film is a series of interviews with illustrator Touko Laaksonen, better known as Tom of Finland, just before his death in 1991 at age 71. In addition there are testimonies by fans and admirers including British director Isaac Julien (*Young Soul Rebels*), and images of the work itself.

Originally influenced by American body building magazines, the young artist submitted his first male erotic images to *Physique Pictorial* in 1957 under the assumed name of Tom. The magazine's editor Bob Mizer is credited with giving the artist the name Tom of Finland. Exaggerated, macho, muscle-bound men in leather in homosexual settings and situations make up the body of work that is explored explicitly and in depth in this fascinating and often-humorous homage.
MPAA Rating: Not rated—Contains full-frontal male nudity both actual and illustrated.
Companion Films: See "Biographies" and

DAMNED, THE ★★
(1969)
Italy-Germany/Color/150 minutes
Director: Luchino Visconti
Cast: Dirk Bogarde *(Friederich)*, Ingrid Thulin *(Sophie)*, Helmut Griem *(Aschenbach)*, Helmut Berger *(Martin)*, Charlotte Rampling *(Elizabeth)*, Umberto Orsini *(Herbert)*, Rene Kolderoni *(Konstantine)*.
Genre: Drama—Helmut Berger made his film debut in this very successful box-office hit. This is a darkly lit film about a dark subject. In Italian with English subtitles.
Plot: Helmut Berger stars as Martin, the grandson of a wealthy and powerful industrialist whose business is being taken over by the Nazi Party.

Martin is an immature, prissy, amoral young man obsessed with his mother (Thulin). He's in love with her; he in fact, desires her sexually. At the same time, he hates her for rejecting him as a child. In the end, he rapes her and gratifies both emotions. She has similar feelings for him and doesn't put up much of a fight.

In the beginning of the film, Martin, to shock his family, performs an impressive and memorable Marlene Dietrich number in drag. But Martin isn't the homosexual in the family. His scheming uncle, Konstantine (Kolderoni), is the closet case who is eventually shot while in bed with a young man.

Konstantine, along with a boardinghouse full of young, gay storm troopers, is murdered by Friederich (Bogarde) and Aschenbach (Griem) in order to take control of the family business. The massacre is especially gruesome after following a long night of gay revelry at the pub downstairs where most of the men spent the evening dancing and singing in drag.

This is a bleak film about the power of evil. The Von Essenbeck family's willingness to betray and murder their own members to gain power and prestige serves as a metaphor for the Nazi's rise to power and eventual self-destruction.

MPAA Rating: R—Contains various scenes of male nudity from behind as well as scenes of incest and violence.

Companion Films: See "Drag Queens" and "Fascists and Nazis" in the "Companion Films Index."

DARLING ★★

(1965)

UK/B&W/122 minutes

Director: John Schlesinger

Cast: Julie Christie (Diana), Dirk Bogarde (Robert), Roland Curram (Malcolm), Laurence Harvey (Miles), Jose Luis De Vilallonga (The prince).

Genre: Drama—About a restless young fashion model looking for love in all the wrong places.

Plot: This was, no doubt, a hip and swinging film in the mid-sixties. Sprinkled throughout the film are gay characters and high-society fringe types that were probably quite risqué and shocking. Three decades later, however, they are simply quaint.

Notable, however, is Malcolm (Curram), a gay photographer whom Diana (Christie) befriends halfway through the film. He seems to be the only happy chap in the film and is certainly the most well-adjusted. He joins Diana on a holiday in Italy. She is there to get away from men; he's there to find one.

As he flirts with the waiter at the local cafe she makes him agree that, "We are not complicating our holiday with any sex-capades." Later that night, however, he slips off with the same waiter. But, as she has done with all the other men in her life, she soon moves on to the next. She continues her unhappy search for love, while Malcolm presumably rides off into the sunset with one of the many hunky young men he has picked up on the streets of this resort.

The performances are the film's strength.

Quotes:

"How lucky it is you're a man after your own heart."

—*Party guest*

"Have you ever been in love?"

"Yes, for as long as I can remember—with myself."

—*Harvey and Christie*

"Your idea of fidelity is not having more than one man in the bed at the same time."

—*Bogarde*

MPAA Rating: PG

Awards: Julie Christie won the *Best Actress* Academy Award for her performance. The film received nominations for *Best Picture, Best Director, Best Story and Screenplay (Written directly for the screen)* and *Best Costume Design* (B&W).

Companion Films: See "Neighbors, Roommates and Best Friends" in the "Companion Films Index."

DEAR BOYS ★★★

(Lieve Jongens)

(1980)

Holland/Color/90 minutes
Director: Paul de Lussanet
Cast: Hugo Netsers *(Wolf)*, Hans Dagelet *(Muskrat)*, Bill Van Dijk *(Tiger)*, Albert Mol *(Albert)*, Jan Hopman *(Wolfie Jr./Fonsje)*, Hans Cornelissen *(Wolfgang Jr.)*, Pleuni Touw *(Corrine)*.
Genre: Drama—Adapted from a novel by Gerard Reve. In Dutch with English subtitles.
Plot: Hugo Netsers plays Wolf, a middle-aged gay man, who is self-absorbed and obsessed with sexual fantasies—and with younger men. An alcoholic and a writer, Wolf is unable to write, spending all of his time making up erotic stories, which he reads to his young men during sex to keep them excited.

The film opens and closes with Wolf masturbating to his erotic fantasies. In between, Wolf and his younger lover of many years, Tiger (Van Dijk), take in Muskrat (Dagelet), a gay friend of Tiger's from school. Muskrat has been living with Albert (Mol) a wealthy but insecure older man. While the two young men share their natural affections they are pursued by the two lecherous older men. Eventually the money and security are not enough to hold either of the young men—when all they really wanted, it seems, was love and a real relationship.

Sarcastic and often humorous, this portrait of desperate, aging men is beautifully photographed, giving it the look of a much bigger production. A memorable score and fine performances make this somewhat dreary tale easy to watch.
Quotes:
"I am a servant of beauty."
—Netsers
MPAA Rating: Not rated—Contains numerous scenes of full-frontal male nudity of most of the cast members from the beginning of the film to the end. The film borders on soft porn and includes numerous gay sex scenes and gay kissing scenes.
Companion Films: See "Men and Boys" and "Unhappy Homosexuals" in the "Companion Films Index."

DEATH IN VENICE ★★
(1971)
US/Color/130 minutes
Director: Luchino Visconti
Cast: Dirk Bogarde *(Aschenbach)*, Bjorn Andresen *(Tadzio)*, Marisa Berenson *(Mrs. Aschenbach)*, Silvana Mangano *(The mother)*, Sergio Garafanolo *(Jaschiu)*, Romolo Valli *(Hotel manager)*.
Genre: Drama—Based on the classic novel by Thomas Mann.
Plot: Visually stunning, this romantic tale of platonic, unrequited homosexual love, is set in Venice, Italy during the cholera epidemic years.

Bogarde plays Gustav von Aschenbach, a composer on holiday who becomes obsessed with a beautiful young boy staying with his family at the same hotel. The boy, Tadzio (Andresen), is aware of the man's attentions and encourages him with his innocent, but flirtatious behavior.

A repressed man in many ways, Aschenbach is unable to act on his feelings and simply spends his days watching the boy from afar. All the while his present situation is causing him to have flashbacks of an unfulfilled, repressed life. In the final scene he sits on the beach admiring his object of desire. Finally deciding to act on

Bjorn Andresen at the beach with a young friend (Sergio Garafanolo) in *Death In Venice* (1971).

Bjorn Andresen plays the object of Dirk Bogarde's desire in *Death In Venice* (1971).

his feelings he is too late—his heart fails him, and he dies unfulfilled.

MPAA Rating: PG—Because of its subject matter, at the time of the film's release it was rated R.

Awards: Received an Academy-Award nomination for *Best Costume Design*.

Trivia: Critic Roger Ebert objected to Visconti's literal interpretation of the book, stating, "His feelings toward the boy are terribly complicated, and to interpret them as a simple homosexual attraction is vulgar and simplistic."

Companion Films: See "Men and Boys" and "Only the Lonely" in the "Companion Films Index."

DEATHTRAP ★★★★

(1982)
US/Color/116 minutes
Director: Sidney Lumet

Cast: Michael Caine *(Sidney Bruhl)*, Christopher Reeve *(Clifford Anderson)*, Dyan Cannon *(Myra)*, Irene Worth *(Helga Ten Dorp)*, Henry Jones.

Genre: Comedy—Based on the long running 1978 Broadway play by Ira Levin, the film is witty, and full of plot twists and fine performances.

Plot: This is a comedy-mystery about a comedy-mystery. The plot begins with Sidney (Caine), a previously successful playwright who has just had another in a series of flops. He is a man who would "kill to have another hit play."

The play he would kill for is "Deathtrap," written by Clifford (Reeve), a former student—only the play isn't just a play, and his student isn't just a former student.

Caine and Reeve are actually sociopathic gay lovers who concoct an elaborate plan to murder Caine's wife Myra (Cannon). The plan is to inherit her home and her fortune, and to live together. Once the deed is done, however, these two deceitful men turn on one another, and in the end their deceit is their own undoing.

Quotes:

"Oh, is that what he was doing. I thought he was finally coming out of the closet."

—*Caine*

"Oh well, nothing recedes like success."

—*Caine*

"I'll tell you how good it is. Even a gifted director couldn't hurt it."

—*Caine*

MPAA Rating: PG—Of the many surprises in this film, the biggest is when Caine and Reeve share a very convincing kiss on the lips.

Companion Films: See "Closet Cases" and "Murderers" in the "Companion Films Index."

DETECTIVE, THE ★★★

(1968)
US/Color/114 minutes
Director: Gordon Douglas

Cast: Frank Sinatra, Lee Remick, Ralph Meeker, Jacqueline Bisset, Jack Klugman, Robert Duvall, William Windom, Horace McMahon, Tony Musante, James Inman.

Genre: Thriller

Plot: Set in New York City, Frank Sinatra plays a detective assigned to solve a brutal murder. James Inman plays a wealthy gay man who is mutilated and murdered by William Windom, who plays a repressed and homophobic homosexual.

Sinatra, more interested in solving the case and making the department look good than in finding the true killer, obtains a confession from an innocent gay man played by Tony Musante.

Windom later commits suicide, leaving a note confessing to the murder. When Sinatra learns that he has sent an innocent man to the electric chair, he's remorseful but cooperates in a coverup by the department to avoid exposing their negligence.

This is a surprisingly graphic and realistic look at the sexual underground of the time by a mainstream film. *Variety* claimed, "Although extremely well-cast, and fleshed out with some on-target dialog, Abby Mann's script is strictly potboiler material."

Quotes:

"I was more ashamed of being a homosexual than a murderer."

—*Windom*

MPAA Rating: Not rated.

Companion Films: See "Closet Cases" and "Murderers" in the "Companion Films Index."

DIAMONDS ARE FOREVER ★★★

(1971)

US/Color/119 minutes

Director: Guy Hamilton

Cast: Sean Connery *(James Bond)*, Jill St. John *(Tiffany Case)*, Charles Gray *(Blofeld)*, Putter Smith *(Mr. Kidd)*, Bruce Glover *(Mr. Wint)*, Bruce Cabot *(Saxby)*, Lana Wood *(Plenty O' Toole)*.

Genre: Action

Plot: Released the same year as *The Boys In The Band*, this ultra-mainstream film's two gay characters on the surface offer quite a contrast to their stereotypical counterparts in the former film.

Putter Smith and Bruce Glover play your average, nerdy diamond thieves. So nonflamboyant are these lovers that not-so-subtle clues to their true identity are dropped throughout the film just to make certain the viewer is set up for the final climax, so to speak.

In the end, however, as so often is the case in Hollywood movies, one stereotype has simply been replaced with another. The two gay characters are turned into cold, calculating, murderers who get theirs in the end—literally. When one of the men's sweet-smelling cologne gives him away as a "tart," 007 does what any hero would do—sets one of the men on fire and plants a bomb between the other's legs.

Even Blofeld, the film's evil mastermind and Bond's arch-nemesis, is forced to don female drag to escape. But he too meets a grisly demise at the hands of our squeaky-clean, skirt chasing, hero.

There's no escaping the not-so-subtle symbolism here—homosexuals and vicious criminals are one and the same—at least in this otherwise-entertaining action pic.

Quotes:

"I must say, Miss Kay seems quite attractive —for a lady."

—*Smith*

"Hi, I'm Plenty."

"But of course you are."

"Plenty O' Toole."

"Named after your father perhaps?"

—*Wood and Connery*

"If we destroy Kansas, the world may not hear about it for years."

—*Gray*

"One of us smells like a tart's handkerchief."

—*Connery*

"I'm afraid you've caught me with more than my hands up."

—*Connery*

"This farcical show of force was only to be expected—the great powers flexing their muscles like so many impotent beach boys."

—*Gray*

MPAA Rating: PG

Companion Films: See "Murderers" and "Sissies" in the "Companion Films Index."

DIFFERENT STORY, A ★★★

(1979)

US/Color/107 minutes

Director: Paul Aaron

Cast: Perry King *(Albert)*, Meg Foster *(Stella)*, Peter Donat *(Sills)*, Valerie Curtin *(Phyllis)*, Glenn Barry *(Ned)*, Doug Higgins *(Roger)*, Lisa James *(Chris)*, Stephen Nichols *(Man at baths)*.

Genre: Drama—Critics loved this comedy-drama about a gay man and a lesbian who fall in love (and presumably grow up and out of their bisexuality) and get married.

Plot: Perry King plays Albert, a gay man who makes his living hopping from one man's bed to another. He's also an illegal immigrant in this country. When his latest sugar daddy, Sills (Donat), throws him out, he hooks up with a free-spirited lesbian who lets him stay in her home.

Their first night together she probes him with questions. Anticipating her three questions he begins, "Alright, yes I have, several, and not particularly." When she looks puzzled, he continues, "Have you ever been with a woman? How many? And did you like it?" This is meant, presumably, to establish that he is bisexual.

Albert does the cooking, the cleaning, the sewing, and before long, a night on the couch has turned into a permanent home. When the nasty homosexual, Sills, decides he wants Albert back he finds he is too late. So of course, he turns him in to the immigration authorities. But before Albert can hit the road, Stella proposes—after all, it's hard to find good domestic help. One thing predictably leads to another and before long, the two have developed sexual amnesia and fallen in love. They even have a baby together.

Albert has a complete change of personality and even lands a real job as a clothing designer. As his career takes off, he stays away from home more often. Suspecting he has slipped and gone back to his old ways, Stella investigates. The big surprise is that he's not with another man, but another woman.

In one of the film's final scenes, Albert begs Stella to forgive him for his affair saying, "I guess that for months I've been trying to prove something. I've been trying to be somebody I'm not." This line could sum up, for many, the entire film. Nevertheless, this light-hearted film is enjoyable and the performances are appealingly fresh.

Quotes:

"My Swedish meatballs are all dried up and my beans are shriveled."

—*King*

"So, what are you going to do when you grow up?"

—*Foster*

"I played the bride, now I get to play the groom."

—*King*

"Who taught you to sew like this?"

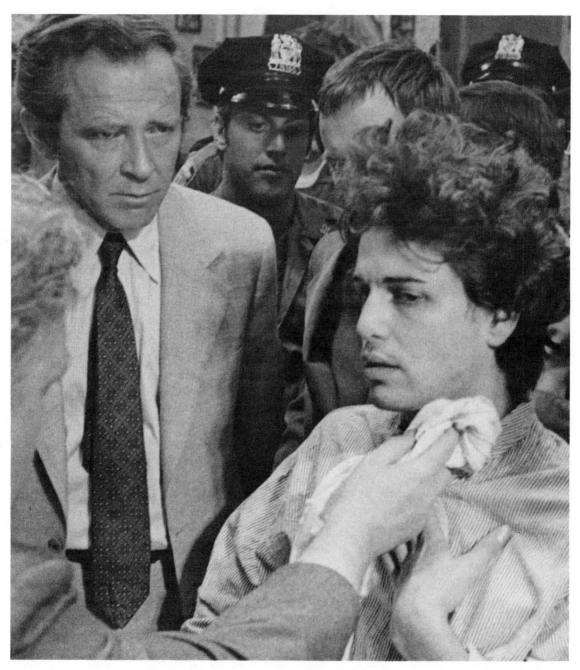

Chris Sarandon plays Al Pacino's mentally unstable gay lover, in Sidney Lumet's *Dog Day Afternoon* (1975)

"My father."

—*Foster and King*

"Can I see your closet?"

—*King*

"You and Ned are really becoming a Batman and Robin."

—*Foster*

MPAA Rating: PG—King appears in one extended scene nude from behind.

Companion Films: See *Green Card* 1990 with Gerard Depardieu and Andie McDowell. While the film does not contain a gay theme, the storylines are nearly identical with one exception.

Also see "Bisexuals" in the "Companion Films Index."

DOG DAY AFTERNOON ★★★★

(1975)

US/Color/125 minutes

Director: Sidney Lumet

Cast: Al Pacino *(Sonny)*, Charles Durning *(Moretti)*, James Broderick *(Sheldon, an FBI man)*, John Cazale *(Sal)*, Chris Sarandon *(Leon)*, Judith Malina *(Sonny's mother)*.

Genre: Drama—Based on an actual incident that occurred August 22, 1972, in New York.

Plot: Pacino stars as Sonny, a very confused, mentally unstable bisexual who attempts to rob a bank for the money to pay for his homosexual lover's sex-change operation. His lover, Leon, is played by newcomer Chris Sarandon. He too is emotionally unstable, and at the time of the robbery is in Bellevue hospital under psychiatric treatment.

From the beginning, Sonny and his mentally deficient partner-in-crime, Sal (Cazale), are in over their heads. The robbery attempt is such a disaster that it becomes humorous. Before long the police arrive, the neighborhood crowds arrive and so does the media—en masse. It seems that the only one who can't make it is Sonny's distraught and emotionally unstable wife, who can't get a baby-sitter.

Sonny becomes a media celebrity. When the media learn the reason for the robbery the scene becomes even more of a circus. Even the gay community shows up to chant their support with, "Out of the closet and into the street." For one very long day, the reluctant robbers hold the bank president and tellers hostage, while they wait for their demands to be met. One of the hostages is Carol Kane, in a small but humorous role.

In the end, the humor turns to desperation and, ultimately, to tragedy, when the FBI and the police get the upper hand.

Quotes:

"His mother and father together are like a bad train wreck."

—*Sarandon*

"Your body's the temple of the Lord."

—*Cazale*

"Forget about it, it's just a freak show to them anyway."

—*Pacino*

"Well, I'm a Christian, and my ears are not garbage cans."

—*A hostage*

MPAA Rating: R—For profanity.

Awards: Earned six Academy Award nominations including *Best Picture, Best Director, Best Actor* (Pacino) and *Best Supporting Actor* (Sarandon). Frank Pierson won an Oscar for *Best Screenplay*.

Companion films: See "Doomed Lovers" in the "Companion Films Index."

DONA HERLINDA AND HER SON ★★

(1986)

Spain/Color/90 minutes

Director: Jaime Humberto Hermosillo

Cast: Guadalupe Del Toro, Marco Antonio Trevino, Arturo Meza, Leticia Lupercia, Guierrmo Alba.

Genre: Comedy—Having the look of a low-budget home movie, the film is not just humorous, it's often laughable. This is mostly because it looks and sounds as if it were made in the 1960s, rather than the late '80s.

Plot: The story is a bit on the quirky side—to say the least. Dona Herlinda's son Rodolfo is a doctor who still lives at home with his mother. Rodolfo's young gay lover Ramon is a music student. Dona invites the young man to move into her home and share her son's bed. At the same time she's trying to set her son up with a potential wife.

To make his mother happy Rodolfo marries a woman, who also moves into the house. This, however, doesn't make Ramon too happy. But he manages to get used to the idea, by the time Rodolfo's new wife gets pregnant and has a baby. The fivesome then live together happily ever after.

MPAA Rating: Not rated—Contains brief male frontal nudity and gay kissing scenes.

Companion Films: See "Men and Boys" and "Men and Their Mothers" in the "Companion Films Index."

DRESSER, THE ★★★★

(1984)

US/Color/118 minutes

Director: Peter Yates

Cast: Albert Finney *(Sir)*, Tom Courtenay *(Norman)*, Edward Fox *(Oxenby)*, Eileen Adkins *(Madge)*, Zena Walker *(Her Ladyship)*.

Genre: Drama

Plot: Albert Finney plays an egotistical, psychologically unstable actor in this story about two men and their mutual dependency upon one another. Tom Courtenay *(Loneliness Of The Long Distance Runner)* plays Norman, a flamboyant, prissy, alcoholic "pansy" who's confidant, nursemaid, and dresser to Finney.

While Norman is secretly in love with his employer, he also has a great deal of resentment towards him. Theirs is a classic love-hate relationship.

In the end, when an exhausted Finney dies, Courtenay becomes emotionally distraught and cries out to Finney's wife, "You think you loved him. What about me?"

Quotes:

"I don't want to go on, night after night, painting my face."

—*Finney*

"Who was that?"

"Just a minion, minioning."

—*Finney and Courtenay*

"You'll have to find another canoe to paddle—ours has holes."

—*Courtenay*

MPAA Rating: PG

Awards:

Received Academy Award nominations for *Best Picture, Best Actor* (Finney and Courtenay), *Best Director* and *Best Screenplay.*

Companion Films:

See "Closet Cases" and "Unhappy Homosexuals" in the "Companion Films Index."

DRIFTING ★

(1983)

Israel/Color/80 minutes

Director: Amos Guttman

Cast: Amos Guttman, Jonathan Sagalle, Blanka Metzner, Ben Levine, Boaz Turjeman.

Genre: Drama—A very low-budget, independent first feature by the late Israeli filmmaker Amos Guttman. English subtitles are annoyingly difficult to read.

Plot: Guttman plays Robi, a bored, frustrated and self-destructive young man desperate to make a film about his sex life and personal struggles. In many ways the film is autobiographical.

Robi lives with his grandmother who's ashamed of him. She calls him a pederast. His father, on the other hand, believes that when he meets the right girl, he'll make the family proud. His mother has simply abandoned him. The point of the story seems to be that contrary to popular belief, not all post-*Boys In The Band* homosexuals are *gay*.

In the end, the film is little more than 80 minutes of therapy for an attractive but bored and unhappy filmmaker and his equally attractive but bored and unhappy friends and family.

MPAA Rating:

Not rated—Contains full-frontal male and female nudity.

Companion Films:

See "Unhappy Homosexuals" in the "Companion Films Index."

EARLY FROST, AN ★★★★★
(1985)
US/Color/100 minutes
Director: John Erman
Cast: Aidan Quinn *(Michael Pearson)*, John Glover *(Victor)*, Gena Rowlands *(Kate Pearson)*, Ben Gazzara *(Nick Pearson)*, D.W. Moffett *(Peter)*, Sylvia Sidney *(Bea)*.
Genre: Drama—A ground-breaking and award-winning, made-for-television AIDS drama.
Plot: While making an effort to be educational, *An Early Frost* is undeniably a powerful and touching film with fine performances.

Aidan Quinn plays Michael, a young man with a promising law career ahead of him. Still in the closet, Michael lives a secret life with his lover Peter (D.W. Moffett)—that is, until the day he discovers that he's HIV positive, and his life turns upside down.

Forced out of the closet, he must deal not only with his family's fears, anger and rejection, but his own, as well. Ultimately, not only do Michael and his family come to terms with his identity and his fate, but they become closer as a result of this tragedy.

Though melodramatic and predictable, this ground-breaking telefilm is both daring and memorable and is one of the few early films to deal with this double-headed-taboo topic.

Quotes:
"I don't talk about sex with them. They don't talk about sex with me."
"Who's talking about sex? I'm talking about us."
>—*Quinn and Moffett*

"I have something to tell you. I'm not a monk."
>—*Quinn*

"When are they going to have the great honor of finding out who you are, after you're dead?"
>—*Moffett*

"I'm not going to apologize for who I am because it's taken me too long to accept it."
>—*Quinn*

"Listen, I wasn't thrilled about it either, thinking I was one of them, but you know it is the only fraternity I ever rushed that let me in."
>—*Glover*

"I've been in and out of this hospital so many times I ought to belong to the Disease of the Month Club."
>—*Glover*

"They're going to be beautiful this year. I only hope an early frost doesn't come along and nip them in the bud."
>—*Sidney*

"My recipes—better burn them lest they fall into the wrong hands."
>—*Glover*

"To nurse Lincoln, a man's best friend, I bequeath Spike's collar. She'll probably look better in it than he ever did."
>—*Glover*

"I'm not the man you wanted me to be. Well, I don't give a damn what you think anymore because I'm a better man than you'll ever be."
>—*Quinn*

MPAA Rating: Not rated—Strictly PG.
Trivia: In a *TV Guide* article by Michael Leahy titled "Why This Young Hunk Risked Playing an AIDS Victim," Aidan Quinn admitted that

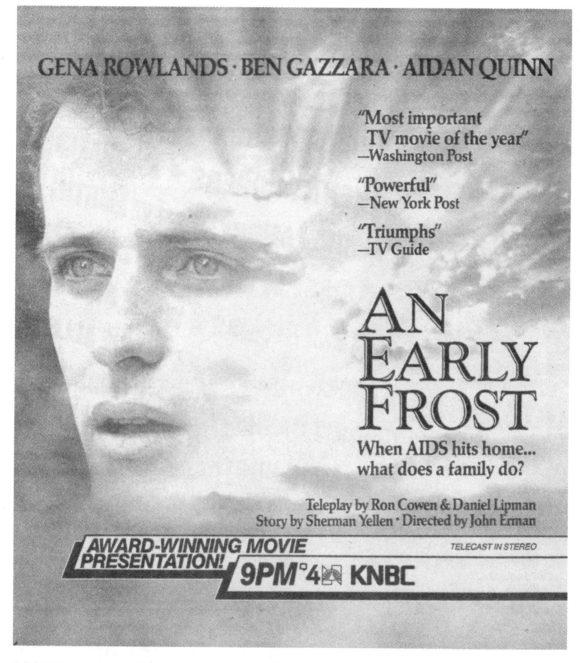

A *TV Guide* ad promoting the ground-breaking made-for-television AIDS drama, *An Early Frost* (1985), starring Aidan Quinn.

friends and advisers were not overly supportive of his decision. "Acquaintances couldn't understand why their gruff friend wanted to play someone so ... unmanly—an outcast with such a vile disease," read the article.

An Early Frost, which originally aired November 11, 1985, ranked number six as the most watched program that week. To say nothing of the fact that it put Quinn on the map and expanded the variety of roles he has since been offered.

Companion Films: See "AIDS" in the "Companion Films Index."

EDWARD II ★★★

(1992)
UK/Color/90 minutes
Director: Derek Jarman
Cast: Steven Waddington *(King Edward II)*, Andrew Tiernan *(Gaveston)*, Tilda Swinton *(Queen Isabella)*, Nigel Terry *(Mortimer)*, Kevin Collins *(Lightborn)*, Jerome Flynn *(Kent)*, John Lynch *(Spencer)*, Dudley Sutton *(Bishop of Winchester)*, Jody Graber *(Prince Edward)*, Annie Lennox *(Singer)*.
Genre: Drama—Believed to be the first openly gay play written in English, director Derek Jarman has adapted this provocative tale of a king who prefers his male lover to his queen and placed it in contemporary times. The story is based on Christopher Marlowe's 16th century Elizabethan tragedy.
Plot: This visually stylized and austere tale of a king brought down by his infatuation with a male lover revolves around a revolt against Edward II (Steven Waddington).

Falling in love with Gaveston (Tiernan), a male lover, the king rejects the affections of his queen (Swinton). Out of jealousy and revenge the queen enlists the aid of palace guard Mortimer (Terry) to help her overthrow the king. They first have Gaveston murdered then imprison the king.

The noblemen and women are equally outraged at the king's preferential treatment and love of Gaveston, a mere peasant, and join the revolt, which turns into a civil war. In the end, the queen orders that Edward be killed. His executioner, however, is gay and falls for him instead. In a humorous final climax, Edward's young son is shown in female drag prancing on top of a cage in which his mother and Mortimer are now imprisoned. Like father, like son?

Updating this tragic play, Jarman cleverly infuses the tale with modern-day gay bashing, attacks on the homophobic church and British press.
Quotes:
"Is it not queer that he is thus bewitched?"
  —Swinton
"Why should you love him when all the world hates him?"
"Because he loves me more than all the world."
  —Executioner and Waddington
MPAA Rating: R—Includes full-frontal male nudity, gay sex scenes, gay kissing scenes, lesbian kissing scenes and violence.
Companion Films: See "Biographies," "Bisexuals" and "Hustlers" in the "Companion Films Index."

EL DIPUTADO ★★★

(Confessions Of A Congressman)
(1979)

Spain/Color/110 minutes
Director: Eloy De La Iglesia
Cast: Jose Sacristan, Ma Luisa San Jose, Enrique Vivo, Queta Claver, Angel Pardo, J. Antonio Bardem.
Genre: Drama—The promotional trailer for this highly acclaimed political thriller stated, "his only crime—a passion more forbidden than his politics." Essentially *El Diputado* is the tragic coming-out story of a politician.

In Spanish with English subtitles.
Plot: "What a rod. Can I hold it," asks Juanito, a young male street hustler and the central char-

acter. The object he is admiring is another man's gun. The gun represents the cold, hard symbol of his deadly desires.

In this intense and tragic political drama set during the post-Franco regime in Spain, homosexuality is a greater crime than Marxism. Unfortunately for the film's protagonist, Roberto happens to be both. Even though he's a happily married man with a bright political career ahead of him, he finds that he can no longer repress his homosexual feelings and begins to seek out male sexual partners. Eventually he falls in love with Juanito, a young male hustler who is only

Edward II (Steven Waddington) kisses the hand of Gaveston (Andrew Tiernan), in Derek Jarman's *Edward II* (1992).

in it for the money.

Juanito, unbeknownst to Roberto, is also bait being used by the political opposition for the purpose of entrapment and blackmail. As their relationship develops over a period of months, the boy falls in love with the man and confesses his betrayal.

In the end, Roberto comes out to his wife and decides to come out to the public. He realizes that he has spent his entire career working to achieve a revolution that would allow everyone to be free to be themselves. He is no longer content living a secret, double life, but before he can come out the opposition puts an end to his relationship, his marriage and his career.

MPAA Rating: Not rated—Contains full-frontal male nudity and gay and straight sex scenes.

Companion Films: See "Blackmail," "Coming Out," "Fascists and Nazis," "Men and Boys" and "Murderers" in the "Companion Films Index."

ENTERTAINING MR. SLOANE ★★★

(1970)

UK/Color/122 minutes

Director: Douglas Hickox

Cast: Peter McEnery *(Mr. Sloane)*, Beryl Reid *(Kath)*, Harry Andrews *(Eddie)*, Alan Webb *(Dadda)*.

Genre: Comedy—This black comedy based on the popular play by Joe Orton has become a cult favorite over the years.

Plot: In this sendup of religion, family and English manners, Beryl Reid plays Kath, a middle-aged, man-hungry flirt on the prowl.

Visiting a local cemetery one afternoon, she picks up a handsome and homeless young stranger, Sloane (McEnery), and rents him one of the rooms in her home. It isn't long before they have seduced one another, and she becomes pregnant. He also manages to seduce her older brother Ed (Andrews), who's quite taken with the young man and offers him a job as his chauffeur.

The only member of the family not smitten with the young charmer is Dadda (Webb). Dadda recognizes him as the murderer of his former boss. Sloane eventually murders Dadda as well.

Following Dadda's death, the siblings fight over possession of Sloane. Each threatens to blackmail the other but decide instead to blackmail their lover. They decide to share Sloane and agree not to turn him into the police if he agrees to marry them both.

A bit tame by today's standards but still enjoyable.

Quotes:

"I was more familiar with Africa than I was with my own body, until I was 15."

—*Reid*

"I have some urgent knitting to do."

—*Reid*

"I'm not marrying a felon. Apart from everything else it would be bigamy."

—*McEnery*

MPAA Rating: Not rated—Strictly PG.

Companion Films: See "Bisexuals," "Hustlers" and "Murderers" in the "Companion Films Index."

ERNESTO ★★★★

(1983)

Italy/Color/95 minutes

Director: Salvatore Samperis
Cast: Martin Halm *(Ernesto)*, Michele Placido *(Stablehand)*, Virna Lisi *(Mother)*, Lara Wendel *(Emillio/Rachel)*.
Genre: Drama—A beautifully photographed-and-acted period piece about a precocious teenage boy who uses his angelic good looks and charm to manipulate others. In the end, however, the tables are turned as he is expected to grow up and be a man.
Plot: Martin Halm stars as Ernesto, a privileged but fatherless Jewish teenager who lives with his mother and wealthy uncle and aunt. An aspiring violinist, he is forced to work as an apprentice to a local merchant.

Seduced by one of the merchant's handsome day laborers (Placido), Ernesto has his first homosexual experience and enjoys it. When the laborer falls in love with the beautiful youth, Ernesto plays hard-to-get. When he suggests that he do to the laborer what the man has done to him sexually, the laborer refuses. He explains that it is natural for a man to have a young boy (before the boy matures and begins to date women) but not the other way around.

Shortly thereafter, Ernesto overhears his uncle discussing a recent scandal. A banker was caught having an affair with a young man and his reputation was ruined. The only thing left for the man to do was to kill himself, which he did. His uncle then explains to Ernesto that, "A man must prove himself," and suggests that Ernesto is no longer an adolescent and must take charge of his life. Having grown more confident, and more manipulative, Ernesto ends his affair, quits his job and confesses the affair to his mother. She is distraught but relieved in part that no one will find out. "Thank goodness you're not a girl," she says. He decides that it is time to

follow his dream, become the master of his own fate and make a living as a violinist.

That very evening he picks up a young boy from a prominent family at a violin recital. The 15-year-old Emillio (Wendel) is taken with the older boy of 17 and asks him to be his tutor. Before they have completed their first lesson they have their first kiss. It is at this point that Emillio's twin sister Rachel (also played by Wendel) walks in on them. Instead of being upset, she is jealous. To entertain Ernesto she suggests that they dress up in each other's clothes to demonstrate how impossible it is to tell them apart in drag.

Rachel does her best to seduce Ernesto and when Emillio discovers them together one night behind closed doors he becomes angered and lashes out at his sister, "Women ruin everything. You're a poor imitation of me!" Ernesto is still very much interested in Emillio, but before he knows what has happened, Rachel has manipulated him into an engagement party sanctioned by both families and friends. Unable to battle society's rigid pressures, Ernesto gives up his dream and his sexual preference, and goes along with the charade—or so it seems.

MPAA Rating: Not rated—Halm appears partially nude briefly from behind and in gay kissing and sex scenes.
Companion Films: See "Bisexuals," "Hustlers" and "Men and Boys" in the "Companion Films Index."

EUROPA, EUROPA ★★★★★
(1991)
France-Germany/Color/115 minutes
Genre: Drama—In German with subtitles.

ACADEMY AWARD NOMINEE
BEST SCREENPLAY
(BASED ON MATERIAL PREVIOUSLY PRODUCED OR PUBLISHED)
AGNIESZKA HOLLAND

EUROPA EUROPA
A TRUE STORY

To pass as one of Hitler's youth, a young Jew (Marco Hofschneider) must hide the fact that he's circumsized in *Europa, Europa* (1992).

Director: Agnieszka Holland
Cast: Marco Hofschneider *(Solomon "Solly" Perel)*, David Hofschneider *(David Perel)*, Klaus Kowatsch *(Schultz)*, Julie Delpy *(Leni)*, Hanna Labornaska *(Leni's mother)*, Hanns Zischler *(Capt. Von Lereneau)*.
Plot: Based on the true story of Solomon "Solly" Perel, a young Jewish boy forced to flee Germany, and his family in the 1930s as Hitler was coming into power.

To survive, Solly learns quickly to blend in, to lie and to betray his past. Able to speak both Russian and German fluently he becomes a master at fitting in and passing. It also helps that he is a beautiful young boy that all are attracted to. When he's adopted by a German unit in the fields, he's used as an interpreter. Befriended by one of the soldiers, the man later tries to fondle the boy while he is bathing. Terrified that the officer will discover that he is circumcised (only Jews were circumcised then), he flees. When the officer finally sees why Solly is putting up a fight he gives the boy his word he will not tell. After all, he has something to hide himself—his homosexuality. His circumcision becomes the one thing he cannot hide and a reminder, should he ever be able to forget, of his real identity. This is a moving and memorable tale.

MPAA Rating: R—For nudity, violence and adult theme. Marco Hofschneider is seen naked a number of times from behind, while bathing, and in full-frontal nudity during the chase scene and capture.

Awards: Winner of the National Board of Review Award for *Best Foreign Film*. Winner of the Golden Globe Award (Hollywood Foreign Press Association) for *Best Foreign Language Film* and the Los Angeles Film Critics Association Achievement *Best Music Award* went to Zbigniew Preisner for *Europa, Europa, The Double Life Of Veronique* and *At Play In The Fields Of The Lord.*

Companion Films: See "Fascists and Nazis" and "Men and Boys" in the "Companion Films Index."

EVERLASTING SECRET FAMILY, THE ★★

(1987)
Australia/Color/93 minutes
Director: Michael Thornhill
Cast: Arthur Dignam *(The senator)*, Mark Lee *(The youth)*, Heather Mitchell *(The senator's wife)*, John Meillon *(The judge)*, Dennis Miller *(Eric)*, Paul Goddard *(Son)*, Beth Child *(Pottery woman)*.
Genre: Drama
Plot: Part *Another Country*, part *El Diputado*, part *Psycho*, part *The Picture Of Dorian Gray* and part *Dona Herlinda And Her Son*, this otherwise well-made film, suffers from a terminal identity crisis.

Lacking a defined beginning or end, the film is difficult to follow, while the characters' motivations are never explained. In addition, the film revolves around a cryptic secret society of homosexuals.

The central character is a wealthy closeted senator who recruits a beautiful young schoolboy into *the family*. The two are lovers for a number of years until the senator decides to marry, for some reason. His former lover reluctantly becomes the baby-sitter to the senator's infant son.

Seeking revenge, the lover seduces the son, not knowing that this is what the senator and the secret society had in mind all along. There are numerous subplots which, like the central theme, go nowhere. In the end, the hope that keeps your interest—that all will be revealed—remains a mystery.

Quotes:

"We've all had our moment of glory and seen it pass."

—*Miller*

"At your age there is no you. You are what people expect you to be. You are personified youthfulness."

—*Dignam*

"Our son is well past puberty and he does not require a baby-sitter."

—*Mitchell*

MPAA Rating: Not rated—Contains male nudity from behind and gay sex.

Companion Films: See "Bisexuals" and "Closet Cases" in the "Companion Films Index."

FAME ★★★★
(1980)
US/Color/133 minutes
Director: Alan Parker
Cast: Paul McCrane *(Montgomery)*, Irene Cara *(Coco)*, Barry Miller *(Ralph)*, Maureen Teefy *(Doris)*, Lee Curreri *(Bruno)*, Eddie Barth *(Angelo)*, Gene Anthony Ray *(Leroy)*, Laura Dean *(Lisa)*.
Genre: Musical—A lively, poignant and entertaining coming-of-age story set in New York City's High School of the Performing Arts.
Plot: "Never being happy isn't the same as being unhappy, is it?" asks Montgomery, the film's lonely gay character played by Paul McCrane. (The actor would go on to play a nearly identical asexual and lonely gay character four years later in *The Hotel New Hampshire.*)

Abandoned by his parents, Montgomery (McCrane) lives alone in New York City with only one friend, his analyst. He eventually befriends Doris (Teefy), an equally shy and sensitive young woman. Doris, however, blossoms and begins to explore her sexuality, as do most of the students, but Montgomery is left alone in his room to write sad songs.

Montgomery isn't the only student struggling with personal problems and self-identity.

Each student must come to terms, over a four-year period, with their talents, ambitions and the realities of the world.

The dancing and singing are all highlights and hold up well, but it's the individuals who make this a warm and appealing human story.
Quotes:
"I guess every boy thinks his mother is very beautiful, but my mother really is."
  —*McCrane*
"I thought I was just going through a stage ... Finally my analyst leveled with me, he said it was probably a life choice."
  —*McCrane*
"It's funny, gay used to mean such a happy kind of word once."
  —*McCrane*
MPAA Rating: R—For profanity, sexual situations and female nudity.
Awards: The title song "Fame" won an Oscar for *Best Song.*
Companion Films: See "Only the Lonely" in the "Companion Films Index."

FAN, THE ★★
(1981)
US/Color/95 minutes
Director: Edward Bianchi
Cast: Michael Biehn *(Douglas Breen)*, Lauren Bacall *(Sally)*, Maureen Stapleton *(Secretary)*, James Garner *(Ex-husband)*, Hector Elizondo *(Inspector)*.
Genre: Thriller
Plot: This psychological thriller revolves around Douglas Breen (Michael Biehn), a deranged young man obsessed with an older actress (Lauren Bacall).

While not explored, many reviewers claimed that Breen is a repressed homosexual. It's not surprising that they would come to this conclusion, since deranged killers in Hollywood normally are homosexuals. Also, it's not an unreasonable assumption, given that he viciously murders two gay men. But it's the actress who receives his undivided attention. Feeling snubbed he begins to stalk her.

When she leaves town to hide from him he stages his own death so she will return. He does this by picking up a young man in a local gay bar and luring him back to his apartment. Once there he murders the young man and sets his body on fire so it can't be identified. He then leaves a suicide note saying this is the only way he can atone for what he has done to the actress. The authorities believe that the body is his. This is truly a revolting scene in an otherwise watchable film. It's unfortunate that we've had to view this type of scene so often.

MPAA Rating: R—For violence.

Companion Films: See "Murderers" in the "Companion Films Index."

FELLINI SATYRICON ★★★

(1970)

Italy/Color/130 minutes

Director: Federico Fellini

Cast: Martin Potter (Encolpio), Hiram Keller (Ascilte), Max Born (Gitone), Salvo Randone (Eumolpo), Magali Noel (Fortunata), Alain Cuny (Lica), Il Moro (Trimalcione), Fanculla (Vernacchio), Capucine (Trifena).

Genre: Drama—The promotional tag line read, "Rome. Before Christ. After Fellini." Described at the end of the film as, "A free adaptation of the Petronius classic," it traces—in the director's stylized vision—the bawdy days of Nero's reign in ancient Rome. In Italian with English subtitles—letterbox format.

Plot: Fellini recreates his distinct version of a self-indulgent, perverse and sexually obsessed ancient Rome, in which human dignity is in shackles.

Martin Potter stars as Encolpio, a beautiful, blue-eyed, blond-haired, homosexual youth, whose young lover and slave Gitone (Born) has been stolen away from him and sold to an older man. He vows to win back the boy he loves and sets out to find him. His journey leads him into a world full of drag queens, dwarfs, hermaphrodites, prostitutes and nymphomaniacs (nothing out of the ordinary for Fellini).

His journey turns into a series of misadventures. At one point along the way, he's captured by an army and enslaved. The military leader falls for the boy and they are married at sea. At this point a woman says to Encolpio, "You, bridegroom, your taste for young boys must be forgotten." But before long the boy's new husband is beheaded and he's once again on his way.

Later, when he tries to make love to a woman he humiliates himself and the entire village. He cries out "My sword is blunted," and "I want to be cured." A sorceress cures the boy of his homosexuality near the end of the film but he meets up with a crew of sailors and sets off for Africa. This perhaps is meant as a test of his newly acquired heterosexuality.

Fans of the director would probably give this film five stars. Less enthusiastic viewers might very well give it one star. This is a "viewer beware" film if ever there was one.

Quotes:

"He's better than any wife."

—*Fanculla*

"When you were a young cock, you crowed too."

—*Moro*

"Happiness is plaguing me."

—*Randone*

"I want to be cured."

—*Potter*

MPAA Rating: R—For subject matter. Contains female nudity.

Awards: Nominated for a *Best Director* Academy Award.

Companion Films: See "Men and Boys" and "Romans" in the "Companion Films Index."

FORTUNE AND MEN'S EYES ★★★

(1971)

US/Color/102 minutes

Director: Harvey Hart

Cast: Wendell Burton *(Smitty)*, Michael Greer *(Queenie)*, Zooey Hall *(Rocky)*, Danny Freedman *(Mona)*, Larry Perkins, *(Screw-*

Michael Greer plays Queenie, a mean queen and female impersonator who bares it all in this scene from *Fortune And Men's Eyes* (1971).

91

Wendell Burton refuses to be raped one more time by Zooey Hall and turns the tables on him in *Fortune And Men's Eyes* (1971).

driver), James Barron *(Holy Face Peters)*, Lazaro Perez *(Catso)*.

Genre: Drama—Based on the popular late 1960s stage play of the same name by John Herbert. The title is derived from a Shakespeare sonnet.

"What goes on in prison is a crime," claimed the movie's advertising tag line.

Plot: For some reason, the horrors of prison life—gang rape, suicide and vicious drag queens—didn't appeal to audiences—gay or straight—in 1971. It's unfortunate because this is a very watchable film with top-notch tech-

nical credits and fine performances.

Director Hart and producer Lester Persky managed to turn Herbert's powerful stage play into an exhibitionistic freak show, claimed many critics. Still, many of the performances, especially Michael Greer's memorable role as Queenie, makes this a film worth viewing.

In this tale of lost innocence, Wendell Burton plays Smitty, a straight, squeaky-clean young man arrested for selling drugs. Thrown in prison, he is forced to share a cell and survive the power struggles among three other inmates. Rocky (Hall) is the power-hungry stud who intimidates the others with force. Jan, or "Mona," is a sensitive gay man and whipping boy of the group. Queenie (Greer) is the scheming vicious queen bee and "mother" of the cell.

Before long Rocky gives Smitty an impossible choice—he can have sex with him or be gang-raped by the other inmates. Rocky eventually rapes Smitty and forces him to become his manservant in return for protection. The jealous Queenie, however, convinces Smitty that he can stand up to Rocky. Full of rage, Smitty turns the tables on Rocky and forces him into the subservient position. Power soon goes to Smitty's head and he becomes no better than the others. Unable to accept his new status, Rocky kills himself.

By the end of the film Smitty, an innocent young man serving six months for a non-crime, has been turned into a hardened criminal by the system. Despite its downbeat plot, the film manages to be quite gripping and entertaining.

Quotes:
"This ain't no garden party."
"Well, I may not know my gardens but I know a pansy when I see one."
—*Prison guard and Greer*
"Look, I don't want to hurt anyone's feelings but I ain't queer."
—*Burton*

MPAA Rating: R—Includes violence, gay rape scenes and full-frontal male nudity.

Trivia:
Actor Don Johnson got his start in the stage play directed by and costarring Sal Mineo in 1970.

Companion Films:
See "Prisoners," "Rape" and "Sissies" in the "Companion Films Index."

FOURTH MAN, THE ★★★★
(1983)
Holland/Color/104 minutes
Director: Paul Verhoeven
Cast: Jeroen Krabbe *(Gerard Reve)*, Renee Soutendijk *(Christine)*, Thom Hoffman *(Herman)*.

Genre: Thriller—Based on the novel by Gerard Reve, this stylishly dark and moody mystery is an original, nightmarish and imaginative take on the genre. Verhoeven, as he often does, uses religious symbolism for bizarre and nightmarish effect.

Filmed in Dutch with English subtitles.

Plot: Jeroen Krabbe stars as Gerard, an alcoholic writer, living with his male lover in Amsterdam. Whether as a result of his clairvoyant powers or simply from alcohol-induced hallucinations, he's haunted by disturbing, surrealistic visions of death and dismemberment.

An adventurous type, Gerard allows himself to be seduced by Christine (Soutendijk), who's a beautiful and wealthy young woman he meets during an out-of-town speaking engagement. To make love to her he pretends that she is a man. To entice him to stay on she sets a trap. The bait is her attractive young boyfriend Herman (Hoffman), whom Gerard falls for. "I've got to have him, even if it kills me," he sighs while looking at the beautiful young man's picture.

Thrown together by Christine, the two men share a very erotic and ironic sex scene in a cemetery. It is in this setting that Gerard discovers the truth. Each of Christine's previous three husbands has died a violent death soon after they were wed. Gerard realizes that his nightmares are real and that either he or Herman is the intended next victim—or the fourth man.

Sex and death are one and the same in this

imaginative and symbol-filled tale of the lethal spider woman. In 1992, the director revisited this theme. The result was the American-made blockbuster hit *Basic Instinct*—the film that catapulted Sharon Stone to stardom.

MPAA Rating: R—Contains full-frontal male and female nudity of all three central characters, as well as gay sex, violence and gore. Krabbe and Hoffman also share a very intense kissing scene.

Companion Films: See "Bisexuals," "Men and Boys" and "Murderers" in the "Companion Films Index."

FOX AND HIS FRIENDS ★★★

(1975)
Germany/Color/123 minutes
Director: Rainer Werner Fassbinder
Cast: Rainer Werner Fassbinder, Peter Chatel, Karlheinz Bohm, Harry Baer.
Genre: Drama—In German with English subtitles.
Plot: Fassbinder plays "Fox, the Talking Head," who works in a carnival. When he wins the lottery, his simple life becomes complicated. A working-class lad, he makes the mistake of becoming involved in a relationship with a snobbish upper-class young man who's only interested in him for his money. It doesn't take long before his new boyfriend has managed to rob him blind. Once the money is gone, the boyfriend dumps him. Dejected and humiliated, Fox again finds himself nearly penniless on the streets. In the end it's the money that drives him to a tragic end.
MPAA Rating: Not rated—Contains numerous scenes of full-frontal male nudity.

Companion Films: See "Unhappy Homosexuals" in the "Companion Films Index."

FRANKIE & JOHNNY ★★★

(1991)
US/Color/118 minutes
Director: Garry Marshall
Cast: Al Pacino *(Johnny)*, Michelle Pfeiffer *(Frankie)*, Nathan Lane *(Tim)*, Hector Elizondo *(Nick)*, Kate Nelligan *(Cora)*, Greg Lewis *(Tino)*, Jane Morris *(Nedda)*.
Genre: Comedy—A very serious and downbeat comedy. The most upbeat character (for a change) is the gay neighbor, Tim.
Plot: This is a fairy tale about romance and loneliness in the big city. Pfeiffer's heart has been broken one time too many, and she's determined not to get involved again. Pacino is just as determined to change her mind. While they're figuring it out, people all around them are involved in a variety of humorous relationships.

David Ansen of *Newsweek* remarked, "The playwright's delicious one-liners detonate with precision timing. The supporting characters, expertly played, have the kind of instant familiarity of regulars on a favorite TV sitcom … Nathan Lane [plays] Frankie's witty gay neighbor and confidant (who gets the best zingers)."
MPAA Rating: R—For language.
Companion Films: See "Neighbors, Roommates and Best Friends" in the "Companion Films Index."

FRIENDS FOREVER ★★★★

(1986)

Denmark/Color/95 minutes
Director: Stefan Henszelmann
Cast: Claus Bender Mortensen, Thomas Sigsgaard, Thomas Elholm, Lill Lindfors.
Genre: Drama—A favorite with gay film festival audiences. In Danish with English subtitles.
Plot: In this coming-of-age story, three 16-year-old school boys explore their sexual identities in open, honest and charming fashion.

Kristian is the new kid in school. To gain popularity and acceptance, this shy and insecure newcomer takes up with Patrick, one of the school's most popular boys. When Kristian later discovers that Patrick is gay, he's forced to examine his own sexuality and feelings. The experience is a positive one that helps him mature and gain self-confidence.

Insightful, humorous, touching and punctuated with fine natural performances, *Friends* is in many ways similar to the equally charming *You Are Not Alone*.
MPAA Rating: Not rated—Contains male nudity.
Postscript: Director Henszelmann died of AIDS in October 1991.
Companion Films: See "Coming Out" in the "Companion Films Index."

GAY DECEIVERS, THE ★★★

(1969)
US/Color/105 minutes
Director: Bruce Kessler
Cast: Kevin Coughlin *(Danny)*, Michael Greer *(Malcolm de John)*, Larry Casey *(Elliot)*, Brooke Bundy *(Karen)*, Jo Ann Harris *(Leslie)*, Sebastian Brock *(Craig)*, Jack Starrett *(Col. Dixon)*, Christopher Riordan *(Duane)*, Jeanne Baird *(Mrs. Conway)*, Mike Kopscha *(The psychiatrist)*, Robert Reese *(Real estate agent)*, Doug Hume *(Corporal)*, Dave Osterhout *(Stern)*.
Genre: Comedy—A low-budget, camp-classic favorite on the gay film-festival circuit.

The advertising tag line read "Wear long hair, tight-fitting pants, lisp a little, put your hands on your hips, quote liberally from Oscar Wilde and Marcel Proust and ask your sergeant if he likes your mascara ... You have nothing to lose but your draft card."

Plot: Heterosexual young men would do just about anything to avoid being drafted and shipped off to Vietnam in 1969. Anything, in this case, involves two straight draft dodgers pretending to be gay lovers.

When the recruiting office decides to investigate, however, the two all-American boys are forced to leave their girlfriends behind and move into a one bedroom apartment together as a cover. As luck would have it, their landlord Malcolm (Greer) is a swishy, mincing, flaming and loveable stereotype, while their next-door neighbor is a gay man having an affair with an army officer.

When the boys' respective girlfriends drop by unannounced, and the parents pop over for a visit, the setting becomes fertile ground for '60s-style sexual confusion and homophobic hijinks. But when Malcolm throws an annual costume party, the film becomes pure camp fun.

As a pre-Stonewall artifact, this gay *Love, American Style* time capsule is a hilarious "trip" to the past. And this one saves the best scene for last.

Quotes:
"Which do you prefer, young boys or mature men?"
"I think that when you really love somebody, age shouldn't matter at all!"
　　—Kopscha and Coughlin
"They asked to see you together."
"What are they, Siamese twins?"
"No, but I get the feeling that they're joined together from time to time."
　　—Hume and Starrett
"Several of my very best friends are members of your faith."
　　—Reese
"I have the most gorgeous peonies in the entire country."
"I'd like to see them sometime."
"I bet you would."
　　—Greer and Casey
"There's something you ought to know. You're not the first man I've ever gone to bed with — when I was a kid I used to sack in with my father."
　　—Casey
"Who's your decorator, Tiny Tim?"
　　—Harris

Kevin Coughlin, Michael Greer and Larry Casey star in the campy farce *The Gay Deceivers* (1969).

"Say no more darling, when Craig and I were first married I didn't know a thing about cooking either. I used to dress a turkey in Levis."
    —Greer

"The wedding was gorgeous. The best man gave the groom away. My father gave the bride away, and the fact that I wanted to be flower girl gave me away."
    —Greer

"Why don't you take your dress off and fight like a man?"
    —Casey

MPAA Rating: R—Contains very brief male nudity from behind.

Trivia: In 1971, Michael Greer played another affected queen—this one nasty, but just as entertaining—in *Fortune And Men's Eyes*.

Companion Films: See "Drag Queens" in the "Companion Films Index."

GILDA ★★★★
(1946)
US/B&W/110 minutes

Director: Charles Vidor
Cast: Glenn Ford *(Johnny)*, George Macready *(Munsen)*, Rita Hayworth *(Gilda)*.
Genre: Drama
Plot: Like many pre-1960s films, *Gilda* can be viewed on at least two different levels. This is one of those films that seems to delight in its own clever ruse. Gay viewers in 1946, however, certainly must have picked up on the double entendres and insider references. At the same time, the intended straight audience of the time enjoyed the film and were none the wiser for its hidden message.

When George Macready saves Glenn Ford's life, the two men become fast friends. Both men are gamblers, and both feel there's no place for women in their lives. Their relationship is exclusive and happy, until Macready goes away on a trip and returns with a wife.

Rita Hayworth plays Macready's new wife Gilda—a spoiled vixen who comes between the men and turns them against each other. Bitchy, witty, biting repartee between the jealous lovers, Hayworth and Ford, comes fast and furious. And although homosexuality is only alluded to, the entire plot seems a thinly veiled subterfuge.

This is high melodrama and camp at its finest. Modern-day, gay-themed films are rarely as tightly written or acted. This is a gem.
Quotes:
"You must lead a gay life."
"I lead the life I like to lead."
—Macready and Ford
"Get this Mr. Munsen. I was born last night when you met me in that alley. That way I'm no past and all future. I like it that way."
—Ford
"I thought we agreed that women and gambling don't mix."

"My wife doesn't come under the category of women."
—Ford and Macready
"I can never get a zipper to close. Maybe that stands for something. What do you think?"
—Hayworth
"Pardon me, but your husband is showing."
—Ford
"I think that's good business—to surround yourself with ugly women and beautiful men."
—Hayworth
"Did you hear about me? If I'd have been a ranch they would have named me the Bar Nothing."
—Hayworth
"Statistics show that there are more women in the world than anything else—except insects."
—Ford
MPAA Rating: Not rated.
Companion Films: See "Closet Cases" in the "Companion Films Index."

GLEN OR GLENDA? ★★★★★
(aka I Led Two Lives, I Changed My Sex and He Or She)
(1953)
US/B&W/67 minutes
Director: Edward D. Wood, Jr.
Cast: Bela Lugosi *(Scientist)*, Daniel Davis *(Glen/Glenda)*, Dolores Fuller *(Barbara)*, Lyle Talbot *(Inspector)*, Timothy Farrell *(Psychiatrist)*, Tommy Haynes *(Alan/Ann)*.
Genre: Drama—Considered one of the best of the very worst films ever made by critics and film buffs the world over—thus earning it a classic five-star rating.

Wood's true claim to fame, however, is the film *Plan 9 From Outer Space,* considered *the* cult film of all time.

Plot: In his first feature film, director Edward D. Wood, Jr., considered *The Worst Director of All Time*, chose to tackle a topic he knew well. A closeted transvestite himself, he chose to star in this no-budget film as Glen, under the pseudonym Daniel Davis.

A brave and daring film for its time, today, 40 years later, it's hysterically camp. In fact, it looks very much like a training film gone awry. Davis plays Glen, a businessman engaged to be married. His dilemma is whether or not to tell his fiancée, Barbara (Fuller), about his *other half* Glenda. As time goes by and the wedding nears, Glen is uncertain whether he's more attracted to Barbara or to her angora sweater.

Glen's story is told in flashbacks by a psychiatrict to a police inspector who has just witnessed the suicide of a transvestite named Patrick/Patricia. The inspector asks if there is any way to help prevent this in the future.

While the doctor explains his theories and pleads the case for tolerance toward transvestites and transexuals, Bela Lugosi appears on screen every now and then as a godlike mad scientist who speaks with a cryptic tongue and says things like, "Beware of the big green dragon that sits on your doorstep, he eats little boys."

In the end, Glen tells Barbara about Glenda, and she gives him her sweater, and they live happily ever after. Tacked onto Glen's story is a brief tale of Alan who has a sex-change operation and becomes Ann. The world is shocked but Ann is thrilled and also lives happily ever after.

This is a film you have to see to believe ... and even then you may not believe it.

Quotes:
"Those fingernails have got to go!"
  —Fuller

MPAA Rating: Not rated—strictly PG.

Companion Films:
See "Drag Queens" in the "Companion Films Index."

HOTEL NEW HAMPSHIRE, THE ★★★

(1984)

US/Color/110 minutes

Director: Tony Richardson

Cast: Beau Bridges *(Father)*, Jodie Foster *(Franny)*, Rob Lowe *(John)*, Nastassja Kinski *(Suzy the Bear)*, Paul McCrane *(Frank)*, Matthew Modine *(Chipper/Ernst)*, Amanda Plummer.

Genre: Drama—Based on the John Irving novel. Like Irving's earlier *The World According To Garp*, *The Hotel New Hampshire* is essentially a quirky tale of sex and death.

Plot: "Sorrow, come on. Get off my bed," pleads Paul McCrane. Sorrow is the family's perpetually flatulent dog. But Sorrow is more than a dog, he's a symbol of life's tragedies and twists of fate in this twisted tale. McCrane plays Frank, a gay adolescent who hardly seems out of place in his off-beat family.

When Frank's brother and sister, John (Lowe) and Franny (Foster), learn that he's gay, they reassure him that it's okay with them. And considering that Franny and John are in love and hot for one another's body, Frank's sexuality really is a minor problem.

When Frank propositions Chipper (Modine) the local football hero, however, it becomes a big deal. Chipper defends his manhood by sexually humiliating Frank. He brings the rest of the football team along to help. Later, Chipper and the team, still needing to prove themselves, rape Franny.

Sometime later, Franny, finds herself in bed with Suzy (Kinski), but only before she ends up in bed with her brother John. But then John has slept with everyone else in the film, so it's only natural that he sleeps with his sister.

In the end, Chipper, the all-American male who started the whole thing, gets a taste of his own medicine. Frank and John, dressed in drag as nurses, rape the surprised Chipper as Franny looks on. But retribution isn't always sweet.

Inbetween all the bed hopping, the family comes face to face with fate and an assortment of oddly entertaining tragedies and triumphs.

Quotes:

"It is hard work and great art to make life not so serious."

—Bridges

"You're as queer as a cat's fart."

—Foster

MPAA Rating: R—Contains profanity, violence and male nudity. Paul McCrane and Matthew Modine appear nude from behind.

Companion Films: See "Only the Lonely" in the "Companion Films Index."

HOURS AND TIMES, THE ★★

(1992)

US/B&W/82 Minutes

Director: Christopher Munch

Cast: Ian Hart *(Lennon)*, David Angus *(Epstein)*.

Genre: Drama—This controversial interpretation and speculation of a real-life event is sure to either shock or fascinate Beatles' fans—and a handful of other curious filmgoers as well.

Plot: Shot in black and white in Barcelona, *Hours And Times* is a fictionalized account of what might have happened between Beatle John Lennon and manager Brian Epstein on a four-day vacation getaway together in 1963.

The filmmaker speculates that Lennon, played by Ian Hart, may have reluctantly become involved sexually with Epstein (David Angus), who was known to be gay and quite taken with the young Lennon. In addition to their sexuality, the film is equally fascinating, as it explores other aspects of their personalities and relationship.

MPAA Rating: Not rated

Companion Films: See "Biographies" in the "Companion Films Index."

I WANT WHAT I WANT ★★

(1972)

US/Color/97 minutes

Director: John Dexter

Cast: Anne Heywood *(Roy/Wendy)*, Harry Andrews *(Father)*, Virginia Stride *(Shirley)*, Jill Bennett *(Margaret)*, Michael Coles *(Frank)*, Paul Rogers *(Mr. Waits)*, Sheila Reid *(June)*.

Genre: Drama—Adapted from the novel by Geoff Brown, this is the story of a man who wants to be a woman. Stiff and unnatural, it has the look of a film made in the early '50s rather than the early '70s.

Plot: For some reason Anne Heywood plays Roy, a man who wants to be a woman. This was done for laughs in *Victor/Victoria*. It seems unclear why it was done here, other than to confuse the viewer, since Heywood never for a minute looks like a man.

When Roy, a young man still living at home with his widowed father, decides to come out and live like a woman, he dresses in his mother's clothes and waits for his father to find him. His father of course finds him, becomes violent and beats him. Roy packs his things and moves— starting a new life as Wendy. One small problem—both women and men are attracted to him and for obvious reasons he must keep them at arm's length.

He turns down a proposition from a lesbian in a bus station restroom, but shortly after falls for a handsome young man who lives in his new boarding house. Wendy is in a no-man's land. When Frank, the man Wendy loves, forces himself upon her he's in for a bit of a shock. When he discovers that he has kissed and fondled another man, he flies into a fit of homophobic rage and beats her. Then in true melodramatic form, Wendy takes a broken piece of glass and cuts off "her" penis. He winds up in a hospital, but within a year has received the transsexual operation he has long desired.

MPAA Rating: R—Presumably for subject matter. Contains one brief shot of Heywood nude from behind.

Quotes:

"What are you for Christ's sake? How long has this been going on?"

"All my life."

　　　—Andrews and Heywood

"I'll have you cured no matter what it costs."

　　　—Andrews

"God made man in his own image and he blew it!"

　　　—Heywood

"Come to think of it, some of the best bank robberies have been done by men dressed as women."

　　　—Heywood

"It's not my mind that's wrong, it's my body."

　　　—Heywood

Companion Films: See "Drag Queens" and "Homophobia" in the "Companion Films Index."

IF ... ★★★★

(1969)

UK/Color & B&W/111 minutes

Director: Lindsay Anderson

Cast: Malcolm McDowell *(Travis)*, Richard

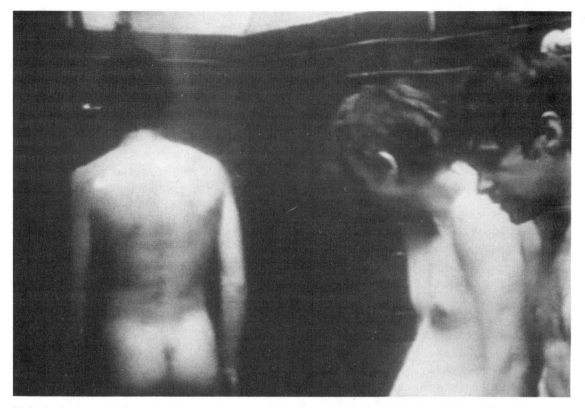

Malcolm McDowell is forced to take a cold shower as punishment as David Wood and Richard Warwick look on in *If...* (1969).

Warwick *(Wallace)*, David Wood *(Knightly)*, Christine Noonan *(Waitress)*, Rupert Webster *(Bobby)*, Peter Jeffrey *(Headmaster)*, Guy Ross *(Stephans)* and Robert Swann, Hugh Thomas, Arthur Lowe, Mona Washbourne.

Genre: Drama—Three teenage boys rebel against the oppressive all-boys military school they attend. This was Malcolm McDowell's film debut.

Plot: "When do we live? That's what I want to know," asks McDowell near the opening of the film. McDowell plays Travis, a free-thinking, spirited and privileged upper-class young man who refuses to conform to rigid rules made by hypocrites in a sexually and spiritually repressed prep school for boys. His only two friends are like-minded Wallace (Warwick) and Knightly (Wood). All three are outcasts in their own way.

The sexual innuendo and the tension are thick, as boys tease one another about their sexuality. Homosexuality is rampant among upper and lower classmen alike, but only in the closet. In this brutal system, disruptions are met with cold showers and harsh beatings.

One very beautiful young lad, Bobby Phillips (Webster), is the slave of one of the upper classmen and the envy of the other boys. Bobby, however, is drawn to Wallace. Their friendship is in sharp contrast to the master-slave relationships encouraged by the school and its traditions. In one very charming scene, they're shown briefly together in bed sleeping.

In a climactic indictment of this oppressive system the three outcasts take up arms against the school and launch a full-scale war. While surreal in nature, the boys' anger and rage are a very graphic metaphor for all the injustices inflicted on man in the name of a higher good.

MPAA Rating: R—Features McDowell, Warwick and Wood nude from behind during a shower scene. After all, what would a movie about a boys school be without a scene of male nudity in the showers. For McDowell, this was the first of many such scenes to come.

Companion Films: See "Boys Schools" in the "Companion Films Index."

I'LL LOVE YOU FOREVER ... TONIGHT ★★★

(1993)

US/B&W/80 minutes

Director: Edgar Michael Bravo

Cast: Paul Marius *(Ethan)*, Jason Adams *(Dennis)*, David Poynter *(Peter)*, Miles Wilshire *(Jeff)*, Roger Shank *(Steve)*.

Genre: Drama—Independent, low-budget feature.

Plot: Paul Marius plays Ethan, a gay man still dealing with an unhappy childhood filled with sexual abuse.

Things are looking especially bleak for Ethan until his best friend and sometimes sex partner, Dennis (Adams), invites him on a getaway weekend trip to Palm Springs.

Once there, however, Ethan discovers that Dennis has more in mind than simply a relaxing weekend. Ethan has been misled. Also staying at the hotel is Peter (Poynter), Ethan's ex and his new boyfriend Jeff (Wilshire).

Dennis, it seems, has plans for each. But in case his plans don't work out, he's got a backup plan—Steve (Shank), a young companion he's brought along as insurance.

While looking for love and sex in all the wrong places, this thirty-something group of gay white men finds companionship and friendship instead.

MPAA Rating: Not rated.

Companion Films: See "Unhappy Homosexuals" in the "Companion Films Index."

IMPROPER CONDUCT ★

(1984)

France/Color/112 minutes

Director: Nestor Almendros and Orlando Jimenez Leal

Cast: Susan Sontag, Herberto Padilla, G. Cabrera Infante, Carlos Franqui, Reynaldo Arenas, Fidel Castro.

Genre: Documentary—Explores the oppression of homosexuality in Castro's Cuba. In Spanish with English subtitles. Also includes occasional English narration.

Plot: From a historical perspective, this is an important documentary of the Cuban concentration camps and prisons designed to house homosexuals and other *undesirables* since the time of the communist revolution.

As a film, it lacks energy, interest, or any of the cinematic techniques that make for an involving documentary. For the most part, this is simply a series of straightforward interviews with camp survivors. Castro's Cuba is likened to Hitler's Germany. The horrors and indignities are corroborated over and over again by talking heads saying essentially the same thing.

It's fascinating and shocking to hear about the moral purges, public humiliation and mistreatment of homosexuals, artists and writers by this communist government. Anyone considered antisocial was either locked up or encouraged to leave the country. Over 1 million Cubans defected. But as a result of the film's pacing and lack of visual interest, it's also easy to lose interest in the message long before the end credits.

Quotes:
"You lack the imagination to be a homosexual."
    —*An interviewee*

MPAA Rating: Not rated.

Companion Films:
See "Documentaries" and "Prisoners" in the "Companion Films Index."

JFK ★★★★★
(1991)
US/Color/188 minutes
Director: Oliver Stone
Cast: Kevin Costner *(Jim Garrison)*, Tommy Lee Jones *(Clay Shaw)*, Kevin Bacon *(Willie O'Keefe)*, Gary Oldman *(Lee Harvey Oswald)*, Joe Pesci *(David Ferrie)*, Donald Sutherland *(X)*, Sissy Spacek *(Liz Garrison)*, John Candy *(Dean Andrews)*, Laurie Metcalf *(Susie Cox)*, Brian Doyle Murray *(Jack Ruby)*, Walter Matthau *(Senator Long)*, Jim Garrison *(Earl Warren)*.
Genre: Drama—In Oliver Stone's version of the JFK conspiracy, communists, the Mafia and an unstable group of gay men are considered the real men behind the assassination. Needless to say, the negative stereotypes portrayed in the film received less-than-glowing reviews from the gay community.

That said, the three strongest performances belonged to the gay characters, played by Jones, Pesci and Bacon.

Plot: Set in New Orleans, in the 1960s, it's a time when you couldn't tell the boys from the girls, as Walter Matthau's character observed, referring to the hippies.

Kevin Costner stars as D.A. Jim Garrison. Unconvinced by the Warren Commission's report that Lee Harvey Oswald single-handedly assassinated the President, he becomes obsessed with the case and launches an investigation.

Garrison's investigation leads him to three prime suspects, all reportedly friends of Oswald's. Jones plays respected businessman and philanthropist Clay Shaw, a wealthy, closeted homosexual. Bacon plays—with flair—Willie O'Keefe, a young gay hustler serving time for male prostitution. O'Keefe, for his own reasons, claims to have met Oswald at Shaw's while attending a private costume-sex party. In flashbacks, Bacon is dressed presumably as Marie Antoinette, surrounded by gold-painted Greek gods—just your typical weekend get-together in the Garden District.

Pesci, wearing Joan Crawford-type painted-on eyebrows and a discount-store, off-the-shelf toupée, plays David Ferrie, a hysterical loose cannon, who eventually confesses everything. Shortly after his friends are indicted, Ferrie turns up dead.

Of all the possible suspects, Shaw is the only one to be officially brought up on assassination conspiracy charges by Garrison.

Quotes:
"God, I'm ashamed to be an American today."
— *Costner*

"Everybody likes to make themselves out to be something more than they are, especially in the homosexual underworld."
— *Bacon*

"You don't know shit 'cause you never been fucked in the ass."
— *Bacon*

"People like you—they just walk between the raindrops."
— *Costner*

"All I wanted in the world was to be a Catholic priest. I had one terrible, fucking weakness and they defrocked me."
— *Pesci*

"Hitler always said, 'The bigger the lie the more people will believe it.'"

—*Costner*

MPAA Rating: R—Includes profanity, violence and adult themes.

Awards: Tommy Lee Jones received an Academy Award nomination for *Best Supporting Actor* for his role. He lost to Jack Palance in *City Slickers*. In addition, the film was nominated for *Best Picture, Best Director, Best Adapted Screenplay* (Stone and Zachary Sklar), *Best Cinematography* (Robert Richardson), *Best Film Editing* (Joe Hutshing and Pietro Scalia), *Best Original Score* (John Williams) and *Best Sound* (Michael Minkler, Gregg Landaker and Tod A. Maitland). Jonathan Demme and *The Silence Of The Lambs* went home with the Oscar for *Best Picture* and *Director*.

Companion Films: See "Murderers" and "Sissies" in the "Companion Films Index."

KENNETH ANGER:
MAGICK LANTERN CYCLE ★★
(1947 through 1980)
US/B&W and Color
Director: Kenneth Anger
Genre: Drama—The works of gay pioneer and avant-garde filmmaker Kenneth Anger are presented in four separate volumes. A collection of short films, you're not likely to see them on television. They do, however, occasionally make the art-house theaters.
Plot: Volume No.1 is 38 minutes long and contains three shorts made between 1947 and 1953: *Fireworks, Rabbit's Moon* and *Eaux D'Artifice*. Volume No. 2 is a 40-minute short, titled *Inauguration Of The Pleasure Dome*, made in 1954. Volume No. 3 is 38 minutes long and includes: *Scorpio Rising*, considered the "definitive" underground film; and *Puce Moment* and *Kustom Kar Kommandos* which were made between 1949 and 1969. Volume No. 4 is 40 minutes long and includes *Invocation Of My Demon Lover* and *Lucifer Rising*, which were made between 1969 and 1980.

Experimental film fans and those simply interested in the first underground expressions of homoerotic love on the screen will find these early and imaginative works worth seeking out.
MPAA Rating: Not rated.
Companion Films: See director Gene Genet's *Un Chant d'Amour.*

KISS OF THE SPIDER WOMAN ★★★★★
(1985)
Brazil/Color/119 minutes
Director: Hector Babenco
Cast: William Hurt *(Molina)*, Raul Julia *(Valentin)*, Sonia Braga (*Spider Woman*).
Genre: Drama—Brazilian drama in English. Based on the novel by openly gay writer Manuel Puig. Like *The Crying Game* nearly a decade later, *Spider Woman* was an unpredictable, intriguing art-house feature that became a popular crossover film and was nominated for a *Best Picture* Academy Award.
Plot: This beautifully photographed and finely acted film takes place almost entirely in the confines of an Argentinean prison. Flashbacks and fantasies provide additional action and mood that prevent the film from being claustrophobic.

William Hurt plays Louis Molina, an effeminate homosexual window dresser, who has been sentenced to eight years in prison for corrupting a minor. Raul Julia plays his cellmate, Valentin, a journalist who has been arrested on political charges. Complete opposites, the men are forced to share their lives in this cramped and intimate setting. Molina passes his days by reenacting melodramatic scenes from his favorite movies. Valentin is his reluctant audience. Molina has spent his life in the shallow pursuit of looking for the perfect man. Valentin has spent his life denying himself pleasure and working to change the world. Molina eventually falls in love with Valentin. In his own way Valentin also loves Molina and they become sexually involved.

This, however, is something the warden never anticipated. Making a deal with Molina for an early release, he's expected to inform on his cellmate in return. When this doesn't work, Molina is released from prison and followed. As expected, he has agreed to give a message to Valentin's girlfriend and political partner. Although he knows that he's being followed, he nevertheless keeps his promise to the man he loves. His love, however, leads to a tragic end that's similar to the fate of the heroines of the movies he loved.

Quotes:

"You really like those Nazi blonds, don't you?"
 —Julia

"Is this propaganda or porno?"
 —Julia

"You atheists never stop talking about God."
"And you gays never face facts. Fantasies are no escape."
 —Hurt and Julia

"If you've got the keys to that door I will gladly follow. Otherwise I will escape in my own way."
 —Hurt

"Do you think it's easy to find a real man?"
 —Hurt

"There's just no talking to a guy about another guy without getting into a fuss."
 —Hurt

Raul Julia and William Hurt share more than a prison cell in *Kiss Of The Spider Woman* (1985). Hurt received the first *Best Actor* Academy Award for a portrayal of a gay character.

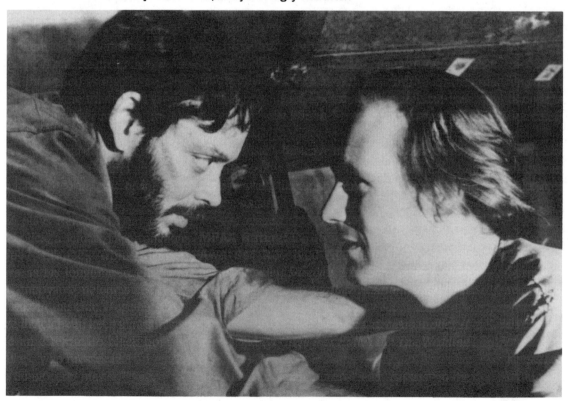

"Working as a window dresser, as enjoyable as it is, sometimes at the end of the day you wonder what it's all about—you feel kind of empty inside."

—*Hurt*

"What's wrong with being like a woman? Why do only women get to be sensitive? Why not a man, a dog or a faggot?"

—*Hurt*

"You wouldn't know reality if it was stuck up your ass."

—*Julia*

"The nicest thing about feeling happy is that you think you'll never feel unhappy again."

—*Hurt*

MPAA Rating: R—Includes a gay kissing scene between Hurt and Julia.

Awards: William Hurt won the *Best Actor* Academy Award, becoming the first actor to win the award for a homosexual role. The film was also nominated for *Best Picture, Best Director,* and *Best Screenplay.*

In 1993, Puig's novel was adapted for the stage and won the year's Tony Award for *Best Musical.* Tony Kushner's *Angels In America: A Gay Fantasia On American Themes,* won for *Best Play* of the year.

Companion Films:

At Play In the Fields Of The Lord (1991) by Babenco features a great deal of male and female nudity including full-frontal scenes with Tom Berenger.

Also see "Prisoners" in the "Companion Films Index."

L' ELEGANT CRIMINAL ★★★

(1990)

France/Color/120 minutes

Director: Francis Girod

Cast: Daniel Auteuil *(Pierre-Francois Lacenaire)*, Patrick Pineau *(Avril)*, Jean Poiret *(Allard)*.

Genre: Drama—A stylish drama based on the real life of one of France's most infamous murderers, Pierre-Francois Lacenaire. The promotional tag line read: "Poet. Thief. Hero. Killer. Truly a man of many convictions."

Plot: Set in 1836, Daniel Auteuil plays Pierre Lacenaire, a 36-year-old man facing the gallows for a string of murders, committed primarily for the thrill.

Highly intelligent, Lacenaire is aware of the hypocrisy of religion and politics from an early age, and rebels. Being homosexual only serves to confirm his outcast status. A roguish sociopath, he's able to charm both men and women to follow him.

After becoming involved with a homosexual inmate, Lacenaire persuades the man to be his partner in crime as well, when the two are released. But since there's no honor among thieves—or murderers—when Avril (Pineau) is turned into the police by a former partner, he in turn informs on Lacenaire. Lacenaire then betrays his lover, Avril.

To ensure his immortality, he pleads his own case and demands the death penalty. While awaiting the trial he writes his autobiography that goes on to become a best-seller.

A fascinating psychological profile that's both chilling and provocative.

Quotes:

"Where there's no murder, there's no pleasure."
—*Auteuil*

MPAA Rating: Not rated—Strictly PG.

Companion Films: See "Hustlers" and "Murderers" in the "Companion Films Index."

L'HOMME BLESSE ★★★

(The Wounded Man)

(1988)

France/Color/90 minutes

Director: Patrice Chereau

Cast: Jean-Hughes Anglade *(Henri)*, Vittorio Mezzogiorno *(Jean)*, Roland Bertin *(Bosmans)*, Lisa Kreuzer *(Elizabeth)*.

Genre: Drama—French with English subtitles.

Plot: Jean-Hughes Anglade plays Henri, a moody and troubled young man from an unhappy home. In a chance encounter he meets a street hustler (Mezzogiorno). He realizes that the hustler is a loser but he continues to seek the man out no matter how many times he's rejected or humiliated. Both men are "wounded."

In the end, Henri's pent-up longing for love and sexual gratification climaxes in a disturbing final scene. In it, he goes to the ultimate extreme and does the only thing he can to hold on to the object of his desire. How many times have we seen this before?

MPAA Rating: Not rated—Contains numerous scenes of male frontal nudity, gay kissing and sex scenes.

Companion Films: For other films with Jean-Hughes Anglade, see *Betty Blue* (1986), featuring Anglade in numerous frontal nude scenes.

Also see "Murderers" and "S&M" in the "Companion Films Index."

LA CAGE AUX FOLLES ★★★
(Birds Of A Feather)
(1979)
France/Color/91 minutes
Director: Edouard Molinaro
Cast: Ugo Tognazzi *(Renato)*, Michel Serrault *(Albin/Zaza)*, Michel Galabru *(Charrier)*, Claire Maurier *(Simone)*, Remy Laurent *(Laurent)*, Benny Luke *(Jacob)*.
Genre: Comedy—This is a gay charade in which everyone pretends to be someone else in order to keep up appearances. In French with English subtitles, the video is also available dubbed in English. It became the highest grossing foreign language film ever released in the U.S.
Plot: Some films age better than others. This film, very popular, among gays and straights alike, appears to have aged quickly beyond its years.

Ugo Tognazzi plays Renato, the gay owner of La Cage Aux Folles, a female-impersonation club in St. Tropez, France. Albin (Michel Serrault) aka Zaza, is his longtime lover and a temperamental, flamboyant, melodramatic drag queen who performs in the club. Together they live in a flat above the club. To keep things interesting they have an effeminate black housekeeper, Jacob (Luke), who dresses like a French maid and calls his employers "master."

When Renato's son Laurent (Laurent), from a previous marriage, announces that he's to be wed, Renato and Albin are a bit put out that it's to a woman. Once they've warmed to the idea, however, Laurent suggests that they hide their lifestyle from his intended in-laws. It seems that Simone (Maurier), the father of the bride to be, is the Minister of the Morality Movement Party and would not let his daughter marry into such a family.

Though Laurent's suggestion causes friction among the lovers, they eventually agree to put his happiness before theirs and to be part of the charade. The meeting starts off a success but soon unravels into a humorous comedy of errors. Before the night is out, the humiliated Minister of Morality must dress in drag to escape the hordes of reporters with cameras who have followed him to the club.

In spite of everything, the wedding day arrives and brings with it a *gay* ending.
Quotes:
"I have been called 'Negro' and 'queer,' but I've never been called 'French.'"
   —*Luke*
"The monster will leave now."
   —*Serrault*
"Try to walk like John Wayne. No, that's John Wayne's sister, Fay."
   —*Tognazzi*
MPAA Rating: PG
Awards: Received Academy Award nominations for *Best Director, Best Screenplay (Based on material from another medium)* and *Best Costume Design.*
Companion Films: See *La Cage Aux Folles II* (1981) and *La Cage Aux Folles III: The Wedding* (1986).

Also see "Drag Queens" and "Sissies" in the "Companion Films Index."

LADYBUGS ★★
(1992)
US/Color/90 minutes
Director: Sidney J. Furie
Cast: Rodney Dangerfield (*Chester Lee*), Jackee (*Julie Benson*), Jonathan Brandis (*Matthew/ Martha*), Ilene Graff (*Bess*), Vinessa Shaw (*Kimberly Mullen*), Tom Parks (*Dave Mullen*), Jeanetta Arnett (*Glynnis Mullen*), Nancy Parsons (*Coach Annie*), Blake Clark (*Coach Bull*), Tommy Lasorda (*Coach Cannoli*).
Genre: Comedy—An incensed reviewer for *Variety* stated, "This picture doesn't deserve any respect. Sexist, homophobic and woefully unfunny to boot, Rodney Dangerfield's latest starring effort is a waste of comic talent."
Plot: Dangerfield stars as Chester Lee, a salesman out to do whatever it takes to impress his boss and get a raise. The boss, of course, is looking for a coach for the company's all-girl soccer team. Chester takes the job, but finds himself on a losing team. His only chance of winning, it seems, is to enlist the help of his fiancee's son Matthew (Jonathan Brandis, *The Never Ending Story*). The only way Matthew can join the team is by dressing in drag. This of course sets the stage for the two to do whatever it takes to play out the charade.

Variety went on to say, "Pic's also inexplicably preoccupied with transvestitism, which extends to a gratuitous scene of Dangerfield dressing up as Brandis' mother."
MPAA Rating: PG
Companion Films: See "Drag Queens" in the "Companion Films Index."

LAW OF DESIRE ★★★
(1986)

Spain/Color/100 minutes
Director: Pedro Almodovar
Cast: Eusebio Ponceta (*Pablo*), Carmen Maura (*Tina*), Antonio Banderas (*Antonio*), Miguel Molina (*Juan*).
Genre: Drama—Often humorous, this melodramatic tragicomedy was Almodovar's first film to gain wide attention in the U.S. The English subtitles are especially difficult to read.
Plot: Eusebio Ponceta plays Pablo, a gay filmmaker living in Madrid. In brief, Pablo is in love with Juan, but Juan cannot express his love for Pablo. Juan is needed in his family business and leaves town, but he and Pablo continue to correspond through letters.

In Juan's absence, Pablo picks up Antonio in a disco, and before long, the young man has fallen for Pablo. Unfortunately for all, Pablo is not in love with Antonio—he's still in love with Juan. Adding to this Spanish soap opera is Tina, Pablo's sister—formerly his brother, before undergoing a sex change operation.

At this point, the film turns abruptly from a comedy into a tragedy. A jealous and obsessive Antonio murders Juan in order to have Pablo to himself. When Pablo turns on him, Antonio sets him up as the murderer. We keep waiting for the humor to return, but the climax turns out to be a tragic cliché. In the end, a melodramatic Banderas proclaims his love for Pablo saying, "Loving you is a crime, but I'll pay for it." Still, the film has its moments.
MPAA Rating: Not rated—Contains nudity, violence and profanity. Opening scene depicts a nude man from behind masturbating. This is a scene from a movie within the movie. After the film has ended, Banderas, who has been watching the film, enters a stall in the men's room, and masturbates. Ponceta appears in full-frontal

nudity, while gay kissing scenes between Ponceta, Banderas and Molina are numerous.

Companion Films: See "Men and Boys" and "Murderers" in the "Companion Films Index."

LEATHER BOYS, THE ★★★★
(1964)
UK/Color/108 minutes
Director: Sidney J. Furie
Cast: Colin Campbell *(Reggie)*, Rita Tushingham *(Dot)*, Dudley Sutton *(Peter)*, Gladys Henson *(Gran)*, Martin Mathews *(Uncle Arthur)*, Betty Marsden *(Dot's Mother)*, Johnny Briggs *(Boy friend)*.

Genre: Drama—Based on a novel by Eliot George.

Plot: In 1964 this was no doubt a shocking, realistic film about rebellious London teenagers with loose sexual morals and dark secrets. Thirty years later it's simply a well-acted, handsomely photographed film that has held up extraordinarily well.

In this scene from *Law Of Desire* (1986), an off-screen director directs a young man, in an erotic film within the film, to turn himself on.

116

Colin Campbell plays Reggie, a strikingly handsome, rugged and painfully naive young motorcycle mechanic. Rita Tushingham plays Dot, his high-school sweetheart who can't wait to get married and move away from her mother's home. Their immature relationship sours, however, halfway through the honeymoon.

Reggie begins to spend more and more of his time away from home with his new "buddy," Pete (Sutton). Pete is an odd-looking, motorcycle-riding leather boy, who has taken a liking to the handsome Reggie. Before long the two have moved in together and are sharing the same bed.

Reggie doesn't understand why he finds it so easy to communicate with Pete and so difficult to get along with Dot. The only thing they don't seem to have in common is an equal interest in picking up girls.

In a desperate attempt to win back her husband, Dot lies about being pregnant. Reggie knows she is lying, however, because they stopped sleeping together long ago. When Pete suggests that she be on her way he says, "Leave the men to mens business." Dot replies, "Men? You look like a couple of queers."

Dot has seen what Reggie refuses to see. In the final scene, the two young men have decided to go off to America together. While waiting for their ship to depart they stop at a bar. When Reggie discovers that this is a gay bar and that his pal is a regular whom everyone knows by name, he feels betrayed. As he walks away from the bar and Pete, he has lost not only a freind, but more important, his innocence.

MPAA Rating: PG

Companion Films:
See "Closet Cases" in the "Companion Films Index."

LIFE IS LIKE A CUCUMBER ★★★
(Affengeil)
(1990)
Germany/Color/87 minutes
Director: Rosa von Praunheim
Cast: Lotti Huber, Rosa von Praunheim, Helga Sloop, Gertrud Mischwitzky, Thomas Woischnig, Hans Peter Schwade, Frank Schafer.
Genre: Documentary—Gay filmmaker Rosa von Praunheim examines his friendship with the eccentric German actress Lotti Huber in this 1990 film.
Plot: A survivor of a concentration camp, the 76-year-old Huber fled to Israel and became a nightclub dancer. In later years she became a TV personality and a flamboyant spokesperson for the gay community. Together they are a bizarre but entertaining twosome, and the film is a warm and witty portrait of a modern-day heroine.
MPAA Rating: Not rated—Seminude gay bedroom scenes.
Companion Films: See "Documentaries" in the "Companion Films Index."

LIVING END, THE ★★★
(1992)
US/Color/92 minutes
Director: Gregg Araki
Cast: Mike Dytri, Craig Gilmore, Mark Finch, Mary Woronov, Johanna Went, Darcy Marta, Scott Goetz, Graig Lee.
Genre: Drama—Underground director, writer, photographer and editor Gregg Araki brings to the screen a quirky, campy, low-budget tragicomic buddy picture whose lead characters are two HIV-positive, angry gay men. The tag line read "an irresponsible movie by Gregg Araki."

Plot: Craig Gilmore plays Jon, a film critic who has just learned that he is HIV-positive. Mike Dytri plays Luke, a drifter who has just blown away three would-be gay bashers. This after he just escapes from two would-be killer lesbians, taking their gun with him.

Jon and Luke meet by chance and discover that they are both members of the "HIV club." Full of rage at society's ignorance and prejudice, and feeling he has nothing to lose, Luke continues his murderous spree. Soon the two young men are on the road running from the law and their own destinies. Somewhere along the way this love story turns sour, however, and they reach the end of their road and quirky romance. Though uneven, this is a film that does have its moments.

MPAA Rating: Not rated—Gay sex scenes are strictly above the belt. Contains violence, profanity and numerous gay kissing scenes.

Companion Films: See "AIDS" and "Murderers" in the "Companion Films Index."

LONG DAY CLOSES, THE ★★★★

(1993)
UK/Color/82 minutes
Director: Terence Davies
Cast: Leigh McCormack (*Bud*), Marjorie Yates (*Mother*), Anthony Watson (*Kevin*), Nicholas Lamont (*John*), Ayse Owens (*Helen*), Robin Polley (*Mr. Nicholls*).
Genre: Drama—Writer-director Terence Davies (*Distant Voices, Still Lives*) brings to the screen a sophisticated, intelligent and complex autobiographical story set in Liverpool, circa 1955.
Plot: Leigh McCormack plays Bud, a lonely young boy who realizes he is attracted to the same sex. Unnable to find reassurance or comfort at home, he spends most of his free time at the movies. It is in this other world of fantasy that he feels safe and happy.

David Ehrenstein in the *Advocate* writes, "Davies knows intelligent moviegoers—both gay and straight—have been longing for years for films half as good as this one."

Armond White, writing in *Film Comment* said, "*The Long Day Closes* is the first great movie about an explicitly gay child, and that particular detail only deepens the film's universality."

MPAA Rating: PG
Companion Films: See "Coming Out" in the "Companion Films Index."

LONGTIME COMPANION ★★★★★

(1989)
US/Color/96 minutes
Director: Norman Rene
Cast: Bruce Davison (*David*), Campbell Scott (*Willy*), Stephen Caffrey (*Allan aka "Fuzzy"*), Dermot Mulroney (*John*), Mark Lamos (*Sean*), Patrick Cassidy (*Howard*), John Dossett (*Paul*), Mary-Louise Parker (*Lisa*), Michael Schoeffling (*Michael*).
Genre: Drama
Plot: In the opening scene, a young Campbell Scott is jogging along the beach. At the end of his run he strips off his running shorts and is seen naked from behind as he runs into the waves for a skinny dip. It's the summer of 1981, and the place is Fire Island. It was a time of disco music, carefree sex, multiple sex partners, parties and fun. It was a time of innocence—before AIDS.

As news of a strange new gay cancer makes

Stephen Caffrey, Campbell Scott and Dermot Mulroney in *Longtime Companion* (1989). The scene takes place at a Fire Island bar in the carefree days before AIDS.

headlines in the *New York Times,* a small circle of gay friends is about to learn firsthand about the disease. Over the course of the decade the group grows smaller as one friend after another succumbs to the disease. The film is more than a story about dying of AIDS—it's a story about living with AIDS. It's about loving friendships, support, companionship and, most of all, about large and small acts of courage.

At the center of this group of friends is Willy (Scott), a gay New Yorker and gym trainer. His best friend is John (Mulroney), the first of their friends to die of the disease. Mary-Louise Parker plays Willy's childhood friend, Lisa, and the only true girl of the group. Willy's lover is "Fuzzy" (Caffrey). In one humorous and embarrassing scene Willy walks in on him as he is lip-synching to the "Dreamgirls." David (Davison) and Sean (Lamos) are longtime companions with a house on Fire Island. David is independently wealthy, while Sean is a writer for TV soap operas. One of the characters on his soap is Howard (Cassidy), a gay actor who's content to pass for straight. Landing a job on the soap is a dream come true—that's until he learns his character is gay. His response, "It's fine for someone like Bill Hurt

A young Tom Berenger in *Looking For Mr. Goodbar* (1977), his second feature film.

to play a gay character, everyone knows he's straight."

At the end of the film, three of the remaining friends, Willy, Fuzzy and Lisa are seen walking along the beach and in a moment of fantasy imagine that all of their friends have come back to life and are celebrating, the way they once did. In a poignant moment Willy says, "I just want to be there if they ever do find a cure. Can you imagine what it would be like?" Lisa answers, "Like the end of World War II." While ultimately heartbreaking, it's also a very funny, tender, warm and moving film. Credit for this can be shared equally by all involved in this rare and authentic film.

Quotes:
"I certainly don't think everyone is going to die who gets it, do you?"
    —*Lamos*
"A lot of peoples' work lives get in the way of their TV viewing."
    —*Lamos*
"He lives with another guy and they both have great bodies. You tell me."
    —*Mary-Louise Parker*
"Who's the president of the United States?"
"Ronald Reagan."
"Who's the vice president?"
"Nancy Reagan."
    —*Dossett and Lamos*
"What do you think happens when we die?"
"We get to have sex again."
    —*Caffrey and Scott*

MPAA Rating: R—Contains profanity, brief nudity and gay kissing scenes between Scott and Caffrey and Cassidy and Dossett.
Trivia: When Craig Lucas and Norman Rene went on to collaborate on the film *Prelude To A Kiss*, David Ansen of *Newsweek* commented,

"Though the film is not about AIDS, it's hard not to think that this deceptively slight romantic comedy was conceived in response to that disease, which, like a witch's curse, can transform a young beauty into a physical beast. From the movie's opening images of a clock tower and a watch, this love story gains poignancy from the pressure of ticking mortality."
Awards: Bruce Davison was nominated for a *Best Supporting Actor* Academy Award for his role.
Companion Films: Also see "AIDS" in the "Companion Films Index."

LOOKING FOR MR. GOODBAR ★★★★
(1977)
US/Color/135 minutes
Director: Richard Brooks
Cast: Diane Keaton (*Theresa Dunn*), Tuesday Weld (*Katherine Dunn*), Richard Gere (*Tony*), Tom Berenger (*Gary*), William Atherton (*James*), Alan Feinstein (*Martin*), Richard Kiley (*Mr. Dunn*), Joel Fabian (*Barney*), Richard Bright (*George*), Levar Burton (*Jackson*), Eddie Garrett (*Bartender*), Alexander Courtney (*Arthur*), Robert Burke (*Patrick*), Tony Hawkins (*Chuck*).
Genre: Thriller—Although not very original (once again the homosexual is a self-hating psycho killer), this is a gripping tale of self-destruction.
Plot: Set in Boston in 1976, Diane Keaton plays a woman with very low self-esteem who's only attracted to men who emotionally and physically abuse her. Brought up in a strict Catholic home she's a teacher and appears to live a model life by day. By night, however, she

cruises the singles bars for men and excitement.

After being dumped-on by a series of men, including Richard Gere, her luck runs out. She has the misfortune to invite back to her apartment a young man with even lower self-esteem.

Newcomer Tom Berenger plays Gary, an ex-con having an identity crisis. Berenger plays an insecure and repressed homosexual who's unable to come to terms with his sexuality. Dressed in drag for a New Year's street party he is attacked by a group of gay bashers. Humiliated he leaves his gay lover and goes to a bar. There he meets Keaton who picks him up. When he is unable to perform sexually, he again feels humiliated. Then when she asks him to leave, he becomes enraged and manages to rape her. His rage escalates from here into an extremely violent and ultimate climax.

Sex, violence and death are all closely linked in this intensely graphic drama. Homophobia also runs rampant in this exploration of sexual perversions that ultimately lead to death. Though difficult to watch, technical credits are topnotch and the performances are memorable all around.

Quotes:
"I'd rather be seduced than comforted."
—Keaton
"Obviously most of you never hope to write anything more literate than a personal check."
—Feinstein
"Confession may be good for the soul, but it's bad for sex."
—Feinstein
"They all think I pee perfume."
—Weld
"I'm not angry, I just can't stand a woman's company right after I've fucked her."
—Feinstein

"It's not very sporting for the mistress of a married man to be jealous."
—Feinstein
"I'm gonna make you an offer you can't refuse."
—Gere
"Nobody tells the truth ever. Well, maybe it's better that way."
"That's the friggin' truth."
—Keaton and Gere
"Hey, your fly's open."
"Of course. I gotta go to work too."
—Keaton and Gere
"Me queer? Jesus, I'm a married man. I got two kids and a very expensive mistress. I'm an animal."
—A trick
"How do you get free of the terrible truth?"
—Kiley
"Don't you ever ask me to wear this crap again. I'm no goddamn nellie, you ought to know that. You know what we are? Look at us, we're a couple of freaks."
—Berenger
"Goddamn it you're the nellie, not me. I'm a pitcher, not a catcher and don't you ever forget that you hear?"
—Berenger
"Can I buy you a drink?"
"Confidentially, with me one's too many and a million's not enough.
"I've got the same problem with men."
—Garrett and Keaton
MPAA Rating: R—Contains graphic violence, scenes of sexuality and female nudity. Gere appears in a lengthy scene in only a jock strap. Berenger has an extended gay kissing scene.
Companion Films: See "Closet Cases" and "Murderers" in the "Companion Films Index."

LOST LANGUAGE OF CRANES, THE ★★★
(1992)
UK/Color/87 minutes
Director: Nigel Finch
Cast: Brian Cox *(Owen Benjamin)*, Eileen Atkins *(Rose)*, Angus MacFadyen *(Philip Benjamin)*, Corey Parker *(Eliot Abrahams)*, Rene Auberjonois *(Geoffrey Lane)*, John Schlesinger *(Derek Moulthorp)*, Ben Daniells *(Robin Bradley)*, Nigel Whitney *(Winston Penn)*, Richard Warwick *(Frank)*.
Genre: Drama—A BBC adaptation of David Leavitt's 1986 novel. Anglophiles will appreciate the setting's relocation from New York City to London.
Plot: Set in suburban London, *Cranes* revolves around Owen Benjamin (Cox), a middle-aged married man struggling to come out of the closet to his wife and son. It's also the poignant and often painful tale of a father and son who discover that they are both gay.

Owen manages to balance his two lives quite nicely until the day his son announces to the family that he's gay. His son's revelation becomes the catalyst that prompts Owen to finally come out of the closet himself. While the news destroys his marriage, father and son bond—as they were never able to in earlier years—and begin a new relationship.

Though a bit melodramatic, performances are natural and handled with warmth and dignity, resulting in a top-notch production.
MPAA Rating: Not rated—MacFadyen and Parker share a gay kiss. UK version contains brief male nudity; a prudish U.S. version has been shot with underwear.
Trivia: The U.S. television premiere on PBS caused quite a controversy in 1992.
Companion Films: See "Coming Out" in the "Companion Films Index."

MACHO DANCER ★★

(1988)

Philippines/Color/136 minutes

Director: Lino Brocka

Cast: Allan Paule *(Pol)*, Daniel Fernando *(Noel)*, Jaclyn Jose *(Bambi)*, Princess Punzalan *(Pining)*, William Lorenzo *(Dennis)*, Bobby Samo *(Greg)*, Charlie Catalla *(Mamma Charlie)*, Joel Lamangan *(Mother)*, Johnny Vicar *(Kid)*, Anthony Taylor *(The manager)*, Lucita Soriano *(The mother)*, Timothy Diwa *(Rolly)*, Angelo Miguel *(Jun)*, Ronald Mendoza *(Customer)*.

Genre: Drama—A low-budget, independent feature light on story and heavy on sexuality. In Tagalog with English subtitles.

Plot: A favorite among festival viewers, this is an erotic tale of a young man's introduction to the sexual underground in Manila. The film opens like soft porn but soon turns into a sentimental, often pristine love story.

In order to earn money to help support his mother and siblings, Pol (Paule), an attractive young man who has just learned he can make money off his looks and body, leaves his rural home for the fortunes to be made in the big city.

Befriended by Noel (Fernando), an attractive young gay man with more experience who earns money as a "macho dancer" (nude male dancer), he's exposed to the seedy, dangerous world of male prostitution, gay porno films, sexual slavery and drugs.

A realistic and absorbing tale, critic Kevin Thomas of the *Los Angeles Times* called it, "One of the top ten films of the year."

MPAA Rating: Not rated—Contains much male nudity from behind as well as brief frontal male nudity. Also contains some violence.

Companion Films: See "Hustlers" in the "Companion Films Index."

MAGIC CHRISTIAN, THE ★★★

(1970)

US/Color/93 minutes

Director: Joseph McGrath

Cast: Peter Sellers *(Sir Guy Grand)*, Ringo Starr *(Youngman Grand)*, Raquel Welch *(Priestess of the Whip)*, Leonard Frey *(Lawrence Faggot)*.

Genre: Comedy—A fast-paced, absurd, farcical, slapstick *Laugh-In*, love-in style fantasy based on the novel by Terry Southern.

Plot: "If you want it, here it is, come and get it, but you better hurry 'cause it's going fast," sings Badfinger in the title song about a fool and his money. The fool in this case is Sir Guy Grand, the richest man in the world, played by Peter Sellers. Bored with making money, he entertains himself by giving away his money and seeing to what lengths people will go to get it. Along for the fun is his adopted son, Youngman (Starr). As they soon discover, there's no limit to which people will go.

Laurence Harvey does a burlesque, strip-tease version of Hamlet, two boxers decide to kiss and make up rather than fight, and Yul Brynner plays a very convincing drag queen

Michael Ontkean, Harry Hamlin and Kate Jackson starred in *Making Love* (1982), the first mainstream-American film devoted entirely to a gay theme.

who picks up Roman Polanski in a bar while singing "Mad About the Boy"—for starters. The film is loaded with gay sight gags and double entendres that make for many cheap thrills and a good time.

Quotes:

"The crowd seemed sickened by the sight of no blood."

>*—Boxing announcer*

"I just wanted to see if you had your price—most of us do."

>*—Sellers*

"In, out, in, out, in, out, in, out."

>*—Welch*

MPAA Rating: PG—Contains female nudity.

Companion Films: See "Sissies" in the "Companion Films Index."

MAKING LOVE ★★★

(1982)

US/Color/113 minutes

Director: Arthur Hiller

Cast: Michael Ontkean *(Zach)*, Harry Hamlin *(Bart)*, Kate Jackson *(Claire)*.

Genre: Drama—The first mainstream-American film to deal openly and honestly with the theme of homosexuality and to feature "normal" gay lead characters. It also features one of the screen's most controversial kisses between two male leads. Screenplay by Barry Sandler.

Plot: Critics praised Hollywood for having the courage to tackle this controversial topic in a big-budget film; however, audiences, for the most part, found it strictly formula. Despite its flaws, however, it did deal with a segment of the gay population honestly and managed to include the rare and elusive (for a gay character or film) happy ending.

In a so-called risk-taking role, Michael Ontkean plays Zach, a young, married doctor who begins a long and painful process of coming out of the closet. Set in West Hollywood, he's equally attracted and repelled by the gay scene. Seeking love and companionship, he instead finds sex and one night stands. Reluctantly, he becomes involved with a male patient. Bart (Hamlin) is an attractive, single, successful gay man and author who is terrified of commitment.

Although Bart is unable to have a lasting relationship with a man, their brief, but painful, encounter helps Zach come to terms with his true sexuality. When he finally decides to leave his loving wife (Jackson) and marriage, it's just as painful. In the end they both find happiness with men able to give them what they want—the happiness they could never have had together.

Quotes:

"I figured, as long as I had to suffer I might as well get a tan."

>*—Hamlin*

"Are you happy?"

"For the most part."

"What about the other part?"

>*—Hamlin and Ontkean*

"Do you do any drugs?"

"Why, you got any to sell? I smoke a little dope once in a while, maybe a line or two of coke, a Quaalude or two now and then, maybe a Percodan once in a while. But if you mean am I *into* drugs, no way."

>*—Ontkean and Hamlin*

"It's not as if I'm gay. I'm just curious."

>*—Ontkean*

"Years from now when you talk about this—and you will—be kind."

>*—Hamlin*

"The most active thing I ever did was jump to conclusions."

—Hamlin

"Since I didn't have anyone to share it with—all the pain and confusion—I shared it with Natalie Wood or Elizabeth Taylor or Marilyn Monroe."

—Hamlin

"Goddamn him. It was going so well. Why did he have to tell me he loved me?"

—Hamlin

MPAA Rating: R—Includes profanity and implied sexuality, not to mention the famous kissing scene.

Trivia: A film buff, Harry Hamlin's character utters the famous line, "Years from now when you talk about this..." which other film buffs will recognize as a direct quote from Deborah Kerr in *Tea And Sympathy*.

Companion Films: See "Coming Out" in the "Companion Films Index."

MASS APPEAL ★★★

(1984)

US/Color/99 minutes

Director: Glenn Jordan

Cast: Jack Lemmon *(Father Tim Farley)*, Zeljko Ivanek *(Mark Dolson)*, Charles Durning *(Tom Burke)*, Talia Balsam *(Liz)*.

Genre: Drama—The fine performances by all the central characters raise this melodramatic morality tale above the level of a television movie of the week.

Plot: Trapped in a moral dilemma, Jack Lemmon plays Father Timothy Farley, a mediocre, alcoholic, hypocrite who's popular with his parish because he tells them what they want to hear.

When Mark (Ivanek), a young, outspoken and idealistic young seminarian with strong convictions, is placed in his charge, Father Farley feels challenged by the young man.

When rumors of homosexuality between two deacon contenders surface, the intolerant and traditional monsignor (Durning) expels them. Mark is outraged and chastises the monsignor, calling him homophobic. He later confesses to Farley that he is bisexual and that his inability to deal with his sexual confusion in the real world is the reason he has chosen celibacy and the priesthood.

The monsignor, out for revenge, is determined to expel Mark. When he learns that he is bisexual, he uses the information to do just that. Mark asks Farley for help, but he cowardly refuses, afraid that his congregation will think that he's gay if he sides with Mark.

In the end, however, Mark's courage and convictions have had an effect on Farley. He decides to risk losing his parish and his position to stand up for Mark who's being persecuted by the Church.

Quotes:

"A harmless lie? I didn't know there was such a thing."

—Ivanek

"As you know, the tricky thing about priests is that they can only live with other men."

"Jesus and St. John dealt with it."

—Durning and Ivanek

"Catholics don't have a patent on guilt."

"No, they're just the number-one manufacturers of it."

—Ivanek and Balsam

"I never liked song-and-dance theology."

—Ivanek

"Let me put my next question in your native

Rupert Graves and James Wilby play gay lovers from different social backgrounds in this adaptation of E.M. Forster's *Maurice* (1987).

tongue. Have you ever seen Paris and if you have seen Paris, were they Parisiettes or Parisians?"

"Both."

—*Lemmon and Ivanek*

MPAA Rating: PG

Companion Films: See "Religion" in the "Companion Films Index."

MAURICE ★★★★★

(1987)

UK/Color/140 minutes

Director: James Ivory

Producer: Ismail Merchant

Cast: James Wilby *(Maurice)*, Hugh Grant *(Clive)*, Rupert Graves *(Scudder)*, Denholm Elliott *(Dr. Barry)*, Ben Kingsley *(Lasker-Jones)*, Simon Callow *(Mr. Ducie)*, Billie Whitelaw *(Mrs. Hall)*.

Genre: Drama—The Merchant-Ivory team again brings to the screen an intelligent, sensitive and beautifully shot period piece based on an autobiographical novel by E.M. Forster. As always, performances are first rate.

Plot: Set in England in the early 1900s, *Maurice* is a story about sexual repression and rebellion. James Wilby plays Maurice, a wealthy, upper-class undergraduate student at Cambridge. His close friend Clive (Grant) is also an aristocrat and a fellow student. Both men are homosexual and eventually discover they are in love. Clive, however, is only interested in a platonic "higher" love. Unfortunately, Maurice longs for a more physical expression of love.

Bowing to the social pressures of the day, Clive ends his relationship with Maurice to marry, and maintain his cover. Maurice is left distraught, but it isn't long before he is in bed with Scudder (Graves), the groundskeeper. Although the two young men have nothing in common but their sexuality, Maurice discovers the physical passions of gay lovemaking for the first time. Though conflicted, Maurice chooses in the end to accept himself and a full sexual life with Scudder and to accept whatever consequences there may be.

MPAA Rating: R—Contains scenes of Rupert Graves in full-frontal nudity. Also contains gay kissing scenes, as well as scenes of gay sexuality.

Companion Films: See "Boys Schools" and "Closet Cases" in the "Companion Films Index."

MENAGE ★

(1986)

France/Color/94 minutes

Director: Bertrand Blier

Cast: Gerard Depardieu *(Bob)*, Michel Blanc *(Antoine)*, Miou-Miou *(Monique)*.

Genre: Comedy—A confused and simplistic sexual farce about a gay thief who disrupts the lives of a down-and-out husband and wife, not to mention a couple of innocent bystanders.

The promotional campaign for this insulting story about homosexuality could easily have read, "Try it—you'll like it."

In French with difficult-to-read English subtitles. Presented in letterbox format.

Plot: Gerard Depardieu plays Bob, a fast talking ex-con who makes his living as a burglar. Antoine and Monique (Blanc and Miou-Miou) are an unhappily married couple whose misfortune it is to cross paths with Bob.

Offering the couple money and a good time, they tag along with Bob on a few house break-ins. But Bob isn't interested in money at the moment, he's interested in Antoine. Antoine, however, has no interest in sleeping with Bob, but Monique does. Bob's persistence and insistence pay off when Antoine eventually relents to sex.

To his surprise, he likes it. In fact, he prefers it to sex with his wife. Bob and Antoine begin a relationship that doesn't include Monique. She eventually leaves, and the two men set up housekeeping. It isn't long before Antoine is feeling taken for granted by his new husband and they quarrel. To make up for his negligence, Bob proposes taking Antoine dancing, after persuading him to dress in drag. At the dance Bob picks up another man for a one night stand. Tempers escalate and eventually lead to violence.

Cut to four years later and the two men have reconnected with Monique and are all three prostituting themselves on the street. The two men are in full drag and makeup. Apparently once they tried it they couldn't go back.

If this film has a message—or a story for that matter—it's as confused as its characters' sexual identities.

MPAA Rating: Not rated—Contains profanity and a brief scene of male nudity from behind.

Depardieu and Blanc share a number of gay kissing and sex scenes together.

Awards: Depardieu and Blanc won the 1986 *Best Actor* award at the Cannes Film Festival for their performances.

Companion Films: See "Bisexuals" and "Drag Queens" in the "Companion Films Index."

MIDNIGHT COWBOY ★★★★★

(1969)

US/Color/113 minutes

Director: John Schlesinger

Cast: Jon Voight *(Joe Buck)*, Dustin Hoffman *("Ratso" Rizzo)*, Sylvia Miles *(Cass)*, Brenda Vaccaro *(Shirley)*, John McGiver *(O'Daniel)*, Barnard Hughes *(Tommy)*, Ruth White, Bob Balaban, Viva, Taylor Meade, Ultra Violet, Paul Morrissey, Jonathan Kramer, Paul Jabara.

Genre: Drama—Based on the novel by James Leo Herlihy.

Plot: Jon Voight plays Joe Buck, a naive, bright-eyed innocent young Texan who decides to move to New York and make his living as a hustler. Joe spends a great deal of time in front of the mirror admiring himself and figures that big-city women will want to do the same.

His first New York City encounter, however, is with a shrewd woman (Miles) who ends up hustling him. Instead of getting paid for his services he gives the woman $20 to keep her from crying. Still stinging from the encounter he finds himself in a bar sitting next to Rico "Ratso" Rizzo (Hoffman) who quickly sizes him up as an easy mark. It doesn't take long before Ratso has scammed him out of another $20 and leaves him stranded. When Joe returns to his hotel room he finds he's been locked out

until he can pay the bill. In desperation, he heads for Times Square where he's just one of many cowboy hustlers out to make a buck. He sells himself to a young gay man in a movie theater only to find out after the fact that the lad has no money.

It would seem that things couldn't get much worse for Joe, but they do. He runs into Ratso once again. But this time, to make amends, Ratso offers him a place to stay. Joe's situation brings on a flashback and we learn that he was raped by a gang of men back in Texas who also raped his girlfriend. This is one of many clues that help explain why Joe would rather have sex for money than get close to a woman in a real relationship.

As Ratso and Joe grow close, their relationship resembles that of husband and wife. It also becomes clear that this clean-cut, wholesome-looking stud is not that different from the slick, sickly cripple—Ratso. Both are emotionally crippled. As Joe becomes more disillusioned he is eventually forced to sell blood to earn money for food. At the same time Ratso's illness is getting worse. When they have just about reached bottom, they decide to leave the city and head for Florida where they dream of better times. On the bus trip, however, Ratso dies.

The film, as fresh today as it was the day it was released, is a compelling story about friendships, loneliness, sex, religion and love in our modern lives.

Quotes:

"You'll be the best-looking cowboy in the parade."

—*Joe's grandmother*

"I ain't a for-real cowboy, but I am one helluva stud."

—*Voight*

"You know what you can do with them dishes, and if you aren't man enough to do it, I'd be glad to oblige."

—*Voight*

"I'm looking for the Statue of Liberty."

"It's up in Central Park taking a leak. If you hurry up you'll catch the supper show."

—*Voight and Miles*

"Frankly you're beginning to smell and that's a handicap for a stud in New York."

—*Hoffman*

"John Wayne? You're gonna tell me he's a fag!"

—*Voight*

MPAA Rating: R—Originally rated X, the video has been edited somewhat and rerated. Voight appears nude from behind in a number of scenes, including the famous shot that catches him running after Sylvia Miles with his pants down around his ankles.

Awards: *Midnight Cowboy* won the Oscar for *Best Picture*. The film also won for *Best Director* and *Best Screenplay (Based on material from another medium)*. In addition, it received nominations for *Best Actor* (Dustin Hoffman and Jon Voight), *Best Supporting Actress* (Sylvia Miles) and *Best Film Editing*.

Companion Films: See "Closet Cases," "Only the Lonely" and "Rape" in the "Companion Films Index."

MIDNIGHT EXPRESS ★★★★

(1978)

US/Color/121 minutes

Director: Alan Parker

Cast: Brad Davis (*Billy Hayes*), Paul Smith (*Camp commander*), Randy Quaid (*Jimmy*), John Hurt (*Max*), Norbert Weisser (*Erich*), Irene Miracle (*Susan*), Bo Hopkins (*Tex*), Mike Kellin (*Mr. Hayes*), Paolo Bonacelli (*Rifki*).

Genre: Drama—The story of an American college student arrested in Istanbul, Turkey while attempting to smuggle hashish to the U.S. The film is based on the autobiographical book by William Hayes.

Plot: Arrested in 1970, Billy, played by Brad Davis, is stripped of all rights in a Turkish prison and subjected to extreme mental and physical abuse. Believing he has only four years to serve, he quietly endures his sentence. With 53 days to go, his sentence is extended and he is used as an example and given a 30-year sentence.

In Turkey, Billy realizes, all foreigners are considered dirty. So is homosexuality, but all the men practice it every chance they get. It's just not discussed. In the book, Billy becomes sexually involved with Erich, a fellow inmate. In Parker's homophobic treatment, Billy and Erich give each other baths, and in one steamy shower scene, kiss—but Billy backs away before it goes any further. The scenes are nevertheless very erotic.

Davis, in a convincing later scene dramatically depicts a man who has been deprived not only of sex but of any human kindness or feeling. When his girlfriend comes to visit, he pleads with her to strip off her top. He masturbates as she does so, in the film's most degrading, yet poignant scene.

In the end, faced with a virtual life sentence, Billy has nothing to lose and manages to catch the *Midnight Express*—the prison word for escape.

Quotes:

"What's legal today is suddenly illegal tomorrow. What's illegal yesterday is suddenly legal today because everybody's doing it. You

can't put everybody in jail."
　　—Davis
"The bad machines don't know that they're bad machines."
　　—Achmed, an inmate
"There will be trouble if you walk this way. A good Turk always walks to the right. You must go the other way."
　　—Achmed, an inmate
"The law is sometimes wrong."
"The law is never wrong here."
　　—Davis and Quaid

MPAA Rating: R—Contains male and female nudity, including Davis, who appears nude from behind while being strip-searched for drugs.

Postscript: Brad Davis died of AIDS in 1991.

Awards: Received an Academy Award nomination for *Best Picture*—lost out to *The Deer Hunter*. Also nominated for *Best Director, Best Supporting Actor* (John Hurt), *Best Screenplay (Based on material from another medium)* (Oliver Stone), *Best Music (Original score)* and *Best Film Editing*.

Companion Films: See "Prisoners" in the "Companion Films Index."

MIKAEL ★★★

(aka Chained: The Story Of The Third Sex)
(1924)
Germany/B&W
Director: Carl Theodor Dreyer
Cast: Benjamin Christiansen *(Zoret)*, Walter Slezak *(Mikael)*.
Genre: Drama—Adapted from the Hermann Bang novel of the same title. The book was reportedly based on the life of French artist Auguste Rodin.

Plot: In this early homosexual love story, Benjamin Christiansen plays Zoret, an artist who falls in love with a young nude male model. Walter Slezak plays Mikael, a calculating young man who uses Zoret and eventually leaves him for a wealthy woman.

In this melodramatic tale, Zoret, on his deathbed, leaves his possessions to Mikael, who's the only person he has ever truly loved. This is a universal story that has been retold many times since.

MPAA Rating: Not rated.

Companion Films: See "Men and Boys" in the "Companion Films Index."

MILLER'S CROSSING ★★★★★

(1990)
US/Color/115 minutes
Director: Joel Coen
Cast: Gabriel Byrne *(Tommy)*, Marcia Gay Harden *(Verna)*, John Turturro *(Bernie)*, Albert Finney *(Leo)*, Jon Polito *(Johnny)*.
Genre: Drama—Sharp, witty, stunning, powerful and a bit bizarre. This is the ultimate story of betrayal and double cross. Everyone in the film is double-crossing someone.

Plot: This mobster film is set in the 1920s. Finney plays Leo, a corrupt political boss. A blowup with his partner and friend (Byrne) pits the two on opposite sides of a violent gang war. In the middle is Bernie (Turturro), a Jewish homosexual or *twist* and the catalyst for the war. Bernie has been cheating Johnny, and Johnny wants him dead. Leo, however, controls who gets hit, and wants him alive.

In the film's most powerful scene—a scene that qualifies as one of the most memorable and moving in film history—Turturro as Bernie, is about to be murdered in the woods. He cries, begs, and humiliates himself as he pleads for his life. He appeals to Tommy's sense of justice when he says, "I'm praying to you, look in your heart." Over and over he pleads, until Tommy has mercy. This is an emotionally wrenching scene that is all the more powerful when we realize later that Bernie is truly a sleazy character who turns around and murders his lover, Mink, and then tries to blackmail Tommy, the man who spared his life. Turturro gives a tour-de-force performance in a first-rate film.

Actor Luke Perry (*Buffy The Vampire Slayer*) described the scene in *Movieline* magazine this way, "Every frame in *Miller's Crossing* is fantastic, but the scene in the woods when John Turturro—who usually plays this 'Fuckin'-A' kind of guy, but here plays a gay in the '20s who's messed people around and has to pay the ultimate price—pleads for his life left me in tears, man. That's why I do what I do. I want one of those moments."

MPAA Rating: R—For language and strong violence.

Companion Films: See "Closet Cases" and "Murderers" in the "Companion Films Index."

MISHIMA: A LIFE IN FOUR CHAPTERS ★
(1985)
US-Japan/Color/121 minutes
Director: Paul Schrader
Cast: Ken Ogata (*Mishima*), Kenji Sawada, Yasosuke Bando, Toshiyuki Nagashima, Mashayuki Shionoya (*Morita*), Junkichi Orimoto.
Genre: Drama—In Japanese with English subtitles. Executive producers were George Lucas and Francis Ford Coppola.

Plot: Directed by Paul Schrader (*American Gigolo*), this ambitious but misguided film flopped at the box office.

A bio pic, the director attempts to tell the story of Japan's celebrated gay writer Yukio Mishima, but nearly forgets to mention that Mishima was homosexual. The result is a cinematically beautiful film without much substance or truth.

Though married, Mishima was open about his sexuality. In the film, however, it's only alluded to briefly, following a failed attempt at a political overthrow he commits ritual suicide, or *seppuku*. Played by Ken Ogata, Mishima, at age forty-five, together with his lover Morita (Shionoya), commits suicide in 1970.

Awards: In 1985 the film won *Best Artistic Contribution* at the Cannes Film Festival.

MPAA Rating: R

Companion Films: See "Biographies" in the "Companion Films Index."

MUSIC LOVERS, THE ★★★★
(1971)
UK/Color/123 minutes
Director: Ken Russell
Cast: Richard Chamberlain (*Peter Tchaikovsky*), Glenda Jackson (*Nina*), Max Adrian (*Bernstein*), Christopher Gable (*Anton Chilovski*), Kenneth Colley (*Madeste*), Bruce Robinson (*Alexi*), Andrew Faulos (*Davidov*).
Genre: Drama—A fantasy, a tragedy and a visual feast, this Ken Russell period film is a stylized biography of tortured Russian composer Peter Tchaikovsky.

Plot: This visually stunning flight of fancy, illusion and delusion asks the question, "Was the 19th-century Russian composer Peter Tchaikovsky driven insane by his love of music, love of men or the love of his mother?"

Richard Chamberlain plays the romantically tragic Peter, a man who lost at an early age the only woman he ever loved—his mother. When society later forces him to kill the relationship he has with the only man he has ever loved (Gable), he's left with only his music.

To fit in with society, he marries a woman, who—unfortunately—is an unbalanced and scheming prostitute. When he eventually leaves her he says, "You wanted a husband. I wanted a marriage without a wife." As sexually insecure as he, she goes mad because of his rejection.

Left with nothing but his music, he catches the ear of a wealthy widow who becomes his patroness. This becomes the happiest time of his life. When she learns from his former lover Anton (Gable), that he is a homosexual, however, she rejects him and cuts off his support. Finally, left with nothing—but his fame and fortune—he chooses a melodramatic

Richard Chamberlain and Christopher Gable play tragic lovers in *The Music Lovers* (1971).

suicide. His death is a slow and torturous one, but, as he says earlier, "To pretend all of one's life is the height of torture."

Performances, while over the top, are fascinating, powerful and memorable.

MPAA Rating: R—Glenda Jackson appears in an extended full-frontal nude scene.

Companion Films: Ten years later, Herbert Ross brought to the screen *Nijinsky* (1980), the life story of an equally tortured artist.

Also see "Biographies," "Closet Cases" and "Unhappy Homosexuals" in the "Companion Films Index."

MY BEAUTIFUL LAUNDRETTE ★★★★

(1986)

UK/Color/93 minutes

Director: Stephen Frears

Cast: Daniel Day-Lewis *(Johnny),* Gordon Warnecke *(Omar),* Saeed Jaffrey *(Nasser),* Roshan Seth *(Papa),* Shirley Anne Field *(Rachel),* Rita Wolf *(Tania),* Neil Cunningham *(Englishman),* Garry Cooper *(Squatter).*

Genre: Drama—Story revolves around the modern-day conflict between lower-class Britons and well-to-do immigrant Pakistanis—with a twist.

Plot: Racism and sexism are opposite sides of the same coin in this often humorous and insightful Stephen Frears film.

Gordon Warnecke plays Omar, a gay Pakistani living with his alcoholic father (Roshan Seth) in London. In need of work, his father convinces his enterprising brother, Nasser, (Jaffrey) to give Omar a job. Uncle Nasser takes Omar under his wing, and before long, he has gone from washing cars to running one of his uncle's laundrettes.

To clean up the business, located in an East Side neighborhood overrun by working-class, racist, out-of-work teenage punks, Omar enlists Johnny, a neighborhood boy and an old friend. As long as Johnny works for Omar the laundrette is safe from the fascist street punks who despise Omar and the other Pakistani immigrants.

Omar and Johnny become lovers as well as partners, and together they turn the laundrette into a beautiful, neon-lite showplace called "Powders" (as in puff). Right before the grand opening, Omar and Johnny retreat to the back room where they have sex, while waiting for Omar's father to arrive.

When the laundrette is a success, it goes to Omar's head, and he turns on Johnny for being like his fascist friends. Both men are now equal, having used one another to get what they want. But when Nasser's arrogant moneyman purposefully runs over one of Johnny's friends, not even Johnny can protect Omar and his shop from the neighborhood's anger and violence.

Fine performances and a fresh new take on a familiar topic make this one of the director's gems.

Quotes:

"Try and fix him up with a nice girl. I'm not sure his penis is in full working order."

—*Seth*

"What do you think I am—your trampoline?"

—*Jaffrey*

"He was to the bottle what Louis Armstrong was to the trumpet."

—*Jaffrey*

"Can I make you a drink?"

"Make him a man first."

—*Cunningham and Jaffrey*

"You're an underpants cleaner!"
　　—Seth
"I thought you two were getting married."
"I'd rather drink my own urine."
　　—Jaffrey and Field
"It's not possible to enjoy being hated so much."
　　—Field
"That country's been sodomized by religion."
　　—Jaffrey
MPAA Rating: R—Contains gay kissing and sex scenes. Also contains female nudity above the waist.
Awards: Nominated for a *Best Screenplay*

Academy Award.
Companion Films: See "Doomed Lovers" and "Fascists and Nazis" in the "Companion Films Index."

MY OWN PRIVATE IDAHO ★★★
(1991)
US/Color/102 minutes
Director: Gus Van Sant
Cast: River Phoenix *(Mike Waters)*, Keanu Reeves *(Scott Favor)*, James Russo *(Richard*

River Phoenix and Keanu Reeves play male hustlers in Gus Van Sant's *My Own Private Idaho* (1991)

Waters), Udo Kier *(Hans)*, William Richert *(Bob Pigeon)*, Grace Zabriskie *(Alena)*.

Genre: Drama

Plot: River Phoenix and Keanu Reeves play teenage male hustlers living on the streets of Portland, Oregon. Although the situations are often comic, director Gus Van Sant *(Drugstore Cowboy)* has brought to the screen a touching and often moving tale about friendship and love. To keep it interesting, Van Sant has thrown in kinky sex, houses that fall from the sky and a little Shakespeare.

Phoenix plays Mike Waters, a vulnerable gay hustler and narcoleptic, obsessed with finding the mother who abandoned him as a child. Reeves plays Scott Favor, Mike's closest friend. A bisexual hustler, Scott only sleeps with men for money and to provoke his wealthy father. Both young men are desperately searching for love and affection. When Mike falls in love with Scott, they share a tender moment; but for Scott, hustling is just a transitional phase. His belief, as he explains to Mike, is that, "Two guys can't love each other."

In the end, Mike is in the same place he was at the beginning of the film—on a lonely, desolate road in the middle of nowhere, still searching for love. While the director's vision is bleak, it's never uninteresting.

MPAA Rating: R—Contains very brief gay kissing scenes between Keanu Reeves and River Phoenix and between Reeves and William Richert. Reeves also appears nude very briefly from behind.

Awards: River Phoenix won the 1991 National Society of Film Critics Award for *Best Actor*. The film was honored with the *Best Film Music*, *Best Actor* and *Best Screenplay* awards from the Independent Spirit Awards, and nominated for *Best Director* and *Best Cinematography*. Reeves won the dubious MTV Movie Award for *Most Desireable Male* in 1992.

Companion Films: See "Hustlers" in the "Companion Films Index."

NAKED CIVIL SERVANT, THE ★★★★
(1980)
UK/Color/80 minutes
Director: Jack Gold
Cast: John Hurt *(Quentin Crisp)*.
Genre: Comedy-Drama-Biography—About the life and times of Quentin Crisp, an outrageous and flamboyant homosexual, coming of age and growing into old age in England.
Plot: In one of the very first lines of the film, Quentin Crisp exclaims, "Any film, even the worst, is better than real life." This statement is a clue to the unrelenting wit, sarcasm and biting humor to follow.

John Hurt puts in a brilliant, touching and memorable performance as the effeminate, outcast homosexual, Crisp. Dressing in drag as a small boy, he grows up to discover he's not the only one of his kind. Instead of hiding his difference he makes it a personal crusade to flaunt it and make a place in the world for others like himself. Unfortunately, he begins his one-man crusade in the 1930s and he must fend off numerous members of a sexually repressed society including hostile police, thugs, parents, neighbors, the draft board, and a few strange bedfellows.

"An exhibitionist has no friends," states an acquaintance. Quentin discovers that this is true even in a local gay club. "Look, ducky, you're spoiling it for the others," says the manager of the club. Quentin replies in so many words that he's out of the closet and is doing it for the cause. The manager responds, "What cause, we're normal."

Throughout the years, faced with hostility, bigotry and physical harm, he courageously remains true to himself, his sense of humor and wit, his only weapons. "Every moment has been agony, but I couldn't have done otherwise," he states at the end of the film. And we understand completely.
Quotes:
"Health consists of having the same diseases as one's neighbors."
    —Hurt
"Do you think a homosexual elephant has a terrible time of it?"
    —Hurt
"Do you intend to spend your entire life admiring yourself?"
    —Crisp's father
MPAA Rating: Not rated—Strictly PG for subject matter.
Awards: John Hurt won the British Academy Award for *Best Actor* in this role.
Companion Films: See "Coming Out" and "Drag Queens" in the "Companion Films Index."

NATIONAL LAMPOON'S LOADED WEAPON 1 ★★★
(1993)
US/Color/82 minutes
Director: Gene Quintano
Cast: Emilio Estevez *(Jack Colt)*, Samuel L. Jackson *(Wes Luger)*, Jon Lovitz *(Becker)*,

The true "Queen of England," Quentin Crisp plays himself in *Resident Alien* (1991).

Kathy Ireland *(Destiny Demeanor)*, William Shatner *(General Mortars)*, Tim Curry *(Jigsaw)*, Phil Hartman *(Comedian)*.

Genre: Drama

Plot: This *Lethal Weapon* spoof is a vehicle for cheap sight gags and endless one-liners, all referring to sex or bodily functions. Gay jokes are numerous, and in the most imaginative sequence Emilio Estevez is shown fantasizing about two of his former male lovers and their romps together on the beach.

Estevez fans will enjoy seeing him in sexy red lingerie, being hit-on by a young black boy and baring his oiled buns in the moonlight. Or, if you just enjoy sophomoric humor, camp and drag, you'll find these 82 minutes loaded with pleasure. And as if that weren't enough, Tim Curry provides a few laughs as a Girl Scout in full drag.

Quotes:

"Say, why did the guy give a name to his penis? He didn't want a stranger making all of his decisions."

—*Hartman*

"Who are you?"

"I'm your worst nightmare."

"No, waking up without my penis is my worst nightmare."

—*Estevez and Curry*

"What do you know about her?"

"I know we wear the same size pumps."

—*Jackson and Estevez*

MPAA Rating: R

Companion Films: See "Drag Queens" in the "Companion Films Index."

NEXT STOP, GREENWICH VILLAGE ★★★
(1976)

US/Color/109 minutes

Director: Paul Mazursky

Cast: Lenny Baker *(Larry Lipinsky)*, Ellen Green *(Sarah)*, Christopher Walken *(Robert)*, Shelley Winters *(Mom)* Dori Brenner *(Connie)*, Lois Smith *(Anita)*, Antonio Fargas *(Bernstein)*, Lou Jacobi *(Herb)*, Jeff Goldblum *(Clive)*, Mike Kellin, John Ford Noonan.

Genre: Drama

Plot: Mazursky's nostalgic tale takes place in 1953. Lenny Baker plays Larry Lipinsky, a 22-year-old aspiring actor who leaves Brooklyn and heads for New York City, fame and fortune. What he ends up with is a lousy job and a pregnant girlfriend, who eventually runs off to Mexico with a mutual friend. Before they leave, he says to his friend played by Christopher Walken, "Underneath that pose is just more pose." But not all is lost, he gets that part he's been waiting for, and in the end, he heads for Hollywood.

One of his quirky friends is a gay black man, Bernstein, who's played by Antonio Fargas. Living in the 1950s isn't easy for anyone. However, it's an especially difficult time for Bernstein. In one scene, a friend kids him about boasting of his heritage. "Tell me," she says, "how did your father, who's an African prince, get along with your mother who's a cleaning woman?" In another scene, Shelly Winters shows up at a party and asks,

"Who are you."

"I'm Bernstein."

"Are you Jewish?" she asks.

"No, I'm gay," he replies.

"I don't care how you feel, you're a great dancer."

In a more somber scene, he believes a female friend's suicide is his fault. He has been dating the man she was hoping to marry. In a depression he tells his friends, "I just want to stay under the covers." And of course he's talking about so much more than how he's feeling on this day. While stereotypical, this portrayal is both sensitive and memorable.

MPAA Rating: R—For language.

Trivia: For film buffs, Jeff Goldblum makes a brief appearance as an aspiring actor in a couple of scenes. Vincent Schiavelli, who played the subway ghost in *Ghost,* is also seen in the crowd during a rent party, while Ellen Green *(Little Shop Of Horrors)* makes her film debut as Larry's girlfriend.

Companion Films: See "Only the Lonely" in the "Companion Films Index."

NIJINSKY ★★★★

(1980)

UK/Color/125 minutes

Director: Herbert Ross

Cast: Alan Bates *(Sergei Diaghilev),* George De La Pena *(Vaslav Nijinsky),* Leslie Browne *(Romola de Pulsky),* Jeremy Irons *(Michael),* Alan Badel *(Patron-Dimitri),* Janet Suzman *(Hera).*

Genre: Drama—A biographical film about the tormented life of ballet legend Nijinsky and his tumultuous relationship with mentor and lover, Sergei Diaghilev. Outstanding performances and beautifully captured images make this a captivating and memorable film.

Plot: Alan Bates plays Sergei, the promoter of a ballet group, and a man with a fondness for younger men. De La Pena plays ballet dancer Nijinsky, who is Sergei's young protégé. Self-centered, dependent and tormented, Nijinsky

has spent his youth in a homosexual relationship with his mentor. Developmentally arrested in many ways, this boy genius is prone to tantrums and outbursts. Unable to accept his sexuality, he begins to wonder what it would be like to be with a woman; what it would be like to make his own decisions. The domineering Sergei reminds him, "We are what we are and we should never forget it." But Nijinsky's dissatisfaction continues to grow, and over a two-year period their relationship begins to deteriorate.

During a difficult separation, Nijinsky is seduced by a young woman, as domineering as Sergei, and without thinking through the consequences, he marries the girl as a way of hurting Sergei. Upon learning of Nijinsky's marriage, however, Sergei has him banned from the ballet troupe and refuses to take him back. In no time, Sergei has discovered a new young protégé. In a selfless act, Nijinsky's wife begs Sergei for forgiveness, "I thought I could save him and make him like other men. I didn't understand," she says. "I've tried to make him what he can't be." But her effort is to no avail.

The film opens and closes with Nijinsky in a symbolic straight jacket that says volumes not only about his life but about the lives of many homosexuals throughout history.

Quotes:

"Not too much culture, please. I'm on my holiday."

    —De La Pena

"The most expensive mistress in the world is art."

    —Bates

"Filthy little pederast whore."

    —Irons to De La Pena

"My taste is impeccable, even when it's bad."

    —Bates

"Do you think I'm a monster?"

—*Bates*

MPAA Rating: R—Presumably for subject matter. Contains only a brief heterosexual love scene.

Companion Films: See "Men and Boys" in the "Companion Films Index."

NITRATE KISSES ★★★

(1992)

US/B&W/67 minutes

Director: Barbara Hammer

Genre: Documentary—An experimental first feature by the controversial director. Her previous work has included similarly-themed shorts.

Plot: Pushing the boundaries of contemporary "queer cinema," the director explores the exclusion of gay men and lesbians throughout history.

Mainstream critics were unanimous in their less-than-favorable reviews. *The Hollywood Reporter*'s Jeff Menell writes, "It's great that in today's world, Hammer is allowed to show oral sex and anal penetration, but in the context of this film it serves no purpose, and the amount of footage devoted to it cannot be justified."

Suzan Ayscough of *Variety* writes, "As in previous work, Hammer's *Nitrate Kisses* is clearly designed to shock. There are numerous closeup shots of genitals ... Graphic docu will

likely be considered pornographic by mainstream standards and enlightened by the radical gay community."

MPAA Rating: Not rated—NC-17, if it were.

Companion Films: See "Documentaries" in the "Companion Films Index."

NOIR ET BLANC ★★

(1991)

France/B&W/80 minutes

Director: Claire Devers

Cast: Francis Frappat *(Antoine)*, Jacques Martial *(Dominique)*, Marc Berman, Josephine Fresson, Christophe Galland, Benoit Regent.

Genre: Drama

Plot: The title of this film translates to "Black and White." Filmed in black and white, it's the story of a sadomasochistic relationship that develops between two very different men.

Inspired by the Tennessee Williams story "Desire and the Black Masseur," the story's central character is Antoine, played by Frappat, who is an accountant at a health club. Dominique (Martial), a sadistic, black masseur at the club becomes Antoine's partner in an ever-increasing ritual of violent massages that leave both men changed forever by the end of the film.

MPAA Rating: Not rated—Violent and sexual.

Companion Films: See "S&M" in the "Companion Films Index."

ONCE BITTEN ★★★

(1985)

US/Color/94 minutes

Director: Howard Storm

Cast: Lauren Hutton *(Countess)*, Jim Carrey *(Mark Kendall)*, Karen Kopins *(Robin)*, Cleavon Little *(Sebastian)*, Thomas Ballatore *(Jamie)*, Skip Lackey *(Russ)*, Alan McCrae *(Man in drag)*, Philip Linton *(Boy in shower)*, Richard Schaal *(Mr. Kendall)*, Peggy Pope *(Mrs. Kendall)*.

Genre: Comedy—Teenage T&A film about a 400-year-old vampire who must drink the blood of young virgin males to retain her youthful appearance. And like most American teenage films about sex, homosexuality—or the fear of it—plays a significant role.

Plot: Carrey plays Mark, a teenage virgin who's doing everything he can to change his sexual status. In one of the film's first humorous scenes Mark is at the drive-in with his girlfriend, Robin (Kopins). When she refuses to have sex with him, he angrily leaves the car and stands in the theater lot. All around cars are bouncing up and down and naked butts are seen in back seats, as everyone in the drive-in is having sex but Mark.

Mark and his two buddies, Russ (Lackey) and Jamie (Ballatore), frustrated by their lack of action at the drive-in, head for Hollywood (of course) looking to score. When Russ gets lucky, Jamie asks if he has protection. Russ brings out an assortment of rubbers saying, "I didn't know what size I'd need." "Try petite," replies Jamie. As it turns out, the girl he gets lucky with turns out to be a guy.

Mark, however, gets picked up by a sexy woman named Countess (Hutton), a vampire in search of a male virgin's blood. Tonight is her lucky night. With the help of her fey chauffeur and servant Sebastian (Little), she takes him home, sucks his blood and he's none the wiser.

Back home on Halloween night, Robin suspects that the Countess has turned Mark into a vampire. She asks Russ and Jamie to check his inner thigh for two telltale signs. In the film's most homophobic and humorous scene, Russ holds Mark down in the shower while Jamie spreads his legs to check for evidence. Of course this shower full of naked teenage boys goes into a panic. The only thing worse than a vampire in the shower room, of course, is a queer.

Humiliated that the entire school suspects that he's gay, Jamie is equally upset that he may have enjoyed the incident in the shower. From this point on, the film becomes a series of slapstick jokes as Robin comes to the rescue and saves Mark. After helping Mark lose his virginity, Robin foils the beautiful Countess, who shrivels up into an old prune before their eyes.

In this age of AIDS, any film about dying for sex, changing in unexplained ways and even dying after sex, takes on additional meanings and becomes a metaphor, even if unintentional.

Quotes:

"Are you a prostitute?"

"I'm whatever you want me to be."

　　　—Carrey and Hutton

"Okay Sebastian, out of the closet."

"I came out of the closet centuries ago."

　　　—Hutton and Little

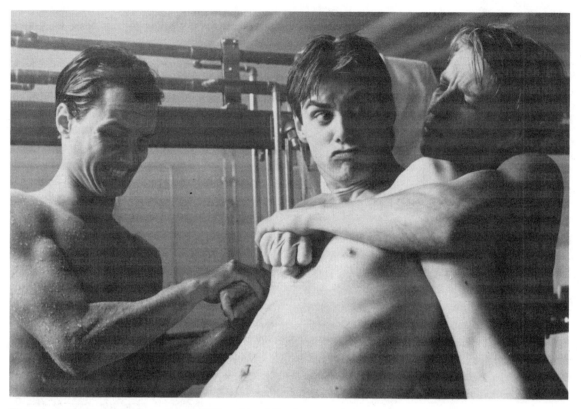

Thomas Ballatore and Skip Lackey hold down friend Jim Carrey in the high school showers and search for evidence that he is really a vampire in *Once Bitten* (1985).

"I haven't had anything this pure since the Vienna Boys Choir hit town."
—*Hutton*
"The whole school thinks we're gay. We might as well move in together and get his and his matching towels."
—*Ballatore*
"Oh my god, I knew it! We enjoyed it! We're homos. We're rump rangers."
—*Ballatore*
MPAA Rating: PG-13—Carrey, Ballatore and Lackey all appear nude from behind in, what else, a shower scene.
Companion Films: See "Homophobia" and "Vampires" in the "Companion Films Index."

OUTCASTS ★★
(1986)
Taiwan/Color/102 minutes
Director: Yu Kan Ping
Cast: Sun Yueh Tai Ling, Su Ming-Ming, Shao Hsin.

Genre: Drama—Based on the novel *The Outsiders* by Shang Yeang. In Mandarin, with difficult-to-read English subtitles.

Plot: A disgrace to his family, Li-Ching is beaten and thrown out of the house by his father because he's gay. Neglected and mistreated by his mother since childhood, his life has been less than happy.

He's found on the street by a kind older man, named Yang, who takes him in and gives him a home. Yang has taken in other young outcasts who have been thrown out for the same reason, and together they live as a family. In their free time, the boys hustle in the park.

Eventually, Yang and his longtime friend and landlady, Man-Yi, decide to go into business together. With the help of the boys, they open Taipei's first gay nightclub, called the Blue Angel.

Disturbing and dark, this moody and senti-mental film will not appeal to everyone.

MPAA Rating: Not rated—Contains graphic violence but surprisingly, lacks any sex or nudity.

Trivia: The ground-breaking first gay-themed film to be licensed by the Republic of China. Considered one of the most controversial films ever released in Taiwan.

Companion Films: See "Coming Out" in the "Companion Films Index."

OUTRAGEOUS! ★★★

(1977)
Canada/Color/96 minutes
Director: Richard Benner
Cast: Craig Russell *(Robin Turner)*, Hollis McLaren *(Liza)*, Richard Easley *(Perry)*, Allan Moyle *(Martin)*, David McIlwraith *(Bob)*, Gerry Salzberg *(Jason)*, Richard Moffatt *(Stewart)*, David Woito *(Hustler)*, Rusty Ryan *(Jimmy)*.

Genre: Comedy—A touching and winning low-budget tale of two outcasts, who don't fit in but manage to make their own place in the world by joining forces. Based on "Butterfly Ward," a short story by Margaret Gibson.

Plot: The late Craig Russell plays Robin Turner, a depressed and frustrated gay hairdresser who longs to perform as a female impersonator, but lacks the confidence. McLaren plays Liza, a schizophrenic escapee from the local mental ward. Longtime friends, Robin and Liza become roommates and obtain the strength and courage they need from one another.

When Robin is finally encouraged by his friends to perform in drag he's a big hit in Toronto—with everyone, that is, but his gay boss at the salon. Afraid that clients will discover that he's gay, Robin's fearful gay boss, Jason (Salzberg), fires Robin. This, as it turns out, forces Robin to sink or swim, and he decides to take the plunge. Once again, with the support of his friends, he heads for New York to see if he really has what it takes. Liza, who has become pregnant, remains in Toronto.

An even bigger hit in New York, the talented performer's success is, however, bittersweet following the news that Liza's baby is stillborn. To rescue her from her depression and from returning to the institution, Robin returns for his friend and brings her to New York, where his inspiration and friendship give her the strength to start over.

Russell manages not only to be outrageous, but a warm, human and a very real character. Per-formances are winning all around, while Russell's impersonations of Streisand, Channing,

147

Garland, Dietrich, Midler, West, Davis and others are first-rate.

Quotes:

"How many Zsa Zsa Gabors can be in a room at one time?"

—*Easley*

"If a caterpillar was afraid of wings, it would never become a butterfly, and people would say, 'Hey look. It's a worm in a tree.'"

—*McLaren*

"Running a beauty salon is very serious."

—*Salzberg*

"Who wants to be felt up by faggots?"

"I can think of two people in this room who would love it."

—*Salzberg and Russell*

"There are three important things in life: sex, movies and my career."

—*Russell*

"Anita Bryant sent me down here to beat some sense into you frozen fruits."

—*Russell*

"I never heard of a *sugar uncle*."

—*Russell*

"Did you want to be a girl when you were little?"

"It was so tragic having to wear mommy's bras to school."

—*A party guest and Russell*

"You're a drag, huh?"

"No, I just like to travel heavy."

—*McIlwraith and Russell*

"Isn't anybody straight anymore?"

"Sure, my father in Montana."

—*Russell and McIlwraith*

"How do you do your tits like that?"

"I usually have someone do them for me."

—*Bar patron and Russell*

"You're alive and sick and living in New York like eight million other people."

—*Russell*

"I've never known anyone worth knowing who wasn't a positive fruitcake."

—*Russell*

MPAA Rating: Not rated.

Companion Films:

See the sequel, *Too Outrageous!* (1987). Also see "Drag Queens" in the "Companion Films Index."

PARIS IS BURNING ★★★★★

(1991)

US/Color/71 minutes

Director: Jennie Livingston

Cast: Pepper Labeija, Willi Ninja, Kim Pendavis, Freddie Pendavis, Octavia Saint Laurent, Angie Xtravaganza and Venus Xtravaganza.

Genre: Documentary

Plot: Controversial documentary filmmaker Jennie Livingston explores the underground world of a group of gay men who dress in drag and compete with one another in the Harlem drag balls. For this subgroup of the gay community, the popular balls are the central focus of their lives. The majority of the men are black or Latino, and many lead harsh, depressing lives. The balls offer a sanctuary for these men to feel special, free to express themselves, and able to escape from reality.

This is a surprisingly candid, touching and moving portrait of a way of life that has evolved over the years into a popular fad. The film was made between 1987 and 1989, and is another example of a bit of the gay "lifestyle" being co-opted by mainstream heterosexual society as it has so often done in the past. *Vogueing*, which originated in the clubs, is now an accepted form of dance in gay and straight clubs around the world.

Quotes:
"I think all men are dogs. All men start barking sooner or later."
—*Saint Laurent*

MPAA Rating: Not rated—Very tame.

Awards: Won *Best Documentary* of the year from The New York Critics Association, as well as The National Society of Film Critics.

Companion Films: See "Drag Queens" in the "Companion Films Index."

PARTING GLANCES ★★★★

(1986)

US/Color/90 minutes

Director: Bill Sherwood

Cast: Richard Ganoung *(Michael)*, John Bolger *(Robert)*, Steve Buscemi *(Nick)*, Adam Nathan *(Peter)*, Kathy Kinney *(Joan)*, Patrick Tull *(Cecil)*, Yolande Bavan *(Betty)*, Andre Morgan *(Terry)*, Richard Wall *(Douglas)*, Daniel Haughey *(Ghost)*.

Genre: Drama—A warm, humorous and uplifting independent feature that takes a look at a group of friends during a 24-hour period, as they confront the reality of AIDS in their lives.

Plot: Set in New York City, Steve Buscemi plays Nick, a young, gay, up-and-coming rock musician dying of AIDS. Richard Ganoung plays Michael, Nick's former lover and longtime friend.

Robert (Bolger), Michael's current lover, is being transferred to Kenya on business for an indefinite period. On the eve of Robert's departure, another mutual friend (Kinney) throws a farewell party. Robert later confesses to Michael that the real reason he's leaving is so that he won't have to watch Nick slowly deteriorate and die.

Faced with losing the two most important men in his life, Michael must come to terms with the fact that Nick is the one he has always loved and is willing to admit it—even though it means risking his own relationship. Throughout the party, friends and acquaintances are each required to confront their feelings about the disease, and in the process, a natural, honest and intelligent film—not to mention an entertaining one—unfolds.

Quotes:

"Do I look too foofie?"

—Ganoung

"Someone should post up signs around New York that say, 'Know thyself, but please don't talk about it.'"

—Buscemi

"What are you going to do when he's gone?"
"Miss him."

—Kinney and Ganoung

"The penis astonishes me. It can give pain and pleasure, it can give life and now it can give death."
"Pesky little devils, aren't they?"

—Party guest and Kinney

"I like the chase. I'm a wolf in Twinkie clothing."

—Nathan

"You know the difference between straight guys and gay guys?"
"I forget."
"There isn't any. Straight guys are jerks. Gay guys are jerks."

—Buscemi and Ganoung

MPAA Rating: Not rated—Contains brief gay kissing scenes and suggested gay sex.

Companion Films: See "AIDS" in the "Companion Films Index."

PARTNERS ★★★

(1982)
US/Color/98 minutes
Director: James Burrows
Cast: Ryan O'Neal *(Benson)*, John Hurt *(Kerwin)*, Kenneth McMillan *(Police chief)*, Robyn Douglass *(Jill)*, Rick Jason *(Douglas)*.
Genre: Comedy—For those who like their stereotypes on the light side.
Plot: Written by *La Cage Aux Folles* scripter Francis Verber, these flamboyant characters seem less offensive than they might otherwise have been if written by another writer.

O'Neal and Hurt play two mismatched undercover cops forced to pose as gay lovers in an effort to track down a murderer who preys on gay men. O'Neal's Benson is painfully straight, while Hurt's Kerwin is just as painfully gay. Renting an apartment in West Hollywood, they eventually begin to grow fond of one another.

To the film's credit, in the final scene, it's Hurt, the passive and wimpy gay man who saves the life of macho O'Neal.

MPAA Rating: R—For nudity, profanity, violence and adult theme. O'Neal appears naked from behind during a photo shoot for a gay beefcake magazine. A gay man he picks up and takes to the beach appears naked from behind and also in dimly lit frontal nudity frolicking on the beach.

Companion Films: See "Cops" and "Neighbors, Roommates and Best Friends" in the "Companion Films Index."

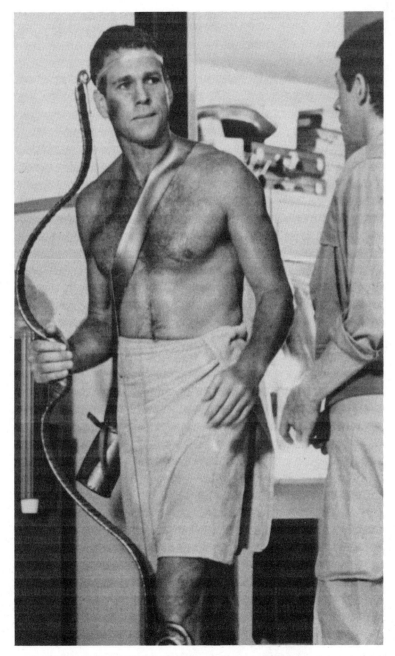

Ryan O'Neal and John Hurt go undercover and pretend to be gay roommates in order to capture a killer in *Partners* (1982).

PAUL CADMUS: ENFANT TERRIBLE AT 80
★★★
(1984)
US/Color/64 minutes
Director: David Sutherland
Genre: Documentary—A conversation with the controversial, very young-looking New York artist at 80.
Plot: Paul Cadmus, an artist whose stylized homoerotic paintings predated the gay movement by many decades, discusses his life and his work.

While he remembers his friendship with E.M. Forster and the influence of W.H. Auden and Christopher Isherwood, little is said of his own personal life. Present throughout the film is John, his nude model for 17 years and presumably his partner, though it's only alluded to.

One of his first paintings completed, while he was working for a public-works project, is titled "Fleets In." Considered at the time an insult to the Navy, it caused a scandal that made him famous overnight. He explains that he owes his career to the admiral who tried to suppress the painting. One outraged viewer wailed, "There will soon be no room in this country for such abortionists of art." Cadmus explains, "I never aimed to be controversial. I suppose it was just my objection to society as it was." It's indeed disheartening to witness how little society has changed in all these years. Cadmus's angry viewer could just as easily be Jesse Helms today.

A thoughtful, introspective, philosophical man, Cadmus has let his work express his emotions in an intoxicating and brilliant way. He quotes Flaubert, who said, "Be regular and ordinary in your life so you can be violent and original in your work." It's obvious that he has taken these words to heart.

You don't need to be an art lover to appreciate this brief but fascinating, pastel portrait of an original talent.
Quotes:
"Peoples' noses should be rubbed in all kinds of things."
—Cadmus

"I believe in exaggeration. If things are not exaggerated, people pass by."
—Cadmus
MPAA Rating: Not rated—Contains male nudity, both illustrated and actual, mostly from behind.
Companion Films: See "Biographies" in the "Companion Films Index."

PIXOTE ★★★★
(1981)
Brazil/Color/127 minutes
Director: Hector Babenco
Cast: Fernando Ramos da Silva (*Pixote*), Jorge Juliao (*Lilica*), Gilberto Moura (*Dito*), Edilson Lino (*Chico*), Zenildo Oliveira Santos (*Fumaca*), Marilia Pera (*Sueli*), Tony Tornado (*Cristal*).
Genre: Drama—In Portuguese with very easy to read English subtitles.
Plot: Fernando Ramos da Silva plays Pixote, an innocent and frightened 10-year-old runaway who quickly learns to survive on the mean streets of San Paulo.

Arrested during a police sweep of the streets, Pixote, the smallest of a group of boys, endures the violence, degradation and corruption of the authorities at a youth detention center. After two of his friends are brutally murdered by the authorities, and another boy is framed for the crimes, Pixote and four friends escape. Once on the street, the friends resume their life of crime, which escalates to violence and death.

The oldest of the group is 17-year-old Lilica (Juliao), a transvestite hustler. Lilica falls in love with Dito (Moura), who is straight. Rejected by Dito, Lilica leaves and goes on his own.

Hooking up with a prostitute, the others rob her johns at gunpoint. Pixote and Dito enjoy the easy money. When one of the johns fights back, Pixote accidentally kills him. He also kills Dito. Pixote is left alone and traumatized by what he has done. In the film's most poignant scene following the murders, Pixote seeks comfort from the prostitute. All he wants is a mother whose breast he can suck. She is the only one left in his life, but she too rejects him. She's looking for comfort herself. It is a powerful scene and says everything there is to say about this moving film.

Sex, and even life itself, is cheap for the children on the streets of this slum. Babenco masterfully captures their desperation and loneliness with a lyrical soundtrack and beautifully shot atmospheric scenes that become a potent counterpoint to this seemingly inescapable existence and environment.

MPAA Rating: Not rated—Contains full-frontal male nudity, gay sex scenes and graphic violence.

Companion Films: See "Drag Queens" and "Prisons" in the "Companion Films Index."

POISON ★★★
(1991)
US/Color/85 minutes

Director: Todd Haynes
Cast: Andrew Harpending *(Young Bolton)*, John R. Lombardi *(Rass)*, James Lyons *(Jack Bolton)*, Tony Pemberton *(Young Broom)*, Scott Renderer *(John Broom)*, Edith Meeks *(Felicia Beacon)*, Larry Maxwell *(Dr. Graves)*, Susan Gayle Norman *(Nancy Olsen)*.
Genre: Drama—A highly polished and imaginative film told in three parts: "Hero," "Horror" and "Homo." All parts are woven together into overlapping stories and were inspired by the novels of Jean Genet.
Plot: More a series of stylized and moody vignettes than a traditional narrative, the film's title seems to refer to sex—in this case sex as a prelude to death.

Haynes, like so many gay filmmakers today, effectively sets his very contemporary story in a different time and place.

In "Hero," set in the not-too-distant past, a young boy—for whom "some felt sorry but most just wanted to hit"—according to a classmate—is remembered as being odd and different. To protect his mother he kills his father and then flies out the window never to be seen again.

"Horror," shot in black-and-white, is a melodramatic spoof of the 1950s science-fiction genre. In it, a young doctor accidentally drinks a sex-drive potion he has invented. In this metaphor for AIDS, his face and body become covered with sores and everyone he kisses becomes grotesquely disfigured, like him, and dies. Ostracized from the community, he's driven to suicide.

"Homo," set in a French prison at the turn of the century, is a poetic exploration of sex and love between two men behind bars. Unable to express true love for one another, humiliation and force are substituted. In the end this unful-filled love also leads to death.

MPAA Rating: NC-17—Contains brief full-frontal male nudity and explicit gay sex scenes.

Awards: Received the *Grand Jury Prize* at the 1991 Sundance Film Festival.

Trivia: The National Endowment for the Arts incurred the wrath of the radical right for having awarded Haynes a grant toward making this film. Their anger came as a result of the film's explicit portrayal of homosexuality.

Companion Films: See "Prisoners" in the "Companion Films Index."

POLICE ACADEMY ★★★

(1984)

US/Color/96 minutes

Director: Hugh Wilson

Cast: Steve Guttenberg *(Carey Mahoney)*, Kim Cattrall *(Karen Thompson)*, G.W. Bailey *(Lt. Harris)*, George Gaynes *(Commandant Lassard)*, Andrew Rubin *(George Martin)*, Scott Thomson *(Chad Copeland)*, Brent Van Hoffman *(Kyle Blankes)*, George R. Robertson *(Chief Hurnst)*, Josef Field and Gary Colewell *(Blue Oyster dancers)*, Leslie Easterbrook *(Sgt. Callihan)*, David Graf.

Genre: Comedy—The tag line promoting this irreverent comedy read, "Be a police officer. All you do is join the farce." If you appreciate the lowbrow humor and sexual sight gags of films like *Airplane!, Naked Gun* and *Hot Shots,* you'll appreciate this very clever sendup of the police force.

Plot: While the setting for this comedy is the police academy, the vehicle that carries it along the fast track is—surprise!—sex.

The stage is set for nonstop fag gags and sexual confusion, when a major metropolitan police force opens its doors to anyone who wants to apply—throwing out all entrance requirements and restrictions. Taking advantage of the new rules, every incompetent, misfit and oddball in town joins the academy. It just so happens that nearly all of them are suffering from sexual-identity confusion. And that includes their pets.

Andrew Rubin plays George Martin, a Latin lover who dresses in drag to slip into the women's dormitory at night. When he gets caught by the equally macho Sgt. Callihan (Easterbrook), he finds the tables are turned.

In another memorable scene, squad leaders Blankes and Copeland (Van Hoffman and Thomson), two strictly by-the-book, regulation-haircut marine types, are tricked into entering a gay leather bar. Once in the "Blue Oyster Bar," the two cadets are startled to find that they fit right in with this room full of hunky macho men. Forced to slow dance the night away to romantic '50s tunes like, "Will You Still Love Me Tomorrow," they eventually even appear to enjoy themselves.

Perhaps the funniest scene of mistaken identity, however, involves Steve Guttenberg, who plays Mahoney, or "Mahomo" as he's called. Switching places with a hooker who has just performed oral sex on the police commandant (Gaynes), the officer believes, to his horror, that Guttenberg is responsible for the act.

In the end, this group of "sissies" manages to rescue the real cops from a life-and-death situation and become heroes in the process. Now that's a rare event in movies worth seeing.

Quotes:

"You men stop that."

—Gaynes

"Back in the old days, there were 'Johnsons' as far as the eye could see."

"And what a lovely sight it was."

—*Robertson and Gaynes*

"Princess! Looks more like a prince to me. He's a queer!"

—*Bailey*

"To me, marriage is a sacred institution. So tell me, you and the wife do it doggy style, or what?"

—*Rubin*

"Son, where did you get this gun?"

"My mom gave it to me."

—*Bailey and Graf*

"You look like the sweet little boy from next door but you don't fool me—you're the devil."

—*Bailey*

"Why do you want to be a cop?"

"I like to dress like a man."

"So do I."

—*Guttenberg and Cattrall*

MPAA Rating: R—Contains female nudity, profanity and sexual situations.

Companion Films: *Police Academy* sequels.

Also see "Cops" in the "Companion Films Index."

PORKY'S ★★★

(1981)

US/Color/94 minutes

Director: Bob Clark

Cast: Dan Monahan *(Pee Wee)*, Mark Herrier *(Billy)*, Wyatt Knight *(Tommy)*, Tony Ganlos *(Meat)*, Roger Wilson *(Mickey)*, Cyrill O'Reilly *(Tim)*, Kim Cattrall *(Honeywell)*, Nancy Parsons *(Ballbreaker)*, Doug McGrath *(Coach)*, Wayne Maunder *(Cavanaugh)*, Alex Karras *(Sheriff Walker)*, Chuck Mitchell *(Porky)*, Jack Makahy *(Frank)*.

Genre: Comedy—While not truly a gay-themed film, *Porky's* is essentially about what it means, or takes, to be a "real man." It was also one of the first teen-exploitation T & A comedies. Most if not all the humor centers on penis size.

Plot: Set in the 1950s, the story revolves around a group of horny young students and their quest for sexual gratification. Pee Wee (Monahan) is the horniest and the nerdiest virgin in the group. Pee Wee bares the brunt of all the small penis jokes and sight gags. At the other extreme, the big man on campus is nicknamed "Meat"—for, you guessed it, the size of his manhood.

"Porky's" is a redneck, strip-joint whorehouse, where the boys go with plans of losing their virginity. What they lose, however, is their dignity, as Porky (Mitchell), the owner of the establishment publicly humiliates them. The remainder of the film is devoted to revenge—which in the end, is sweet.

To the film's credit, it includes a subplot involving a bigoted student (Maunder) who attacks a new Jewish student (Colomby). Cavanaugh, the bigot, eventually realizes he's wrong and stands up to his father, whom he was trying to emulate and please all along.

"I'm gonna make a man of you yet," declares his father as he beats his son in public.

"If being a man means being what you are I'd rather be queer!," cries Cavanaugh.

Cavanaugh and Brian, the Jewish student, soon become fast friends and actually become the heroes of the film.

Quotes:

"I need a rubber—It's too big."

"We don't have any training rubbers."

—*Monahan and student*

A practical joke finds a group of boys tricked into taking off their clothes and waiting to visit a hooker. Their night of sexual gratification turns into a night of embarrassment and humiliation in *Porky's* (1981).

"Man is not known by inches alone."
  —*Monahan*
"I'd recognize that penis anywhere."
  —*Parsons*
"You're too stupid to even be a good bigot."
  —*Colomby*
"Can we call it a tallywacker? 'Penis' is so personal."
  —*School principal*
MPAA Rating: R—Contains profanity and numerous scenes of male and female full-frontal nudity.

Companion Films: See "Homophobia" in the "Companion Films Index."

PRICK UP YOUR EARS ★★★★★
(1987)
UK/Color/111 minutes
Director: Stephen Frears
Cast: Gary Oldman *(Joe Orton)*, Alfred Molina *(Kenneth Halliwell)*, Vanessa Redgrave *(Peggy Ramsay)*, Wallace Shawn *(John Lahr)*, Lindsay

Duncan *(Anthea Lahr)*, Julie Walters *(Elsie Orton)*, James Grant *(William Orton)*.

Genre: Drama—A biographical drama about the life and death of British homosexual writer Joe Orton and his lover Kenneth Halliwell.

Plot: "Oh dear, oh dear, oh dear," exclaims a cop at the beginning of the film," Someone here's been playing silly buggers." The cop is referring to Joe Orton (Oldman) and his long-time lover Kenneth (Molina), whose bloody bodies are discovered in their single room apartment. Kenneth, after years of resentment towards Joe, has bludgeoned him to death and then killed himself when it looks as if Joe is about ready to end their relationship.

Opening and closing with this scene, Kenneth states at the end of the film, "I loved him. I must have loved him. I chose him to kill me." In-between, the story of their relationship and lives together is told in a series of flashbacks.

The time is the 1960s. The place—London. From the beginning, theirs is a mismatched relationship. Joe is young, sexually adventurous, self-centered and the more talented of the two. Kenneth is older, balding, sexually timid and apparently content to live vicariously through Joe—all the while encouraging him as a writer while sacrificing his own writing. As Joe grows into a celebrated writer with the hit plays *Loot* and *Entertaining Mr. Sloane*, his need for Kenneth simultaneously diminishes. Over the years Kenneth feels more and more left out of Joe's life and his success—a success he helped create. In the end, his revenge is a senseless act that made sense only to a desperate and angry man.

This is a fascinating and powerful film, due in great part to the fine performances all around.

It's perhaps Orton's finest and most memorable.

Quotes: The screenplay written by Alan Bennett contains many humorous and memorable lines including:

"Sleep together do you?"

"No, but we have sex."

—An interviewer and Molina

"Writing is one-tenth perspiration and nine-tenths masturbation."

—Oldman

"Normal sex is still a novelty to most people."

—An editor

"I always wanted to be an orphan. I coulda been, if it hadn't a been for my parents."

—Oldman

"Have a wank? It would be easier to raise the Titanic!"

—Molina

"This may come as a surprise to you, but I suspect your friend may be a homosexual."

—A psychologist

MPAA Rating: R—For language, gay kissing scenes and suggested gay sex scenes. Oldman appears nude from behind in one scene.

Companion Films: See "Biographies" and "Men and Boys" in the "Companion Films Index."

PRINCE OF TIDES, THE ★★★

(1991)

US/Color/132 minutes

Director: Barbra Streisand

Cast: Nick Nolte *(Tom Wingo)*, Barbra Streisand *(Susan Lowenstein)*, George Carlin *(Eddie Detreville)*, Blythe Danner *(Sallie*

Wingo), Kate Nelligan (Lila Wingo Newbury), Jeroen Krabbe (Herbert Woodruff), Melinda Dillon (Savannah Wingo).

Genre: Drama—Based on Pat Conroy's best-selling novel of the same name.

Plot: "I didn't know it could happen to a boy—all I wanted to do was die," reveals Nick Nolte to his sister's therapist in a painful and powerful scene. He's talking about being raped by a man when he was a child.

Nolte plays Tom Wingo, a middle-aged man who has harbored this family secret that has haunted him and his twin sister, Savannah, (Dillon) all their lives: As a 13-year-old boy he was raped by an escaped convict who broke into his parent's home. His sister and his mother were also raped by two of the three convicts.

When the violent and deadly incident was over, his mother's way of dealing with the horror was to pretend that it never happened. Savannah's way of dealing with the pain was to turn it inward and to become suicidal.

The most recent suicide attempt lands her in the hospital in New York City. When Tom is summoned by her psychiatrist, Dr. Lowenstein (Streisand), he finds the courage, with her help, to confront and overcome his past. At the same time, he helps his sister begin a new life.

Playing Savannah's gay next-door neighbor Eddie, George Carlin's character is a warm, caring individual who just happens to be gay. In fact, he seems to be the only character in the film who isn't psychologically tortured. Now that's a rare and refreshing switch in the movies that's worth noting.

A 1991 film, Frankie & Johnny, also featured a "normal" gay next-door neighbor, as did 1992's Single White Female. Only time will tell whether this is a fluke or a trend.

Quotes:
"You look terrible, Tom. I mean you're not even cute anymore."

"If that's your idea of seduction, no wonder you're alone."
    —Carlin and Nolte

"Oh, you do have a sense of humor. I was beginning to think you had it surgically removed."
    —Nolte

"Just because I don't know how to cook doesn't mean I don't know how to eat."
    —Streisand

"Who taught you to be so cruel?"
"You did mama, you did."
    —Nelligan and Nolte

MPAA Rating: R—Contains profanity, violence and a gay rape scene.

Awards: Nominated for seven Academy Awards including Best Picture, Best Actor (Nick Nolte), Best Supporting Actress (Kate Nelligan), Best Adapted Screenplay (Pat Conroy and Becky Johnston), Best Art Direction (Paul Sylbert and Cary Heller), Best Cinematography (Stephen Goldblatt) and Best Original Score (James Newton Howard).

Companion Films: See "Neighbors, Roommates and Best Friends" and "Rape" in the "Companion Films Index."

PRIVATE RESORT ★★★
(1985)
US/Color/82 minutes
Director: George Bowers
Cast: Rob Morrow (Ben), Johnny Depp (Jack), Dody Goodman (Mrs. Rawlings), Hector Elizondo (Maestro), Leslie Easterbrook (Bobbie

Sue), Andrew Dice Clay (*Curt*), Michael Bowen (*Scott*).

Genre: Comedy—Teenage, slapstick, sexual comedy with lots of male and female nudity and sexual confusion.

Plot: Rob Morrow (TV's *Northern Exposure*) and Johnny Depp (*Cry Baby*), play Ben and Jack, two horny teenagers ready for action on a sun and fun-filled private resort vacation.

This sophomoric romp comes complete with a gigolo jewel thief (Elizondo), a wealthy widow proficient in the martial arts (Goodman), a womanizing two-timer (Clay) and an assortment of other screwball characters that keep this comedy on the very light side.

The trouble and sexual hijinx begin when Ben and Jack step on the toes of Maestro, the con-man crook out to steal Mrs. Rawlings' jewels. Each young man gets caught without his clothes at the most inopportune moment. In one scene Ben ends up in a bubble bath with a very surprised Maestro.

Later in the film, Ben dresses up in drag to escape from Maestro. Maestro develops a crush on this very bad drag queen and chases him through the hotel. Trapped in an elevator with Maestro and Curt, both men proceed to fondle Ben's fanny. When the two men end up holding hands (this setup first appeared in the silent films) they react with homophobic rage. If only they knew whose ass they were fondling!

This is mindless, good-natured gender-bender fun that will appeal to a select audience.

MPAA Rating: R—For nudity and profanity. Depp and Morrow appear in extended nude scenes from behind while numerous young women drop their tops and bottoms every few frames or so.

Companion Films: See "Drag Queens" and "Homophobia" in the "Companion Films Index."

PRIVATES ON PARADE ★★
(1981)
UK/Color/107 minutes
Director: Michael Blakemore
Cast: John Cleese (*Major Giles Flack*), Dennis Quilly (*Captain Dennis*), Patrick Pearson (*Steven Flowers*), Michael Elphick (*Reg Drummond*), Simon Jones (*Eric Young-Love*), Joe Melia (*Len Benny*), John Standing (*Captain Savory*), Bruce Payne (*Kevin Cartwright*), David Bamber (*Charles Bishop*), Nicola Pagett (*Sylvia Morgan*), John Quayle (*Henry Cox*), Julian Sands (*Climbing sailor*).

Genre: Comedy—The most outrageous thing about this film is the title. Alternating between a deadly serious drama and a flippant comedy, this film about a group of British soldiers who "perform" for the troops is a bit schizophrenic and a truly wasted opportunity. Yet it has its moments and is worth viewing.

Plot: John Cleese plays Major Flack, the dimwitted, religious-fanatic leader of an unusual song-and-dance unit. Stationed in Singapore during WWII, the army is short on women, so the unit is made up mostly of soldiers in drag. The director of the troupe, Capt. Dennis (Quilly), is an old queen whose every word is a sexual double entendre.

The funniest scenes revolve around the troupe as they sing and dance their way through the war. Their show is called the "Jungle Jamboree," and in one number, Capt. Dennis does a very enjoyable Carmen Miranda routine. In another he's joined by two fellow soldiers, as

Zero Mostel and Gene Wilder look on, as Andreas Vomtsinas helps Christopher Hewett dress for a party in *The Producers* (1968).

they do a variation on the Andrew Sisters. Just when the plot begins to look bright, however, the film switches gears, and the troupe is ambushed in the jungle by terrorists. Nearly everyone is either shot, maimed or killed in a very bloody scene that appears to be from another film. Then, before you know it, the film has ended as abruptly as it began.

Quotes:
"No perfume on guard duty."
  —*Cleese*

"I must say, the way some people will creep and crawl just for a little tiara and their bangle."
  —*Quilly*

MPAA Rating: PG-13

Companion Films: Bruce Payne, who plays Capt. Cartwright and one of the Andrew Sisters in drag, demonstrated quite a range when he went on to star with Wesley Snipes in 1992's *Passenger 57*, as an evil hijacker and terrorist.

Also see "Drag Queens" and "Military Men" in the "Companion Films Index."

PRODUCERS, THE ★★★★

(1968)

US/Color/90 minutes

Director: Mel Brooks

Cast: Zero Mostel *(Max Bialystock)*, Gene Wilder *(Leo Bloom)*, Kenneth Mars *(Franz Liebkin)*, Dick Shawn *(LSD/Hitler)*, Christopher Hewett *(Roger Debree)*, Andreas Vomtsinas *(Carmanghia)*, Lee Meredith *(Secretary)*, Renee Taylor, Barney Martin, Frank Campanella.

Genre: Comedy—The first film directed by Mel Brooks, *The Producers*, is a sexual farce considered by many to be a classic of the genre.

Plot: Zero Mostel plays Max Bialystock, a washed-up Broadway producer. His neurotic accountant, Leo (Wilder), suggests that it would be possible to make more money from a flop than a hit play—by scamming investors. From this suggestion a partnership is born.

Once they've located the world's worst play, they go in search of the world's worst director—who just happens to be an over-weight drag queen with an assistant named Carmanghia (Vomtsinas). Carmanghia, suffice it to say, makes your average flaming drag queen look like a librarian.

Roger Debree (Hewett), the director, adores the idea of directing the play titled "Springtime For Hitler," but suggests that they produce it as a musical. This would seem to rule out any possibility of the play's succeeding, but unfortunately for Max and Leo, their scheme back-fires and the play is a huge hit. The Busby Berkley sendup alone is a show-stopper.

Roger and his assistant are extreme stereo-types, but then everyone in this irreverent slap-stick comedy is equally ridiculed—but all in good fun. In the end, the two partners in crime find themselves in the state penitentiary selling shares of their new musical, "Prisoners Of Love."

Quotes:

"If we get caught we'll go to prison."

"You think you're not in prison now?"

    —Wilder and Mostel

"He who hesitates is poor."

    —Mostel

"I want everything I've ever seen in the movies."

    —Wilder

"I'm supposed to be the grand duchess Anastasia, but I think I look more like Tugboat Annie."

    —Hewett

"It's gorgeous. Let's face it Roger, that dress is you."

    —Mostel

"Will the dancing Hitlers please wait in the wings. We are only seeing the singing Hitlers."

    —Hewett

"Don't be stupid, be a smarty. Come and join the Nazi party."

    —Dancer

"Will you shut up? You shut up. You are the audience; I am the author—I outrank you."

    —Mars

"Next time I produce a play—no author."

    —Mostel

MPAA Rating: PG

Companion Films: See "Drag Queens" and "Sissies" in the "Companion Films Index."

PROTOCOL ★★★

(1984)

US/Color/96 minutes

Director: Herbert Ross

Cast: Goldie Hawn *(Sunny Davis)*, Chris Sarandon *(Michael)*, Cliff De Young *(John)*, Gail Strickland *(Ambassador St. John)*, Kenneth Mars *(Lou)*, Joel Brooks *(Ben)*, Grainger Hines *(Jerry)*, Ed Begley, Jr. *(Pat)*, Jean Smart, Richard Romanus, Kenneth McMillan, Andre Gregory, James Staley.

Genre: Comedy—Goldie Hawn plays Sunny Davis in this farcical variation on the *Mr. Smith Goes To Washington* classic.

Plot: When Sunny, a Washington, D.C., cocktail waitress, saves the life of a visiting Arab dignitary from an assassin's bullet, she becomes a national hero.

Like Dustin Hoffman in *Tootsie*, Sunny's face appears on the covers of magazines and newspapers, on talk shows, and she grabs the nation's heart. But where Tootsie only had one roommate, Sunny has two—and hers just happen to be gay. Ben and Jerry (Brooks and Hines) are gay lovers who share their home with Sunny. All are trying to make ends meet. When Sunny is offered a job at the State Department, it is not because of her diplomatic expertise, but that doesn't stop her from taking the position.

The two men are supportive of Sunny and her new position, and even help her entertain her foreign diplomats. In the film's most memorable scene the threesome take the visiting Arab dignitaries on a gay night on the town that turns into a riotously funny scandal that rocks the capital.

When she discovers she's being used as a pawn by the American government, she manages to turn the tables, but not before she turns Washington upside down and has them rolling on the floor—literally.

This is light entertainment with a few normal homosexuals thrown in for good measure.

Quotes:
"What do you expect for christsakes? This is Washington, D.C. The men are all married or gay, or they work for the government."
  —*Smart*

"Come on, can you be that dumb and run for office?"
  —*Begley, Jr.*

"You know more queens than I do."
  —*Brooks*

"Oh, I have the napkins that match your hat."
  —*Hawn*

"Now remember, it's BYOL—bring your own leather."
  —*Smart*

"What the hell is this place? Must be one of those gay, Arab, biker sushi bars."
  —*Bar patron*

MPAA Rating: PG—For violence, partial female nudity, and adult situations.

Companion Films: See "Neighbors, Roommates and Best Friends" in the "Companion Films Index."

PSYCHO ★★★★★

(1960)
US/B&W/109 minutes
Director: Alfred Hitchcock
Cast: Anthony Perkins *(Norman Bates)*, Janet Leigh *(Marion Crane)*, Vera Miles *(Lila Crane)*, John Gavin *(Sam Loomis)*, John McIntire *(Chambers, the Sheriff)*, Simon Oakland *(Dr. Richmond)*, John Anderson *(Car salesman)*, Frank Albertson *(The millionaire)*, Patricia Hitchcock *(Secretary)*.
Genre: Thriller—The Alfred Hitchcock masterpiece that was panned by critics when it first

arrived in the theaters.

Plot: Anthony Perkins plays Norman Bates, an attractive, sensitive young man who lives with his mother. He also dresses in drag and hates women. Because of this, many reviewers refer to this as a gay-themed film. That he's also a psychopathic murderer is the final proof, they might argue. After all, in Hollywood, psychopathic murderers are usually homosexuals.

On the surface, Norman isn't expressly a homosexual and in fact, at the film's end, a psychiatrist explains that he isn't a transvestite. He doesn't dress in drag to be *like* his mother but because he thinks he *is his mother*. But for homosexual moviegoers of the time, *Psycho* came extremely close to expressing a gay sensibility. And considering the director's other films containing homosexual characters, it's safe to say that this film can be read on many levels.

But despite any hidden meanings, the film is a masterpiece of suspense, and the shower scene alone is probably the most memorable moment in any film of the past 50 years. In addition, Perkins' character remains both appealing and frightening, even today—much the same way as homosexuality on the screen.

Quotes:
"You know what I think? I think that we're all in our private traps. I was born in mine."
　　—Perkins
"A boy's best friend is his mother."
　　—Perkins
"You make respectability seem disrespectful."
　　—Leigh
"I will not hide in the fruit cellar. You think I'm fruity?"
　　—Perkins
"A son is a poor substitute for a lover."
　　—Perkins

MPAA Rating: Not rated.

Awards: Received Academy Award nominations for *Best Supporting Actress* (Janet Leigh), *Best Director, Best Cinematography* and *Best Art Direction (B&W)*.

Postscript: Anthony Perkins died of AIDS in August, 1992 in Hollywood, California.

Companion Films: See "Drag Queens" and "Murderers" in the "Companion Films Index."

QUEENS LOGIC ★★★
(1991)
US/Color/112 minutes
Director: Steve Rash
Cast: John Malkovich *(Elliot)*, Kevin Bacon *(Dennis)*, Ken Olin *(Ray)*, Joe Mantegna *(Al)*, Tony Spiridakis *(Vinny)*, Jamie Lee Curtis *(Grace)*, Linda Fiorentino *(Carla)*, Chloe Webb *(Patricia)*.
Genre: Drama—A coming-of-age comedy-drama referred to by critics as a pale version of *The Big Chill*.
Plot: Set in Queens, New York, the film opens just days before Ray's (Olin) wedding. Ray's cousin Al (Mantegna) and his wife are in the middle of a separation and Ray gets cold feet about his own wedding. The action centers on these two men and their group of friends, who are also having a difficult time with relationships, commitments and growing up.

Elliot (Malkovich) is the group's repressed homosexual. Sensitive and a bit introverted, he rejects an obnoxious gay man putting the make on him. It seems that he would rather be celibate. Eventually he forms an uneasy alliance with a neighbor who's also "sensitive," but like all the other relationships in this film, it's difficult to know if it will last.
MPAA Rating: R—For language and brief nudity during a skinny-dipping scene.
Trivia: Kevin Bacon, during a *Movieline* interview (December 1992), talked about the filming of a nude skinny-dipping scene for the film. "They said they'd hired a male dresser for the night because they thought it'd be weird for a girl to be doing this for us. Well, they got, like the gayest guy in New York City to do it. Which is, you know ... a good job for him," claimed Bacon. Bacon goes on to explain that they had to wear a sock over their genitals for the scene. The interviewer asks, "Why couldn't you just do the scene naked?" "Because there were cops there, and New York City law prohibits it. Our asses could be hanging out, but for some reason our dicks had to be covered," explained Bacon in a very humorous interview.
Companion Films: See "Neighbors, Roommates and Best Friends" and "Only the Lonely" in the "Companion Films Index."

QUERELLE ★★★
(1982)
Germany/Color/106 minutes
Director: Rainer Werner Fassbinder
Cast: Brad Davis *(Querelle)*, Franco Nero *(The Lieutenant)*, Jeanne Moreau *(Lusianne)*.
Genre: Drama—Fassbinder's adaptation of Jean Genet's story "Querelle Of Brest," a bizarre story of man's conflict between love and sex. Filmed in English, this was Fassbinder's final film.
Plot: Degradation, humiliation, and abandonment are the themes of this highly stylized and offbeat exploration of masculinity and sexuality.

Brad Davis plays Querelle, a French sailor who is stationed in the port of Brest. To Querelle, sex and murder are the same—passionless activities. When he discovers his true sexual nature in a local brothel he's unable to accept it

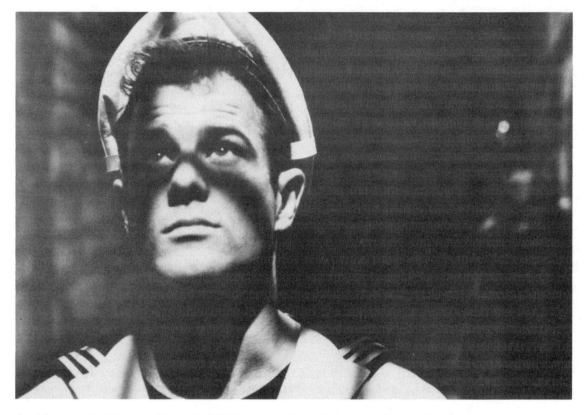

Brad Davis in the title role of *Querelle* (1982), adapted from the homoerotic Jean Genet novel.

as anything more than just meaningless fun. Eventually he's unable to deny it and falls in love with a man who has murdered a fellow sailor. That both men are murderers is the basis for their love. But Querelle betrays his love and turns him in to the authorities. In the end, Querelle has chosen death over the love of another man.

Querelle is not the only man in this film suffering from an identity crisis. The naval lieutenant, played by Nero, is in love with Querelle but prefers to pour out his heart to a tape recorder, rather than to act on his feelings. The owner of

the brothel, with bulging muscles, is as masculine-looking as they come, but he prefers to have sex with men rather than his wife.

Moreau is madam of the house and mournfully sings the film's theme song, "Each man kills the thing he loves," as she's used by the men to make one another jealous.

Disturbing, violent and often cryptic, this is nevertheless one of the director's more engaging and daring films.

Quotes:

"All you ever look at is yourselves."
 —*Moreau*

"You know for a little girl, you sing that song just like a big boy."

    —*Gil character*

"That cop is covered with jewels. I've got my jewels but I don't show them off."

    —*Davis*

"I never loved a boy before. You're the first one."

    —*Davis*

"He made fun of me in front of everyone, including myself."

    —*Gil character*

"You know I've dreamt a lot about your prick lately."

"Was it nicer in your dreams?"

    —*Moreau and Davis*

"If I were to say I felt for you, that would be a lie. I've never understood how anybody could fall in love with a man."

    —*Nono character*

MPAA Rating: R—Includes profanity, brief nudity from behind, simulated gay sex and gay kissing scenes involving Davis.

Trivia: Frank Ripploh (*Taxi Zum Klo*) receives film credit.

Companion Films: See "Murderers" and "S&M" in the "Companion Films Index."

REFLECTIONS IN A GOLDEN EYE ★★

(1967)
US/B&W/109 minutes
Director: John Huston
Cast: Elizabeth Taylor *(Leonora Penderton)*, Marlon Brando *(Major Weldon Penderton)*, Brian Keith *(Mr. Langdon)*, Julie Harris *(Alison Langdon)*, Robert Forster *(Pvt. Elgee Williams)*, Zorro David *(Anacleto)*, Irvin Dugan *(Murray Weincheck)*.
Genre: Drama—Based on the novel of the same name by Carson McCullers.
Plot: Oozing hypocrisy, hysteria and homophobia, this slow-moving and ever-so-serious melodrama boasts an all-star cast.

Marlon Brando plays the closeted homosexual, one of a sextet of bizarre characters. Julie Harris plays a tortured soul driven to mutilate her breasts, while Robert Forster plays a voyeur and an exhibitionist. Then there's Zorro David, Harris' nelly houseboy. Taylor and Keith are the practicing heterosexuals.

Weldon (Brando), an unhappily married military officer, is terminally repressed—and obsessed. The object of his obsession is Private Williams (Robert Forster), a young man who likes to go for moonlit horseback rides in the nude.

Williams, however, is obsessed with the Major's wife (Taylor). Driven by desire, the Major would rather see Williams dead than with his wife, and kills the man he loves.

If it weren't for the presence of such powerhouse stars, this fiasco would have faded into obscurity long ago.
Quotes:
"Is it better because it is morally honorable for the square peg to keep scraping around the round hole, rather than to discover and use the unorthodox square that would fit it?"
　—Brando
MPAA Rating: Not rated.
Companion Films: See "Closet Cases" and "Military Men" in the "Companion Films Index."

RESIDENT ALIEN ★★★

(1991)
US/Color/85 minutes
Director: Jonathan Nossiter
Cast: Quentin Crisp, Sting, John Hurt, Holly Woodlawn, Fran Lebowitz, Emile DeAntonio, Robert Patrick, Michael Musto, Felicity Mason and Paul Morrissey.
Genre: Documentary
Plot: The *alien* in this memorable and engaging documentary is the flamboyant Quentin Crisp. He refers to himself as "England's stateliest homo." Now in his 80s, he's a long-time resident of New York City.

This portrait of the self-proclaimed homosexual who wrote the internationally acclaimed, witty autobiography, *The Naked Civil Servant*, is revealed by friends, acquaintances and by himself.

Possessing style, claims Crisp, is a matter of "being yourself, but on purpose." This is certainly a film with style.

MPAA Rating: Not rated.
Companion Films: For other films of interest about Quentin Crisp see *The Naked Civil Servant* (1980).

Also see "Drag Queens" in the "Companion Films Index."

REVENGE OF THE NERDS ★★★★

(1984)
US/Color/89 minutes
Director: Jeff Kanew
Cast: Robert Carradine *(Lewis)*, Anthony Edwards *(Gilbert)*, Larry B. Scott *(Lamar)*, Ted McGinley *(Stan)*, John Goodman *(Coach Harris)*, Bernie Casey *(U.N. Jefferson)*, Curtis Armstrong *(Booger)*, Timothy Busfield *(Poindexter)*.
Genre: Comedy—This is one of those rare finds, a sophomoric teenage T&A film with a conscience, sensitivity and a heart.
Plot: Robert Carradine and Anthony Edwards star as Lewis and Gilbert, nerdy best friends who go away together to college. When they and the other freshmen are thrown out of the dorm by the campus jocks, they are forced to find another place to live. Resourceful and smart, they rent a house together.

When they can't get into the fraternities, they decide to start their own and they pledge not to discriminate like they have been discriminated against. The name of their fraternity is Lambda, Lambda, Lambda. Gilbert assures their sponsor that they will be open to all races and creeds. Lamar Latrell (Scott), the gay black member of their new fraternity, adds "sexual orientation" to the list.

Lamar is a non-threatening stereotypical sissy who wears a leotard and seems to live to do aerobics, but he fits right in and is completely accepted among this group of non-jocks. He also has pride and in the end helps win an athletic contest against the jocks. The contest is part of an annual homecoming carnival that determines which fraternity will have control over the student council the following year. Not only do they get their revenge on the jocks for all of the abuse they have taken, but Lewis becomes president and Gilbert wins over the head cheerleader.

The jocks, led by star quarterback Stan Gable (McGinley), have always held control in the past, so when they lose to the nerds they are humiliated and trash the nerds fraternity. As the new president, Gilbert decides to stand up to the team. He fearlessly addresses the team and the large crowd gathered for the celebration. "No one's really gonna be free until nerd persecution ends ... I'm a nerd and I'm here tonight to stand up for the rights of other nerds. All our lives we've been laughed at and made to feel inferior. Why, because we're different? Because we're smart?" he asks with tears in his eyes.

Gilbert is pleading the case of everyone who has ever been discriminated against and it is a speech that wins the entire school to his side—because everyone can relate on some level.
Quotes:
"The nerds are a threat to our way of life."
　　—*McGinley*
"What was the dirtiest thing ever said on television?"
"I don't know."
"Ward, I think you were a little hard on the Beaver."
　　—*Two jocks*

MPAA Rating: Contains male nudity from behind and full-frontal female nudity.
Companion Films: See "Heroes" and "Sissies" in the "Companion Films Index."

RITZ, THE ★

(1976)
US/Color/91 minutes
Director: Richard Lester
Cast: Treat Williams *(Detective Brick)*, Rita Moreno *(Googie)*, F. Murray Abraham *(Patron)*, Jack Weston *(Geatano Proclo)*, Kay Ballard *(Wife)*, Jerry Stiller *(Carmine)*.
Genre: Comedy—This low-budget gay bathhouse farce, is a desperate attempt at comedy that trips over itself every step of the way. Only recommended for viewers with a strong constitution.
Plot: Jack Weston plays Geatano, a naive garbage man from the Midwest being pursued by a hit-man. His brother-in-law wants to keep him from inheriting the family fortune, it seems. Geatano heads for New York in search of the last place anyone would look for him. To his surprise, he ends up hiding out in a gay bathhouse. It takes him a while, but he eventually discovers that this isn't the Cincinnati Jack La Lane's.

From here on out, the film is a series of chase scenes, mistaken identities and sophomoric sexual innuendo and humor. The only bright spot in this charade is Treat Williams. Spending the entire movie in nothing but a towel, he plays a dimwitted, straight man whose voice never changed during adolescence.

Eventually, almost everyone in the place turns up in bad male or female drag. Even Moreno, who plays an obnoxious cabaret singer, is mistaken believed to be a transvestite. This is a film only for the most adventuresome. It will make younger viewers rejoice that they never lived through the '70s.
Quotes:
"You're not gay? What are you—a social worker or something?"
　　—Bathhouse attendant
"What do you think—this is the YMCA?"
　　—Bathhouse attendant
"It's just a phase you're going through. Last year it was miniature golf."
　　—Ballard
MPAA Rating: R—For profanity.
Companion Films: See "Drag Queens" and "Sissies" in the "Companion Films Index."

ROCKY HORROR PICTURE SHOW, THE
★★★★★
(1975)
US/Color/100 minutes
Director: Jim Sharman
Cast: Tim Curry *(Dr. Frank-n-Furter)*, Susan Sarandon *(Janet Weiss)*, Barry Bostwick *(Brad Majors)*, Richard O'Brien *(Riff Raff)*, Patricia Quinn *(Magenta)*, Little Nell *(Columbia)*, Jonathan Adams *(Dr. Everett V. Scott)*, Peter Hinwood *(Rocky Horror)*, Meatloaf *(Eddie)*, Charles Gray *(The Criminologist)*.
Genre: Musical—The ultimate midnight movie and campy cult classic. It's not unusual for fans to have seen this film more than 100 times.

An outrageously witty sendup of the science-fiction, horror, late-night "double-feature" picture shows made famous by studios like RKO.

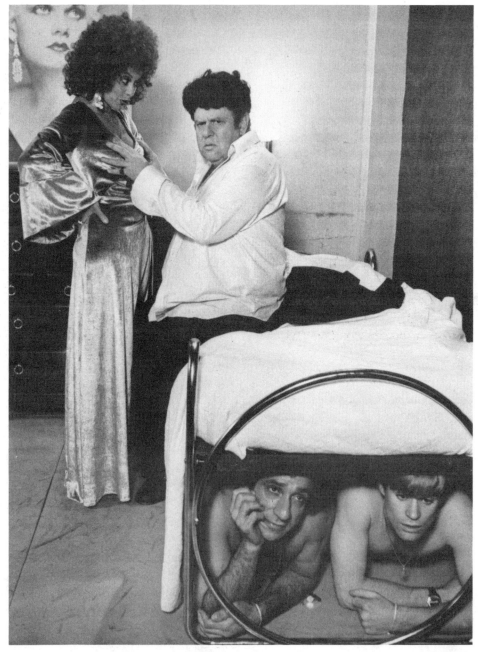

Rita Moreno, Jack Weston, F. Murray Abraham and Treat Williams in the farcical *The Ritz* (1976).

Based on the popular 1970s stage play, also starring Tim Curry.

Plot: "Society must be protected," exclaims Dr. Scott near the end of the film. Sexual deviants from outer space have landed and are about to corrupt two innocent earthlings.

Tim Curry plays the sexually mad Dr. Frank-n-Furter, a bisexual transvestite from the planet of Transsexual in the galaxy of Transylvania. When naive, all-American virgins Brad and Janet (Bostwick and Sarandon) have a flat tire one stormy night, they hike to the nearest castle to make a phone call.

Before the night is through, they have both gratefully lost their virginity to the mad scientist. They have also witnessed the unveiling of the Doctor's new creation, Rocky Horror (Hinwood). The only thing frightening about this bare-chested blond, however, is his bulging—uh—biceps.

It isn't long before everyone finds themselves dressed in red- and black-satin lingerie. And then there's the swimming pool orgy. But before the fun can really begin, Frank-n-Furter's sexual excesses cause his sidekicks to revolt.

In the end, this monster of a sex fiend is destroyed by his own kind, and the human race has been saved from cross-dressing—all set to clever rock-and-roll music and lyrics.

Quotes:
"Yes, Janet, life's pretty cheap for that type."
    —*Bostwick*
"They're probably foreigners with ways different from our own."
    —*Bostwick*
"He carries the Charles Atlas seal of approval."
    —*Curry*
"It's not easy having a good time."
    —*Curry*
"Now really, that's no way to behave on your first day out!"
    —*Curry*
"I ask for nothing."
"And you shall receive it in abundance."
    —*Quinn and Curry*

MPAA Rating: R—Includes profanity, violence and sexuality.

Companion Films: See "Drag Queens" in the "Companion Films Index."

ROPE ★★★

(1948)
US/Color/80 minutes
Director: Alfred Hitchcock
Cast: James Stewart *(Rupert Cadell)*, John Dall *(Brandon Shaw)*, Farley Granger *(Philip)*, Cedric Hardwicke *(Mr. Kentley)*, Constance Collier *(Mrs. Atwater)*, Joan Chandler *(Janet Walker)*, Douglas Dick *(Kenneth Lawrence)*, Edith Evanson *(Mrs. Wilson, the governess)*, Dick Hogan *(David Kentley)*.

Genre: Thriller—*Rope* was Hitchcock's first color film, and the first time he worked with Jimmy Stewart. The film, based on the play by Patrick Hamilton about the Leopold-Loeb murder case, was adapted by Hume Cronyn. The script was written by Arthur Laurents.

Plot: Surprisingly suspenseful, this briskly paced parlor drama is unintentionally humorous in retrospect, but nonetheless engaging. Because of the time in which it was made, this film about two homosexual killers is covert in its sexual innuendo. The only references to homosexuality are intended to be read between the lines—in both dialogue and manners.

Dall plays Brandon, a cold-blooded, dominating killer, who believes that he's superior to other people and therefore has the right to kill them. Granger plays Philip, Brandon's sensitive, emotionally unstable lover, who goes along with the murder to please his mate. Strangling David (Hogan), a college chum, they hide the body in a chest in the parlor. To heighten the thrill of the killing, Brandon invites the dead man's fiancé and parents to a dinner party in which the chest is used as a dining table.

Stewart plays Rupert, Brandon's former professor, who's also invited. During the evening, David's absence becomes conspicuous. When Brandon and Philip's behavior becomes suspicious, Rupert unravels the mystery.

In one of the most telling scenes, just after the two men have strangled their victim, an exhilarated Dall lights up a cigarette and exhales with a long languorous sigh. We have all seen this scene many times before, but it usually follows sex, not death. Hollywood, however, has often equated homosexuality with murder and death, so in many ways, this scene made perfect sense.

Quotes:
"You strangled the life out of a human being that could live and love like you never could."
    —*Stewart*
"Pity we couldn't have done it with the curtains open."
    —*Dall*
"How queer, I never heard of anyone who didn't eat chicken."
    —*Chandler*
"Oh, we all do strange things in our childhood."
    —*Dall*
"Cat and mouse, cat and mouse. Which is the cat and which is the mouse?"
    —*Granger*

"It's what you wanted isn't it—someone else to know?"
    —*Granger*
"You frighten me. Part of your charm—I imagine."
    —*Granger*
"Being weak is a mistake."
    —*Dall*
"What would you say to champagne? 'Hello, champagne.'"
    —*Chandler*

MPAA Rating: Not rated.

Companion Films: Other films about the Leopold-Loeb case include *Compulsion* (1959), featuring Dean Stockwell and Bradford Dillman and *Swoon* (1992).

Also see "Closet Cases" and "Murderers" in the "Companion Films Index."

ROSE, THE ★★★

(1979)
US/Color/134 minutes
Director: Mark Rydell
Cast: Bette Midler (*Rose*), Alan Bates (*Rudge*), Frederic Forrest (*Dyer*), Barry Primus (*Dennis*), David Keith (*Mal*) and Harry Dean Stanton (*Billy Ray*).
Genre: Drama—A realistic and depressing story of self-destruction based loosely on the life and death of 1960s rock singer Janis Joplin.
Plot: Bette Midler plays Rose, a self-destructive, alcoholic, drug-addicted rock star of the 1960s on a downward spiral to a tragic end.

This is a realistic on-the-road-with-a-rock and-roll-band movie. It's about a rock star's desperate attempt to get out of the business at the same time that she's addicted to it. It's about her inner battles and her battles with her promoter-manager (Bates), who has no interest in her mental well-being.

Inbetween the self-destructive behaviors are a number of light and humorous moments. The lightest and most humorous moment occurs after Rose and Dyer (Forrest) are kicked out of a diner by rednecks with an unnatural fear of hippies. The next stop is a gay nightclub for some fun. During a drag show, female impersonators do Streisand, Mae West, Diana Ross, Bette Davis and finally Rose. This is especially funny, since Bette is so often impersonated in real life.

Rose has a special fondness for these friends, it seems, since she's bisexual herself. In a very brief scene, a former lesbian lover shows up wanting to rekindle their relationship. This only would complicate her life further, however, and she flees.

In the end, Rose's addictions lead to a lonely and tragic end.

Quotes:
"You wanna eat some Chinese?"

"Yeah, all 900 million of them."
—Bates and Midler

"What are we, ladies? I'll tell you what we are: waitresses at the banquet of life."
—Midler

"Holy shit! Your hair has a hard on."
—Midler

"I love how you say 'fuck.' It sounds like tea and crumpets at the Ritz Carlton."
—Midler

MPAA Rating: R—Contains strong language and brief nudity in an older-men's bathhouse.

Awards: Midler received an Academy Award nomination for *Best Actress*. Forrest received a nomination for *Best Supporting Actor*. The film was also nominated for *Best Sound* and *Best Film Editing*.

Postscript: Female impersonator Kenny Sacha, one of the performers at the club, died of AIDS in 1992.

Companion Films:
See "Drag Queens" in the "Companion Films Index."

SALO: 120 DAYS OF SODOM ★
(1975)
Italy/Color/115 minutes
Director: Pier Paolo Pasolini
Genre: Drama—The director's final film before his violent and controversial death. In Italian with English subtitles.
Plot: Set in Salo, a town in northern Italy during the Nazi-fascist occupation of 1944-45, Pasolini uses the writings of the Marquis de Sade to tell a story of the horrors of humanity.

Most of the action takes place in a countryside villa. Everything is beautiful on the surface—the countryside, the young men and women and the estate. But it's all just a facade.

Four powerful fascist leaders round up young orphan boys and girls, victims of the war, and hold them captive on the estate. At first they're used by the men for their sexual pleasures. No sexual act is taboo. Anal sex at the dinner table is welcomed. There is no distinction between sex with boys or with girls—it is all the same to these men.

As their desires become progressively insatiable, the boys and girls are humiliated, degraded, brutally tortured and eventually murdered. This is as close as one will come to a living hell in the cinema.

Sex has replaced religion, love and values in this metaphor for society's sickness, and the ultimate gratification seems to be death and destruction. Those familiar with Pasolini will only be slightly unprepared for this grim film.
MPAA Rating: Not rated—NC-17 by today's standards. Contains numerous full-frontal male and female nudity throughout the film as well as soft-porn sex scenes and violence.
Trivia: The film was banned in Australia for 17 years, only to be lifted in 1993 upon revising their film rating system.
Companion Films: See "Fascists and Nazis" and "S&M" in the "Companion Films Index."

SALOME'S LAST DANCE ★★★
(1987)
UK/Color/89 minutes
Director: Ken Russell
Cast: Glenda Jackson (*Herodis/Lady Alice*), Stratford Johns (*King Herod/Alfred*), Nickolas Grace (*Oscar Wilde*), Douglas Hodge (*John the Baptist/Bosey*), Imogen Millais Scott (*Salome/Rose*), Dougie Howes (*Phony Salome*), Kenny Ireland (*1st soldier*), Michael Van Wuk (*2nd soldier*), Russell Lee Nash (*Pageboy*), Alfred Russell (*Cappadocian*).
Genre: Comedy—An outrageously dark and stylized comedy and homage to Oscar Wilde.
Plot: Set in London in the 1890s, a group of actors stages the premiere of "Salome," a new play by Oscar Wilde. The performance is held in a brothel.

In this unconventional telling of the story of Salome, few of the women wear tops to cover their breasts and most of the men are scantily dressed as well. Among the odd characters populating this play are dancing midget Jews and bitchy drag queens.

Salome (Scott) is a spoiled, selfish brat who

wants the only man she can't have, John the Baptist (Hodge). When he rejects her advances, she vows revenge. To get what she wants, she makes her lecherous stepfather, King Herod (Johns), promise he'll do whatever she wishes and in return she'll do the dance of the seven veils. He agrees. After she has performed, she demands the head of John the Baptist. Herod, witnessing her kiss the beheaded John, realizes that she is a monster and has her killed—and so ends the tragedy.

However, it's just beginning for Wilde (Grace). While the play is taking place, Oscar is having his way with Bosey's (also played by Hodge) young boyfriend. Witness-ing this, John summons the police and has Wilde and Alfred (also played by Johns), the owner of the brothel, arrested on charges of corrupting a minor.

In the end, just before being taken away by police, Wilde jokes, "We've had one melodramatic ending tonight. Two might be an indulgence."

Quotes:
"Since when has it been a crime to play charades?"
—*Jackson*
"I can resist anything but temptation."
—*Grace*
"You took advantage of my position."
"And I might be tempted to do so again if you don't close your mouth."
—*Hodge and Grace*

MPAA Rating: R—For scene of Dougie Howes in full-frontal male nudity, gay kissing scenes, profanity and full female nudity.

Companion Films: Other films with similar theme: *Salome* (1912), *Salome, Where She Danced* (1945), *Salome* (1953) and *Salome* (1985).

Also see "Biographies," "Drag Queens" and "Romans" in the "Companion Films Index."

SCARECROW ★★★

(1973)
US/Color/115 minutes
Director: Jerry Schatzberg
Cast: Al Pacino *(Lion)*, Gene Hackman *(Max)*, Richard Lynch *(Jack Riley)*, Dorothy Tristan *(Coley)*, Ann Wedgeworth *(Frenchy)*, Eileen Brennan *(Darlene)*.
Genre: Drama
Plot: Pacino and Hackman play drifters who become buddies in search of a dream. They plan to one day own their own car wash. As they travel across the country they rely on one another for survival. At the outset, Hackman, who plays Max, asks Pacino if he has a middle name because he has "a little trouble with Francis," Pacino's real name. His middle name is Lionel, so Max calls him Lion.

When they're thrown into prison together for fighting, their cellmate is a calculating inmate named Jack Riley (Lynch). Riley takes a liking to Lion and pulls strings to get him the softest jobs in the lockup. Before long, however, he expects a payback. In a brief but gruesome scene, he corners Lion, attempting to force him into sex. When Lion refuses, Riley nearly beats him to death. When confronted by Max, Riley says, "I had my laughs." But Max gets the last laugh.

Once again, the gay character is evil and, in this case, used as a catalyst to reunite the two pals, who have been on the outs.

MPAA Rating: R—Contains profanity and violence.

Awards: Pacino and Hackman shared the 1973 *Golden Palm Award* at the Cannes Film Festival.

Companion Films: See "Closet Cases," "Prisoners" and "Rape" in the "Companion Films Index."

SCENES FROM THE CLASS STRUGGLE IN BEVERLY HILLS ★★★

(1989)

US/Color/103 minutes

Director: Paul Bartel

Cast: Jacqueline Bisset *(Clare)*, Ray Sharkey *(Frank)*, Robert Beltran *(Juan)*, Mary Woronov *(Lisabeth)*, Ed Begley, Jr. *(Peter)*, Wallace Shawn *(Howard)*, Arnitia Walker *(To-Bel)*, Rebecca Schaeffer *(Zandra)*, Barret Oliver *(Willie)*, Edith Diaz *(Rosa)*, Paul Bartel *(Mo)*, Paul Mazursky *(Sidney)*.

Genre: Comedy—The promotional tag line read, "Just another weekend of shameless sexual adventures, ill-fated romance and accidental death."

Plot: Jacqueline Bisset plays Clare, a newly widowed sitcom star and Beverly Hills resident. Lisabeth (Woronov) is her just-divorced next-door neighbor and best friend. Their servants, Frank and Juan (Sharkey and Beltran) are also friends. Having her home fumigated, Lisabeth, her son Willie (Oliver), her visiting brother Peter (Begley, Jr.) and his new wife, To-Bel (Walker), are invited to spend a quiet weekend with Clare, her daughter Zandra (Schaeffer) and her dead husband Sidney (Mazursky).

This sets the scene for a nonstop, cleverly written, two-day sexual romp through the mansion that eventually finds everyone in the wrong bedroom at least once. Now that the women's husbands are out of the way, Frank and Juan are making plans to improve their stations in life. Frank, a gay hustler who also sleeps with women for money, initiates a $5,000 contest with Juan. He bets Juan that he can have sex with Juan's boss, Clare, and that Juan can sleep with Frank's boss, Liz. Since Juan has no money, he asks what Frank wants if he loses, "To get to know you better," he responds. Juan comes back with one of the film's funniest lines—"How many times."

The two men eventually sleep with the two women, but Juan also falls in love. To protect Liz from finding out about the bet, he agrees to sleep with Frank—and discovers it's not so bad. In another memorable line he says to Frank, "No music. No tequila. You ain't gonna get no second date, that's for sure."

In the end, Frank gives Juan the money to pay off his gambling debts and they part friends.

Quotes:

"Look at his basket—hard as a stale baguette."
—*Woronov*

"Did you see the lipstick on his collar?"
"At least they got it off his fly."
—*Bisset and Bartel*

"I never saw one so small."
—*Sharkey*

"The way I see it, you spend $3,000 on a bathrobe, you deserve to die."
—*Beltran*

"What do I look like, a midnight cowboy?"
—*Beltran*

"I've had more virgins than you've had crabs."
—*Sharkey*

"Gertrude Stein was right. A mouth is a mouth is a mouth."
—*Sharkey*

"Would you believe I was a virgin when I got married."

"So was I according to my publicist."

—*Woronov and Bisset*

"I don't think you're setting your sights low enough."

—*Bisset*

"I can waltz in like Ozzie, or I can waltz in like Harriet, but I can't waltz in like Ozzie and Harriet. It's just too taxing."

—*Shawn*

"The man has no morals. He's a moral psychopath."

—*Begley, Jr.*

"Playwrights make good pets. And God knows, Peter's nearly house-broken by now."

—*Bartel*

"It was so degrading. I felt like some fabulous farm animal."

—*Walker*

"My idea of taking a risk is shopping at Saks without a sale."

—*Schaeffer*

"It's been my lifelong ambition to sell out to TV."

—*Begley, Jr.*

MPAA Rating: R—For sexual humor and adult subject matter. Robert Beltran bares his buns, and a number of women bare their breasts. Other than this, the film is tame.

Companion Films: See "Bisexuals" and "Hustlers" in the "Companion Films Index."

SEBASTIANE ★★★
(1976)
UK/Color/82 minutes
Directors: Paul Humfress and Derek Jarman

Cast: Leonardo Treviglio, Richard Warwick, Barney James, Ken Hicks, Janusz Romanov, Neil Kennedy, Steffano Massari, David Finbar, Donald Dunham.

Genre: Drama—A homoerotic version of the St. Sebastian legend set in Rome in the year 303 A.D. In Italian with difficult-to-read English subtitles.

Plot: When Emperor Diocletian decides to persecute all Christians, he spares his favorite, Sebastian (Treviglio), the captain of the palace guard, but sends him to a deserted outpost with fellow guards to think and repent.

In this deserted land, the men have nothing to do but play and wait. The men, wearing little or nothing throughout the movie, skinny dip, bathe together, sleep together and have sex together. Two athletic gay lovers, Anthony and Adriani, are teased by the others, who only have sex with each other because there are no women around.

The new leader, Severus (Warwick), falls in love with Sebastian, but each time he approaches him he is rebuffed. Sebastian is in love with only one man—God, and he would rather die than renounce his Christianity. Alternating between torturing Sebastian and longing for him, Severus proclaims his love for the dark-haired young man. But it's futile, and having been given many opportunities to have a change of heart, Severus is forced to make a martyr of the man he loves.

Beautifully photographed on location in England and Sardinia, this highly erotic tale of persecution, punishment, sex and love is at times difficult to follow, but worth the effort in the end.

Trivia: In an interview with Patrick Z. McGavin during the Sundance Film Festival in Park City,

John Phillip Law slugs Rod Steiger, who has just kissed the young soldier in *The Sergeant* (1968).

Utah in 1992, Jarman commented on his place in gay cinema. "I think of all the British filmmakers from my generation I'm the only one making films that had to be made. People congregate around the films for validation. When *Sebastiane* came out, we had these lines around the block of people going to the cinema because there was this gay movie, and people were wondering, are we finally going to see ourselves portrayed in the cinema."

MPAA Rating: R—For graphic scenes of sex and torture. For most of the film, a group of Roman soldiers cavorts in the nude and near-nude including much full-frontal male nudity.

Companion Films: Also see "Biographies," "Doomed Lovers," "Only the Lonely" and "Romans" in the "Companion Films Index."

SERGEANT, THE ★★
(1968)
US/Color and B&W/107 minutes

Director: John Flynn
Cast: Rod Steiger *(Sgt. Albert Callan)*, John Phillip Law *(Pfc. Tom Swanson)*, Ludmila Mikael *(Solange)*, Frank Latimore, Elliott Sullivan.
Genre: Drama—The advertising tag line read, "Just one weakness. Just one."
Plot: "To say that this is a story about a homosexual," reported *Variety*, "is like claiming that an iceberg floats completely on the surface of water. The pic is about a total, pervading enslavement of one person to another." Other critics were not as kind. They claimed it was about Hollywood's inability to deal with the subject of homosexuality in an open and honest way.

Rod Steiger plays Master Sergeant Albert Callan, an intensely repressed and hostile homosexual who's unable to express the true feelings he has for one of his men. The setting is a U.S. base in France. The year is 1952.

John Phillip Law plays Private First Class Tom Swanson, a naive young officer who allows himself to be pursued by the Sergeant. When Callan can no longer control his hidden desire for the young man, he kisses him. The stunned GI rebuffs his advance. Desperate and humiliated, the Sergeant, in a melodramatic turn, takes his own life. Now *that's* original.

As a relic of its time and for its otherwise fine performances, the film is, after all is said, worth viewing.
MPAA Rating: R—At the time, the subject matter alone was risqué enough to warrant such a rating.
Companion Films: See "Closet Cases" and "Military Men" in the "Companion Films Index."

SERVANT, THE ★★★
(1963)
UK/B&W/117 minutes
Director: Joseph Losey
Cast: Dirk Bogarde *(Barrett)*, James Fox *(Tony)*, Sarah Miles *(Vera)*, Wendy Craig *(Susan)*.
Genre: Drama—Screenplay written by Harold Pinter. Pinter also appears in a restaurant scene as a society man.
Plot: Like many films of this period, the topic of homosexuality is discreetly veiled in insider references, so that the film can be "enjoyed" on two different levels without offending the sensibilities of mainstream audiences. On one level, *The Servant* is about a destructive, sadomasochistic relationship between two men. On another level, it's simply the story of a domineering servant who takes advantage of his employer.

In an early and curious scene, two patrons of a restaurant pub appear to be talking about Oscar Wilde. The woman says, "He's a wonderful wit. I'm dying to see him again." "You won't for a while," replies her male companion. "He's in jail." In the same restaurant two women are dining. One of the women is jealous of the attentions her companion is receiving from another woman. At a nearby table two priests are enjoying a meal and perhaps something more. The entire restaurant scene appears to be a tip off to what is to come—that things aren't always what they appear to be.

James Fox plays Tony, a well-to-do young man who hires a servant to take care of him and his newly acquired London flat. Dirk Bogarde plays Hugo Barrett, the servant who helps him decorate and attends to his masters every whim. Tony's fiancé, Susan (Wendy Craig), and Barrett take an immediate dislike to one another. Both see the other as competition.

In time, Barrett is revealed to be a master manipulator with an elaborate scheme to humiliate his boss and drive away his fiancé. Although succeeding in his scheme, he unfortunately loses his job in the process. But it isn't long before the lonely, dependent Tony forgives his tormentor and allows him to come back to work. Only Barrett has no intention of working. From this point on, the two are involved in a master-servant relationship where the roles have been reversed.

Near the end, Bogarde reveals, "You know sometimes I get the feeling that we're two old pals." Tony replies, "That's funny, I got the same feeling myself." They both agree that they had the same feeling once before in the Army. Barrett knows that Tony is a latent homosexual and uses his knowledge to browbeat and degrade his new "pal."

"You're hiding. You'll be caught. You've got a guilty secret, but you'll be caught," claims Barrett as he searches for Tony in a drunken game of hide-and-seek. He finds him cowering in a dark closet. Tormenting the innocent homosexual has rarely been as demented or sinister as it is in this psychological drama.

MPAA Rating: Not rated.

Companion Films: See "Closet Cases" and "S&M" in the "Companion Films Index."

SHORT EYES ★★

(1977)
US/Color/100 minutes
Director: Robert M. Young
Cast: Bruce Davison *(Clark Davis)*, Jose Perez, Curtis Mayfield, Freddie Fender.

Genre: Drama—A tough prison drama based on the book by Manuel Pinero.

Plot: Davison plays Clark Davis, a frail, young white man thrown into prison on charges of child molestation. In prison, child molesters are called "short eyes" and are considered by all to be the lowest of the low. Davis becomes a pariah among his cellmates, a hardened group of black and Hispanic convicts.

Tensions between the racial groups confined to these tight quarters are high. Sexual tension also permeates the cellblock. A young heterosexual Hispanic named Julio is nicknamed "cupcakes" by the group who all want to have sex with him. In one shower scene he narrowly escapes being raped.

Clark is the match that ignites a fire among the men. Clark is derided as a faggot, a freak, stuff and squeeze. The men decide to rape him, but in his struggle to avoid being gang-raped, the violence escalates, and his throat is slit.

Following the incident, the prison labels the death a suicide. The captain later gathers the men to explain that Clark was not identified by his attacker and that he has been mistakenly jailed.

Quotes:

"Your soul may belong to God, but your ass is mine."

　—*An inmate*

"There's gonna be blood on my knife and shit on my dick."

　—*An inmate*

"Don't you know what justice means? Just us white folks.'"

　—*An inmate*

"Just 'cause I kiss you doesn't mean you're a faggot."

　—*An inmate*

"You are not my judge. I'm sick of people judging me."

—*Davison*

MPAA Rating: R—For violence and language.

Companion Films: For other films with Bruce Davison see *Longtime Companion* (1989), *Last Summer* (1969) and *The Strawberry Statement* (1970)—the latter two featuring Davison in nude scenes from behind.

Also see "Prisoners" and "Rape" in the "Companion Films Index."

SILENCE OF THE LAMBS, THE ★★★★

(1991)

US/Color/116 minutes

Director: Jonathan Demme

Cast: Jodie Foster *(Clarice Starling)*, Anthony Hopkins *(Dr. Hannibal Lecter)*, Scott Glenn *(Jack Crawford)*, Anthony Heald *(Dr. Frederick Chilton)*, Ted Levine *(Jame Gumb)*, Kasi Lemmons *(Ardelia Mapp)*, Brooke Smith *(Catherine Martin)*, Diane Baker *(Senator Ruth Martin)*.

Genre: Thriller—The film opened to gay protests that once again the central character was a homosexual psychopath. This time, just for variety, he was also a serial killer who skinned his female victims.

Plot: Jodie Foster plays Clarice Starling, an FBI trainee, who's asked to assist FBI special agent Jack Crawford (Glenn) in solving a series of grisly murders committed by a psychopath (Levine). The demented homosexual killer is known as "Buffalo Bill" because he tortures and skins his victims.

Starling is recruited to seek help from Dr. Hannibal Lecter, or "Hannibal the Cannibal" (Hopkins), who's the American prison system's No.1 homicidal maniac. Hannibal, they believe, is the only one ruthless enough to put together a psychological profile that will help catch the killer.

As "Buffalo Bill" is slowly being cornered, Lecter manages an inconceivable escape. The FBI then finds themselves with an even more diabolical foe to deal with—if that's possible.

Trivia: *Film Comment* remarked that the protests were misdirected. It claimed the protests should have been about the less obvious and more harmful hidden characteristics. It also observed, "Demme's three protagonists demonstrate a range of gay archetypes, but so subtly encoded ... that their *difference* makes no difference. The characters' lack of sexual affect makes them unresonant. Their gayness remains unempowered, hidden."

MPAA Rating: R—For violence, nudity and profanity.

Awards: Won the 1991 Academy Award for *Best Picture, Best Director, Best Actress* (Foster), *Best Actor* (Hopkins), and *Best Adapted Screenplay* (Ted Tally), among many other national and international awards.

Companion Films: See "Murderers" in the "Companion Films Index."

SILVERLAKE LIFE: THE VIEW FROM HERE ★★★

(1993)

US/Color/120 minutes

Directors: Tom Joslin and Peter Friedman

Cast: Tom Joslin and Mark Massi

Genre: Documentary—Shot on video and transferred to film.

Plot: As the AIDS pandemic enters its second

decade, the filmmakers, Tom Joslin and Mark Massi, lovers for over 20 years, manage to personalize this human tragedy by documenting their final days.

At times painful to witness, *Silverlake* is an intimate and intense love story, presented as a first-person diary. Originally begun by Joslin as a way of dealing with his lover's HIV-positive status, Joslin eventually becomes the focus when he develops full-blown AIDS himself. Unable to bring the film to completion, the filmmakers enlist Peter Friedman, a former film student of Joslin's, to co-direct, edit and complete the film.

When the film was released, not all the reviews were positive. Many theaters declined to book the film because of its difficult topic. Despite the inevitable end, as the title suggests, this is a testament to life, not death, and succeeds not so much in entertaining, as in inspiring.

MPAA Rating: Not rated.

Awards: Received the *Grand Jury Prize* and *Freedom of Expression Award* at the Sundance Film Festival, January 1993.

Companion Films: See "AIDS" in the "Companion Films Index."

SINGLE WHITE FEMALE ★★★★★
(1992)
US/Color/107 minutes
Director: Barbet Schroeder
Cast: Bridget Fonda *(Allison)*, Jennifer Jason-Leigh *(Hedra)*, Stephen Tobolowsky *(Myerson)*, Steven Weber *(Sam)*, Peter Friedman *(Graham Knox)*.
Genre: Thriller—Director Barbet Schroeder's *(General Idi Amin Dada, Barfly, Reversal Of Fortune)* psychological thriller is a masterwork of style and intelligence. It's hard to say which is more impressive, the first-rate technical credits or the outstanding lead performances—all are award-winning caliber.

Plot: Bridget Fonda plays Allison, a single, upper-West-Side New York fashion designer. Following a split with her fiancé, Sam (Steven Weber, *Wings* TV series), Allison fears living alone and advertises for a roommate. When Ally invites Hedra (Jennifer Jason-Leigh), a meek and unassuming young woman to move in, she has unknowingly opened her door to a monster. Hedra is really a mentally unstable woman who never stopped blaming herself for her twin sister's death. In Ally, she believes she has found her other half. When Ally decides to reconcile with Sam, Hedra begins to unravel at the psychological seams and turns all of their lives into a nightmare.

The three men in Ally's life are a fiancé she can't trust, a would-be rapist client and a gay neighbor. Peter Friedman plays the gay upstairs neighbor, who ends up saving her life in the end. It is a small role, but for the most part he isn't a stereotype or a plot device used for laughs. Though he does have the funniest line in the film when he claims, "I can be butch when I have to—I get it from my mother."

Despite a formula-driven ending, genre fans and a large mainstream audience turned this *Hand That Rocks The Cradle* and *Unlawful Entry*-like thriller into a late summer hit.

MPAA Rating: R—For male (Steven Weber from behind) and female nudity, strong sexuality, language and violence.

Companion Films: *Apartment Zero* (1989) features a strikingly similar theme with men in the lead roles.

Also see "Neighbors, Roommates and Best Friends" in the "Companion Films Index."

SLEEPER ★★★★★

(1973)
US/Color/88 minutes
Director: Woody Allen
Cast: Woody Allen *(Miles Monroe)*, Diane Keaton *(Luna)*, John Beck *(Urno)*.
Genre: Comedy—A classic Woody Allen sexual farce and slapstick, sci-fi spoof.
Plot: In this futuristic Rip Van Winkle tale, Woody Allen plays Miles Monroe, a man who wakes up from a cryogenic sleep, 200 years in the future. Considered an alien, he spends most of his time on the run from the authorities. Along the way, he runs into a gay couple whose futuristic home is full of antiques and comes complete with a gay robot.

In this future world, there are no sexual problems because everyone is frigid (except men of Italian ancestry). Sex between two people is rare, since nothing can compare with the ultimate orgasm received while standing inside an *orgasmatron*. It's an appliance no household would want to be without.

There are other memorable sight-gags, scenes and characters throughout the film, but it's Allen who provides most of the laughs. When he's eventually captured and brainwashed by the government, he takes on a new persona—that of a Miss America beauty queen. Later he's kidnapped by the resistance underground and deprogrammed. This time he believes he is Blanche Dubois.

This is a film not to be missed.

Quotes:
"My brain? It's my second-favorite organ."
—*Allen*
"I'm sorry, I never get involved in anything where I can be tortured. It's this practice of mine. I'm a screamer, and it's embarrassing."
—*Allen*
"I think we should have had sex, but there weren't enough people."
—*Keaton*
"Do you think it's easy to run when you're holding a banana the size of a canoe?"
—*Allen*
"What's it feel like to be dead for 200 years."
"Like spending a weekend in Beverly Hills."
—*Keaton and Allen*
"Do you want to perform sex?"
"Perform sex? I don't think I'm up to a performance, but I'll rehearse with you, if you like."
—*Keaton and Allen*
"It's hard to believe that you haven't had sex in 200 years."
"Two hundred and four if you count my marriage."
—*Keaton and Allen*
"Arlene and I have to get a divorce. She thinks I'm a pervert because I drank the waterbed."
—*Allen*
"I'm not knocking Urno. He's great if you happen to like a tall, blond, crushing, Nordic, Aryan, Nazi type."
—*Allen*
"What do you believe in?"
"Sex and death—two things that come once in a lifetime, but at least after death you're not nauseous."
—*Keaton and Allen*
"I've got a Ph.D. in oral sex"

Jack Lemmon (fifth from left) plays Daphne in the classic *Some Like It Hot* (1959).

"Did they make you take any Spanish with that?"

—*Keaton and Allen*

MPAA Rating: PG

Companion Films: See "Sissies" in the "Companion Films Index."

SOME LIKE IT HOT ★★★★★
(1959)
US/Color/105 minutes
Director: Billy Wilder

Cast: Marilyn Monroe *(Sugar)*, Tony Curtis *(Joe/Josephine)*, Jack Lemmon *(Jerry/Daphne)*, George Raft *(Gangster)*, Pat O'Brien *(Cop)*, Joe E. Brown *(Osgood)*.

Genre: Comedy—A zany, farcical comedy classic about two men who hide out from the mob by dressing in drag.

Plot: Set in Chicago in 1929 during prohibition, Curtis and Lemmon play musicians Joe and Jerry, two pals who accidentally witness a St. Valentine's Day massacre. Managing to escape the gangsters, the two men dress in drag—as Josephine and Daphne—and join an all-girls band heading for a gig in Florida. This, of course, sets the stage for hilarious sexual innuendo and double entendres.

On the train trip to Florida, Josephine unfortunately falls for the group's sexy singer and ukulele player, Sugar Cane (Monroe). Sugar doesn't realize he's a man, however, complicating matters even further. At the same time, Josephine is being pursued by an amorous and persistent hotel bellboy, and Daphne is being romanced by Osgood (Joe E. Brown), an admiring millionaire. Daphne gets so confused that he accepts a proposal of marriage.

Just when things look like they can't get any more confusing or amusing, the Chicago gangsters arrive in Florida for a convention and just happen to bump into their witnesses, who are still in hiding. This is when things really get hot. When Josephine kisses Sugar on the lips in public, it's especially funny. After all, the sight of Marilyn Monroe kissing another woman is a not so subtle irony.

But it's the final scene that steals the show. Daphne tries to break off her engagement to Osgood by reciting all of her negative qualities. When none of this matters to the lovesick millionaire Daphne decides to reveal the truth— that she's a man. Daphne says, "You don't understand, I'm a man." Osgood replies with a wry smile, "Well, nobody's perfect."

Time magazine called it "The best comedy of the year."

Quotes:
"Pull in your reel, Mr. Fielding, you're barking up the wrong fish."
 —*Lemmon*
"I've got this thing about girls—they just sort of leave me cold."
 —*Curtis*

"Why would a guy want to marry a guy?"
"Security."
 —*Curtis and Lemmon*
"Are you out of your mind? We're up the creek; and you want to hock the paddle."
 —*Lemmon*
"I feel like everyone's staring at me."
"With those legs, are you crazy?"
 —*Lemmon and Curtis*
"I tell you it's a whole different sex."
 —*Lemmon*
"I always get the fuzzy end of the lollipop."
 —*Monroe*

MPAA Rating: Not rated.
Awards: Jack Lemmon received an Oscar nomination for his role but lost out to Charlton Heston who won that year for *Ben-Hur*. The film also received nominations for *Best Screenplay, Best Cinematography, Best Art Direction* and won the award for *Best Costume Design.*

Another film receiving nominations that year was *Suddenly, Last Summer.*

Companion Films: See "Drag Queens" in the "Companion Films Index."

SOME OF MY BEST FRIENDS ARE ...
★★★
(1971)
US/Color/89 minutes
Director: Mervyn Nelson
Cast: Nick DeNoia (*Cheri/Phil*), Gary Sandy (*Hustler*), Candy Darling (*Karen*), Rue McClanahan (*Lita*), Fannie Flagg (*Mildred Pierce*), Sylvia Sims (*Sadie*).
Genre: Drama—A low-budget independent feature originally titled *The Bar.*
Plot: Taking place in a single night, the setting for the film is the Blue Jay bar, on Christmas eve.

During the course of an evening, a large group of unhappy homosexuals and an assortment of hangers-on spend an evening of psychotherapy disguised as a gay night out on the town. Drag queens, fag hags and sissies make up this stereotyped group of lonely hearts with nowhere else to go.

The straight-owned Blue Jay represents the only refuge these gay men have from a homophobic world. In a more insidious way, however, the bar turns out to be as oppressive as the outside world.

This cliché-ridden, melodramatic relic of the past no longer has the power to offend as it did when it first premiered. As a campy and telling period piece, it hits the mark like few other films of its type.

Quotes:
"You boys make me feel like a queen."
—*Sims*

MPAA Rating: Not rated.

Companion Films: See "Drag Queens" and "Unhappy Homosexuals" in the "Companion Films Index."

SOMETHING FOR EVERYONE ★★★
(1970)
US/Color/112 minutes
Director: Harold Prince
Cast: Michael York *(Conrad)*, Angela Lansbury *(Countess Orenstein)*, Anthony Corlan *(Helmut)*, Jane Carr *(Lotte)*, Heidelinde Weis *(Analisa)*.
Genre: Comedy—This black comedy based on Henry Kressler's novel, *The Cook*, over the years has become a cult classic.
Plot: The homosexual in this film (oh, what a surprise) is an amoral, manipulative opportunist who murders and sleeps his way to the top.

York plays Conrad, an attractive country boy with big dreams. Charming his way into the household of a widowed Austrian countess (Lansbury), he lands a job as footman. The countess, however, has lost her fortune and has had to close up the castle. Before long he's in charge of running the entire house and, like a modern day Robin Hood, has devised a scheme to rob from the rich and give to the poor countess.

All the while he's having an affair with Helmut (Corlan), the countess's son. At the same time he's also sleeping with the daughter (Weis) of a wealthy socialite. His plan, in fact, calls for his two lovers to marry. Once the fortune of the new bride has been willed to her new husband, Conrad arranges for an accident.

The countess is so impressed that she seduces the seducer, and they plan to marry. Lotte (Carr), the countess' precocious young daughter, however, has other plans. Jealously watching and waiting in the wings for her turn, the young girl turns the tables on the young opportunist in an ironic final scene and proves that Conrad has met his match.

Quotes:
"There are no men anymore ... facsimiles, that's all, facsimiles."
—*Lansbury*

MPAA Rating: R—Michael York and Anthony Corlan share an intense gay kissing scene.

Companion Films: See "Bisexuals" and "Hustlers" in the "Companion Films Index."

SPARTACUS ★★★
(1960)
US/Color/196 minutes

Director: Stanley Kubrick
Cast: Kirk Douglas, Laurence Olivier, Charles Laughton, Tony Curtis, Jean Simmons, Peter Ustinov, John Gavin, John Ireland, John Dall.
Genre: Drama
Plot: Laurence Olivier plays Crasius, the bisexual emperor. Tony Curtis plays his poor, young slave, who runs away to join up with Spartacus (Douglas) after Olivier puts the make on him during the famous bathtub scene.

Life magazine wrote in 1992, "The creators of *Spartacus* never thought audiences would see the infamous four-minute "bath sequence"—in which Laurence Olivier attempts to seduce Tony Curtis by asking him if he prefers snails or oysters—censored and left on the cutting room floor." "Some people," Olivier notes, "like both." When the restored version appeared in theaters this year [1991], moviegoers couldn't imagine what all the fuss was about."

This is a classic film epic that can be appreciated on many levels.

Awards: Peter Ustinov won a *Best Supporting Actor* Academy Award for his performance. The film also won for *Best Cinematography, Best Art Direction (Color), Best Costume Design (Color)* and was nominated for *Best Film Editing.*
MPAA Rating: Not rated.
Companion Films: See "Romans" in the "Companion Films Index."

SPECIAL DAY, A ★★
(1977)
Italy/Color/110 minutes
Director: Ettore Scola
Cast: Marcello Mastroianni *(Gabriel)*, Sophia Loren *(Antonette).*

Genre: Drama—Italian drama takes place during a single day. It's the day Hitler arrives in Rome to meet with Mussolini. It's also the day two strangers meet and share a brief encounter. Dubbed in English.
Plot: Sophia Loren plays Antonette, an underappreciated mother of seven children with an insensitive husband. When Hitler comes to Rome it's considered a national holiday, and the entire city attends the parade. Everyone, it seems, but Antonette, who's left at home to take care of the house.

When her bird flies out the window, Antonette enlists the help of Mastroianni, who plays Gabriel, a stranger across the hall, to retrieve it. Lonely and depressed, Gabriel welcomes her company. Reluctantly she agrees to spend time with him. Also lonely, and attracted to this stranger, she begins to seduce him, to no avail. When he explains that he's queer, she's repulsed and rejects his friendship.

Later in the day she apologizes, and they get to know each other all over. He describes how he lost his prestigious job after his homosexuality was discovered and that the fascists forced his lover to leave. Before long, she's comforting him, and herself, and they make love. What they share together isn't real for either of them—it only substitutes for the love and warmth they're both missing in their lives.

Though only for a moment, these two sensitive people, trapped in this totalitarian, fascist state, find love and acceptance. By the end of the day, however, her family returns, Gabriel is taken away by the police, and all they have is the memory of this special day.
MPAA Rating: Not rated.
Companion Films: See "Coming Out," "Fasc-

ists and Nazis" and "Only the Lonely" in the "Companion Films Index."

SPETTERS ★★★

(1980)

Holland/Color/115 minutes

Director: Paul Verhoeven

Cast: Hans van Tongeren *(Reen)*, Toon Agterberg *(Evelyn)*, Maarten Spanjer *(Hans)*, Renee Soutendijk *(New girl in town)*, Marianne Boyer *(Maya)*, Rutger Hauer *(Gerrit Witkamp)*, Jeroen Krabbe *(Announcer)*.

Genre: Drama—A cult classic.

Plot: A coming-of-age story centering around three friends, as they deal, none too successfully, with their identities and sexuality.

The central focus of their lives is motorcycle racing. That is, until a sexy new girl (Soutendijk) moves to town with her gay brother. Their lives are, at least temporarily, refocused on her, and it doesn't take long before she's made a play for each.

Within a very short time, these attractive, carefree young men come up against a number of unpleasant realities of life revolving around religion, money and sex. One of the boys painfully discovers his homosexuality, another faces humiliation, and the third young man meets with a tragic end.

Toon plays Eve, a fag basher who realizes after he is gang-raped by Soutendijk's gay brother and his pals, that he also is gay.

In the very next scene he has gone from a homophobe to a gay activist, proclaiming his sexuality to his religious-fanatic father. "Father," he says, "I'm gay. You can pray the house down, but I am what I am."

MPAA Rating: Not rated—Contains violence, profanity and nudity. All three young men appear in complete frontal nudity in a number of scenes. One scene in particular has them measuring the size of their "manhood" in a three-way competition. The one with the longest penis gets to screw the new girl in town.

Companion Films: *Murmur Of The Heart* (1971): Features another scene in which three boys measure their penises with a ruler to see who is largest.

Also see "Coming Out" and "Rape" in the "Companion Films Index."

STAIRCASE ★★

(1969)

US/Color/101 minutes

Director: Stanley Donen

Cast: Richard Burton *(Harry)*, Rex Harrison *(Charlie)*, Cathleen Nesbitt, Beatrix Lehmann, Gordon Heath, Stephen Lewis.

Genre: Comedy—Based on the dramatic Broadway stage play by Charles Dyer.

Plot: Set in the suburbs of London, the film's two central characters are aging, unhappy, stereotypical gay hair stylists.

Both men are middle-aged. Rex Harrison plays Charlie, a swishy, self-hating man, whose life is one long regret. His partner, Harry (Burton), is a bitter, acid-tongued man whose life is also filled with disappointment.

Although they've been roommates for some 20 years, there seems to be no love between them. They hold one another in the same contempt they hold themselves, but nevertheless cling to each other out of neurotic fear and loneliness. Before the end of the film, Harry has

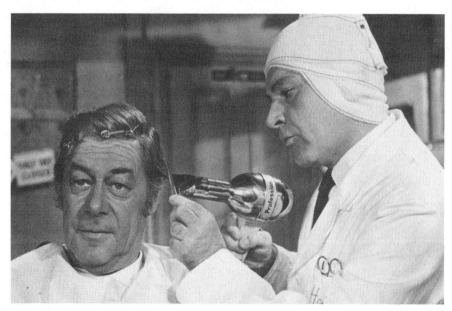

Richard Burton and Rex Harrison play aging and unhappy homosexuals in *Staircase* (1969).

even attempted suicide.

Gay and mainstream critics alike found the film an insult. Time has been even less kind to this exercise in self-hate. As camp, however, it deserves to be seen, if not appreciated.

MPAA Rating: Not rated.

Companion Films: See "Only the Lonely" in the "Companion Films Index."

STATUE, THE ★★

(1971)

UK/Color/84 minutes

Director: Rod Amateau

Cast: David Niven *(Alex Bolt)*, Virna Lisi *(Rhonda Bolt)*, Robert Vaughn *(Ray Whiteley)*, John Cleese *(Harry)*, Ann Bell *(Pat)*, Tim Brooke-Taylor *(Hillcrest)*, Hugh Burden *(Sir Geoffrey)*, Erik Chitty *(Mouser)*, Derek Francis *(Sanders)*.

Genre: Comedy—Dated, sophomoric, sex comedy with a few winning moments. Most viewers would have to admit that an entire movie devoted to comparing penis sizes has some humorous possibilities—and so this movie does.

Plot: David Niven plays a Nobel-Prize winning linguist obsessed with uncovering the identity of the man who posed nude for his wife's statue.

Commissioned by the United Nations to do a statue of her husband, she's inspired to sculpt him in the nude. When Niven sees the larger-than-life-size work he realizes that not all the parts are his. She refuses to divulge the man's identity, and he assumes it's her lover. He spends the remainder of the film convincing all the men in his wife's life (and there are a considerable number, since she is an internationally-known artist) to drop their drawers so that he can determine who posed for the statue. This leads to much homosexual humor and double entendre.

Much of it is inane, but occasionally the situations are quite comical—such as a series of meetings Niven sets up in a local steam room. There he manages to remove each of his guest's towels for a discreet peek. When the manager of the establishment realizes what's going on, he throws him out on his ear. Niven becomes known as "a steam room cowboy." In fact, his reputation quickly turns from respected scholar to notorious homosexual.

Later in the film, he manages to convince the U.S. that it would be in its best interest to help him in his search. Embarrassed by the prospect of a nude sculpture displayed in a very public place, they readily agree, and a worldwide search is on. In the end Niven accidentally discovers his wife's inspiration in Florence, Italy—his name is David. At the same time, a group of schoolgirls spots the naked statue of David and begins to giggle. One of the girls then remarks, "If that's David, I'd like to see Goliath!"

MPAA Rating: R—Contains numerous bare bottoms and a few full-frontal nudes in some unedited versions of the film.

Companion Films: See "Homophobia" in the "Companion Films Index."

STRANGE ONE, THE ★★

(1957)

US/B&W/90 minutes

Director: Jack Garfein

Cast: Ben Gazzara *(Jocko De Paris)*, Paul E. Richards *(Perrin "Cockroach" McKee)*,

George Peppard *(Robert Marquales)*, Pat Hingle *(Harold Koble)*, Arthur Storch *(Simmons)*, James Olson *(Roger Gatt)*.

Genre: Drama—A dated, military boys-school melodrama. In retrospect, while certainly not intended, the film is very humorous.

Plot: A very young Ben Gazzara plays Jocko De Paris, a sadistic, sociopathic bully, who upsets the balance in a military academy.

Bent on tormenting and persecuting his enemies, those weaker or with less authority, he eventually alienates everyone in the school. When he taunts a shy freshman about not liking girls, it appears that he may be overcompensating for his own sexual insecurities. As the film unfolds, it appears that Jocko's problems may stem from the fact that he is a closeted homosexual, unable to accept himself or others.

Later, he's intrigued, when Perrin (Richards), nicknamed "Cockroach," a sensitive young writer and effeminate homosexual sent to military school by his parents to "straighten him out," reveals that he worships Jocko. Since Cockroach has information to blackmail Jocko, he feels safe revealing his true feelings. He has written a novel about Jocko titled *Nightboy*. Cockroach caresses Jocko's hand and asks, "Do you like my style?" Jocko replies that he does, but quickly escorts him out of the room before things become any more intimate.

When Jocko's schemes jeopardize the other cadets' careers, they band together and run him out of town. In the end, this bully turns into a weeping, pleading coward, thus revealing his true self.

This fascinating and melodramatic morality tale introduced a young George Peppard in a memorable role.

Quotes:
"What's the matter, don't you like women?"
  —*Gazzara*

"Tell me the truth, don't you have any wicked thoughts?"
"Very seldom, sir."
  —*Gazzara and Storch*

"I promised my mother on her deathbed that I would not go out with any girls."
  —*Storch*

"If I didn't know you, I'd think you were telling the truth."
  —*Peppard*

"I'll be back."
  —*Gazzara*

MPAA Rating: PG

Companion Films: See "Closet Cases" and "Military Men" in the "Companion Films Index."

STRANGERS ON A TRAIN ★★★★

(1951)
US/B&W/101 minutes
Director: Alfred Hitchcock
Cast: Farley Granger *(Guy Haines)*, Robert Walker *(Bruno Anthony)*, Ruth Roman *(Mother)*.
Genre: Thriller
Plot: "You're spoiling everything. You're making me come out into the open," complains Robert Walker to Farley Granger. Walker plays Bruno Anthony, the stranger who befriends the unsuspecting Guy Haines (Farley Granger) on a train.

Bruno is a wealthy, scheming, affected, sociopathic momma's boy—and Guy's worst nightmare. Though never directly mentioned in the film, Bruno's relationship with Guy is often referred to by film critics as a sexual one. From his actions (when he's not obsessing over Guy he has his mother file his nails), it's reasonable to conclude that Bruno was at the very least a closeted homosexual, but viewers will have to judge for themselves.

This is a Hitchcock classic worth seeing, if only for the famous climactic out-of-control merry-go-round scene.

Quotes:
"I may be old fashioned but I thought murder was against the law."
　—Granger
"Are you out of vitamins?"
"I took a bottle yesterday ma. A whole fifth."
　—Roman and Walker
MPAA Rating: Not rated.
Companion Films: See "Closet Cases," "Hustlers" and "Murderers" in the "Companion Films Index."

STREAMERS ★★★★

(1983)
US/Color/118 minutes
Director: Robert Altman
Cast: Matthew Modine *(Billy)*, Michael Wright *(Carlyle)*, Mitchell Lichtenstein *(Richie)*, David Alan Grier *(Roger)*, Guy Boyd *(Rooney)*, George Dzundza *(Cokes)*, Albert Macklin *(Martin)*.
Genre: Drama—This intensely intimate drama is an adaptation of the David Rabe play about a group of Vietnam-bound soldiers waiting in their barracks for orders to ship out.
Plot: "Do some push-ups. It'll straighten you out," exclaims Roger (Grier), an enlisted man

who doesn't know how to deal with another young man's homosexuality.

Mitchell Lichtenstein *(The Lords Of Discipline)* plays Richie, an intelligent and witty, effeminate young man who teases the others that he's homosexual and that they may be as well. He's especially suspicious of Billy (Modine), the most homophobic of the group.

When Carlyle (Wright), a confused and angry young black man, wanders into the barracks, his presence is a disruption to the group and a catalyst for the rage and violence that follow.

Though aware of his emotional instability, Richie propositions Carlyle, who accepts. When they ask Billy and Roger to give them some privacy, Billy explodes. Carlyle is much more unstable than anyone realized and goes on a killing rampage as a result.

Following the tragic incident, Sergeant Cokes (Dzundza) comes in search of his pal, who unbeknownst to him has been killed. He asks Richie, "Why you crying soldier?"

Roger replies, "He's crying 'cause he's a queer."

The sergeant, in one of the most touching scenes of the film, says that there are worse things than being queer. And considering all that has happened, this is a very profound statement.
MPAA Rating: R—For language, violence and nudity. Mitchell Lichtenstein appears nude from behind in a shower scene. Matthew Modine also appears nude from both front and behind, but obscured by shower steam.
Awards: Matthew Modine first gained attention with the critics in this, his second feature film. For the first time in its history, the Venice Film Festival jury gave the entire cast its *Best Actor* award.

Companion Films: See "Military Men" and "Murderers" in the "Companion Films Index."

STRIP JACK NAKED (NIGHTHAWKS II) ★★★

(1991)
UK/Color/96 minutes
Director: Ron Peck
Cast: Nick Bolton, Derek Jarman, Ken Robertson.
Genre: Documentary—Consisting of outtakes from his 1978 film *Nighthawks*, plus new footage, the film is dramatic and personal.
Plot: Gay filmmaker Ron Peck provides first-hand reflections of what it was like to be a young boy who realizes he's gay. As the voice-over for the boy, Peck explores the ostracism and anguish experienced as a result of his sexual preference. In addition, he touches on the problem of AIDS today. The setting is England in the 1960s and 1970s.
MPAA Rating: Not rated.
Companion Films: See *Nighthawks* (1978).

Also see "Coming Out" in the "Companion Films Index."

SUDDENLY, LAST SUMMER ★★★

(1959)
US/B&W/112 minutes
Director: Joseph Mankiewicz
Cast: Elizabeth Taylor (*Catharine Holly*), Katharine Hepburn (*Violet Venable*), Montgomery Clift (*Dr. Sugar*).
Genre: Drama—This Southern Gothic melodrama is based on Tennessee Williams' play about homosexuality and cannibalism. In the film, scripted by Williams and Gore Vidal, the cannibalism has been deleted and the homosexuality becomes the big mystery.
Plot: Katharine Hepburn plays Violet, a hysterically deluded woman who must live with the memory of her son Sebastian's bizarre murder the previous summer. Taylor plays Catharine, Sebastian's companion on his final summer vacation.

Unable to cope with her son's death, Violet goes on a mission to silence Catharine—a constant reminder of the tragedy. Violet, who cannot admit the awful truth wants to silence Catharine forever by having her lobotomized. It is up to the surgeon, Dr. Sugar, played by Montgomery Clift, to decide if Catharine is indeed insane as Hepburn insists. (Dr. Sugar's homosexuality has been removed from the film.)

The doctor eventually forces a confrontation between the women and allows the truth to be told. Violet, it seems, had traveled each summer with her son, so that he might write. For inspiration she would find and lure in young men for his pleasure. When Violet was no longer able to attract men, her son enlisted the services of his sexy cousin, Catharine. On this final trip he is murdered by a group of young men whom he had presumably propositioned earlier.

While the murder is a grisly one, cannibalism isn't mentioned. At this point in the tale it becomes clear that Catharine isn't the woman in need of a lobotomy.

MPAA Rating: Not rated—What was considered risqué at the time, is simply amusing and arch by today's standards.
Awards: Received Academy Award nomi-

nations for *Best Actress* (Katharine Hepburn) and *Best Art Direction (B&W)*.

Companion Films: See "Closet Cases" in the "Companion Films Index."

SUMMER WISHES, WINTER DREAMS

★★★

(1973)
US/Color/95 minutes
Director: Gilbert Cates
Cast: Joanne Woodward *(Rita)*, Sylvia Sidney *(Rita's mother)*, Martin Balsam *(Harry)*, Ron Rickards *(Bobby)*, Dennis Wayne *(Bobby's friend)*, Dori Brenner *(Anna)*.
Genre: Drama—This film would have been more accurately titled "The Invisible Homosexual." It's essentially about a mother coming to terms with her son's homosexuality.
Plot: Joanne Woodward plays Rita, a Manhattan housewife in the middle of a mid-life crisis. Her mother's death causes her to confront her own regrets and mistakes, and to try to make amends.

Her biggest regret is that she rejected her son, Bobby (Rickards), when she discovered that he was gay. In an early black-and-white flashback sequence we learn how Rita discovered her son's secret. When she walks in on him with a ballet-dancer friend in his room, he questions her, "How did you know it wasn't locked?" "I touched the knob, is that such a crime?" she answers. "I don't think mommys are allowed to go around touching their little boy's knobs," he answers angrily. This and one other brief moment are the only times we see the infamous Bobby.

Later in the film, Rita and husband Harry (Balsam) take a trip to Europe with the intention of making amends with their son, who now lives in Amsterdam. When Bobby doesn't respond to their telegrams, Harry informs his wife, "Bobby is living with a man in Amsterdam ... it's what those people call a 'lover.' Like that kid he brought home before."

"You said that was just a phase," she responds.

After she gains her composure he continues, "He also said that he's very happy for the first time in his life, and he sends us his love. And you're right, he doesn't want to see us."

Woodward is distraught by the news, and finally breaks down and confides in her husband. The pain of regret has taken its toll, and she laments, "I can't show anything to the ones that mean the most to me ... I know I drove Bobby away ... I keep telling myself that maybe I didn't have anything to do with why he is the way he is." Harry eases his wife's guilt by explaining, "Bobby was Bobby the day he was born, and if he wasn't, then you can't do better than your best. You did your best."

For an early 1970s film this was a pretty sensitive treatment of the topic. It was a refreshing change to find that the tortured monster was not the homosexual. It's too bad, however, that he was confined to status of "Invisible Man."

Quotes:
"Growing up is harder than learning to fly. One requires truth, the other only fairy dust."
   —*Woodward*
"You look fine. Look at your color."
"How can you tell what color I am under all this makeup? I could be dead, and I'd still look like I'd just gotten back from a cruise."
   —*Woodward and Sidney*

"My fat is my own accomplishment so don't go giving credit to mom."
—*Brenner*

"I may love you, but I don't like you at all."
—*Woodward*

"You pay your way through life as if every relationship were a toll booth."
—*Sidney*

"They give you a cupful of time. You either drink it or spill it all over the floor."
—*Balsam*

MPAA Rating: PG

Companion Films: See "Coming Out" in the "Companion Films Index."

SUNDAY BLOODY SUNDAY ★★★★
(1971)
UK/Color/110 minutes
Director: John Schlesinger
Cast: Glenda Jackson *(Alex Greville)*, Peter Finch *(Dr. Daniel Hirsh)*, Murray Head *(Bob Elkin)*, Peggy Ashcroft *(Mrs. Greville)*, Maurice Denham *(Mr. Greville)*, Tony Britton *(Businessman)*.

Peter Finch, Glenda Jackson and Murray Head are lovers in *Sunday Bloody Sunday* (1971).

Genre: Drama

Plot: Murray Head plays Bob, a bisexual artist living in London who's involved with two lovers. Glenda Jackson plays his thirty-something female lover, Alex. The late Peter Finch plays his forty-something male lover Daniel. Bob has been open and they both know about one another; each is satisfied to have half a lover over no lover at all. All the characters are sophisticated and accepting of their lifestyle and arrangement. The problem arises when Bob decides to leave for New York and ends both relationships.

Film critic Roger Ebert said at the time, "I think *Sunday Bloody Sunday* is a masterpiece, but I don't think it's about what everybody else seems to think it's about. This is not a movie about the loss of love, but about its absence."

MPAA Rating: R—Peter Finch and Murray Head have a kissing scene that was pretty risqué at the time.

Awards: Peter Finch became the first actor to be nominated for an Academy Award for an openly gay role. Glenda Jackson also received a nomination for her role in the film.

Other nominations included *Best Director* (John Schlesinger) and *Best Screenplay (Based on another medium)*.

Companion Films: See "Bisexuals" in the "Companion Films Index."

SWOON ★★★
(1992)
US/B&W/85 minutes
Director: Tom Kalin
Cast: Daniel Schlachet *(Richard Loeb)*, Craig Chester *(Nathan Leopold, Jr.)*, Ron Vawter *(State's Attorney Crowe)*, Michael Kirby *(Detective Savage)*, Michael Stumm *(Dr. Bowman)*, Valda Z. Crabla *(Germaine Reinhardt)*.

Genre: Drama—More than anything this crime drama has the look of a feature-length Calvin Klein commercial. It's so breathtakingly beautiful that one almost forgets to notice the story as it unfolds.

Plot: A low-budget, highly stylized film shot in black and white on 16mm and blown up to 35mm, it has the look of a much more expensively made film. In this dramatization of the notorious 1924 Leopold and Loeb murder case, first-time feature director Tom Kalin probes the topic from a contemporary point of view. Reviewers called this version of the true story revisionist. Daniel Schlachet and Craig Chester play the wealthy, spoiled, intellectually brilliant, Richard "Dickie" Loeb and Nathan "Babe" Leopold, Jr. As homosexual lovers and as Jews, their contempt for society, mixed with feelings of superiority, lead the two young men to calculate and coldly murder a young boy whom they know, simply for the thrill of it. It's called "the crime of the century," and they're represented by Clarence Darrow during their trial.

During the trial the prosecutor claims that the people had a right to know of their perversions. They are lumped together with bootleggers, dope fiends and perverts. And because their perversions are so scandalous and offensive, women are ordered under protest to clear the courtroom.

MPAA Rating: Not rated—Contains brief gay kissing scenes between the two leads, and suggested sex.

Trivia: Critic Jay Maeder of the *New York Daily News* had this to say: "In this, there is material for a landmark exploration of psycho-sexual social history. Filmmaker Tom Kalin has mostly squandered a potentially scalding picture, choosing instead to work the fringes of the gay-film genre. That said, it also is the case that *Swoon* is cinematographically miraculous, that Craig Chester's eerily dead-ringer Leopold is an extraordinary performance, and that this is going to be one of the season's most-discussed features."

Companion Films: Two previous films dealing with this topic are Alfred Hitchcock's *Rope* (1948) and Richard Fleischer's *Compulsion* (1959).

Also see "Closet Cases," and "Murderers" in the "Companion Films Index."

T

TASTE OF HONEY, A ★★★

(1961)
UK/B&W/94 minutes
Director: Tony Richardson
Cast: Rita Tushingham *(Jo)*, Murray Melvin *(Geoff)*, Dora Bryan *(Helen)*.
Genre: Drama—Based on the hit 1958 play of the same name written by Shelagh Delaney.
Plot: Set in London, Rita Tushingham plays Jo, a rebellious, working-class girl who's estranged from her man-chasing, alcoholic mother (Bryan). When Jo becomes pregnant by a black sailor, the only person she can turn to is Geoff (Melvin), a sensitive gay young man she has befriended.

Geoff is an effeminate, stereotypical outcast, who knows the pains of being ostracized. He is more than willing, for the companionship and affection, to move in and take care of Jo. She's more than willing to accept, and the two live a sheltered, fairy-tale life together free of adult concerns—at least for a while.

When Jo's mother learns that Jo's pregnant and living with a homosexual, she moves back into the flat and throws the young man out. Both Jo and Geoff are forced to grow up.

This is about as realistic and natural as you could ask for in 1961.
MPAA Rating: Not rated.
Companion Films: See "Neighbors, Roommates and Best Friends" in the "Companion Films Index."

TAXI ZUM KLO ★★

(Taxi To The Toilet)
(1981)
Germany/Color/107 minutes
Director: Frank Ripploh
Cast: Frank Ripploh, Dieter Godde, Orpna Termin, Peter Fahrni.
Genre: Drama—A low-budget independent feature about a man living a double life as a straight-laced elementary-school teacher by day and a sexually obsessed gay man by night.

In German with English subtitles.
Plot: Filmmaker and star Ripploh plays a 30-year-old teacher who one day tires of his double life and comes out to his students. He subsequently loses his job and becomes a full-time filmmaker.

The title of the film comes from Ripploh's fear that he will grow into an old man who must hang around the public toilets to find sex. His more pressing fear, however, is that he will be forced into a "normal" monogamous relationship with his jealous lover.

Not ready to settle down, Frank is a sexually promiscuous man who's into S&M, drag and public sex. Graphic, honest and at times humorous, *Taxi* is a portrait of a gritty slice of gay life.
MPAA Rating: Not rated—Contains graphic gay sex scenes bordering on hard-core porn and includes full-frontal male nudity.
Companion Films: Making a film as therapy was employed with less success, but a similar effect, by Amos Guttman in *Drifting* (1983).

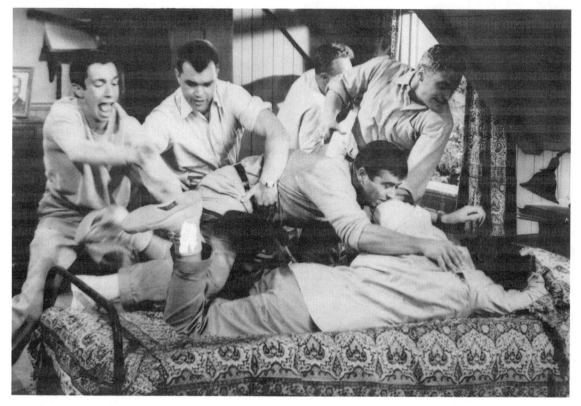

In *Tea And Sympathy* (1956) the other boys in the boarding house attack John Kerr for being a sissy.

Also see "Unhappy Homosexuals" in the "Companion Films Index."

TEA AND SYMPATHY ★★★★

(1956)
US/Color/122 minutes
Director: Vincente Minnelli
Cast: Deborah Kerr *(Laura Reynolds)*, John Kerr *(Tom Robinson Lee)*, Leif Erickson *(Bill Reynolds)*, Edward Andrews *(Herb Lee)*, Darryl Hickman *(Al)*, Norma Crane *(Ellie Martin)*, Dean Jones *(Ollie)*, Tom Laughlin *(Ralph)*, Ralph Votrain *(Steve)*.
Genre: Drama—About a sensitive young man who's wrongly suspected of being a homosexual and cruelly persecuted as a result. The film was based on the play by Robert Anderson.
Plot: Five decades after its release, it's startling to observe how little society has changed in its lack of tolerance for individuals who don't fit in. The monster in this film is a gentle young man who refuses to act cruel or callous towards others, and is ostracized as a result.

In this melodramatic morality tale set in New England in the '50s, John Kerr plays Tom

Lee, a sensitive 17-year-old boy living in a college dorm. Having a crush on Laura (Deborah Kerr), the house mistress, he prefers to spend his time with her rather than join the rest of the boys in sporting activities.

Subtle is not a word one would use to describe the plot. In one of the film's first scenes Laura helps Tom hem a dress he's to wear in the school play. It seems the only role he could get was that of Lady Teasle in "The School For Scandal." Tom, having been raised without a mother and having an absent father, learned to cook and sew and take care of himself and considers such things normal. When the boys in his dorm later discover him sewing a button on a shirt he is ridiculed and nicknamed "sister boy."

On a visit to the school, his father Herb (Andrews), an alumnus, discovers that Tom is being shunned by the other boys and is humiliated. Tom's father quickly suggests that he "oughta get a crew cut like the other fellas." Things were apparently a lot simpler in the 1950s. The dialogue and many of the situations are very humorous, though unintentional, by today's standards.

As a form of hazing, the boys participate in a ritual pajama-bonfire game. Tom is this year's guest of honor. When Laura asks her husband Bill (Erickson) to explain what goes on during these games he explains, "all the new boys put on their pajamas and the older boys try to tear them off." Many today would not consider this a punishment!

The thought of Tom being a homosexual (the word is never mentioned) has all the men, young and old, in a panic. Their fears, anguish and contempt eventually turn to cruelty. To prove himself to the others, Tom visits Ellie (Crane) the local prostitute. But when she too humiliates him he flies into a rage, grabs a knife from the kitchen and makes an unsuccessful suicide attempt.

When Laura learns what has happened she decides that it's time to end Tom's misery by reciprocating his love. Sleeping together—off screen of course—Laura has courageously saved Tom's life while ruining her own.

The not-too-subtle irony here is that her own husband refuses to sleep with her. Tom is the only decent, caring, three dimensional character in the film. Best of all, the screenwriter has gone to great pains to make it clear that he's the only real man in this movie.

Quotes:
"Boy, my dad's going to hit the roof when he hears I'm playing a girl."
 —*J. Kerr*
"What's the matter, are women *verboten*?"
 —*D. Kerr*
"He's going to have to learn to run with the other horses."
 —*Andrews*
"Why must the test of everything be its durability?"
 —*D. Kerr*
"In trying to prove he was a man, he died a boy."
 —*D. Kerr*
"Years from now when you talk about this—and you will—be kind."
 —*D. Kerr*

MPAA Rating: Not rated—Strictly PG.
Trivia: Dean Jones, best known for his roll in *The Love Bug* (1970) and other Disney comedies, made his film debut in 1956. That year he appeared in seven films, including *Tea And Sympathy,* playing Ollie, one of the varsity boys

John Kerr is the reluctant center of attention at the annual hazing In *Tea And Sympathy* (1956)

who torments Tom.

Companion Films: See "Sissies" in the "Companion Films Index."

"10" ★★

(1979)

US/Color/122 minutes

Director: Blake Edwards

Cast: Dudley Moore *(George)*, Julie Andrews *(Samantha)*, Bo Derek *(Ginny)*, Robert Webber *(Hugh)*, Sam Jones *(David)*, Dee Wallace *(Mary)*.

Genre: Comedy—A buxom Bo Derek (in her film debut) plays a dream-come-true vision who turns into a nightmare for a 42-year-old man going through a mid-life crisis.

Plot: In this sex comedy, Dudley Moore plays George, an Academy-Award-winning songwriter with everything a man could want but youth—his and any of a number of girls he longs to be with throughout the film.

George's song writing partner is Hugh (Webber), a middle-aged, gay man with a young male lover, whom he supports. In an early scene, George asks Hugh about his lover, Larry, "Doesn't he do anything except swim and jog on the beach?" "Oh yes, he makes me happy," Hugh replies in a defensive tone. The fact is that George is jealous. Shortly thereafter, George confides in his psychiatrist that he would gladly trade places with Hugh if he could be with someone as young as Larry. *This* gets the psychiatrist's attention.

There are other references to George's possible bisexuality, just as there are cheap-shot lines like George's description of Hugh's friends as "The Malibu chapter of the sugar plum fairies." All of this takes a back seat to the film's main theme.

George is a man in the middle of a mid-life crisis. He leaves his girlfriend Sam (Andrews), for a fantasy woman he happens to meet the day after his 42nd birthday. The only problem is that it's her wedding day. Obsessed with her youth and beauty, he follows her on her honeymoon. When he finally gets what he thought he wanted, sex with this fantasy turns into a fiasco, and he discovers that he had what he wanted all along with Sam.

Upon losing his young fantasy and returning home, he discovers that Hugh's young man has left him and gone to Europe. The message here seems to be that whether gay or straight, a man's better judgment goes out the window when it comes to youth and sex.

Trivia: Sam Jones plays David, Bo Derek's new husband. Film buffs will remember him as Buck Rogers. He'll also be remembered as a *Playgirl* centerfold in the late 1970s.

Quotes:

"Some of us just don't bring out the man in men."

　　—*Wallace*

"Sometimes you really are a pain-in-the-ass fag."

　　—*Moore*

MPAA Rating: R—Contains numerous scenes of male and female nudity—full-frontal female nudity, as well as Moore in the nude from behind. Jones keeps his clothes on in this one.

Companion Films: See "Men and Boys" in the "Companion Films Index."

TEOREMA ★

(Theorem)

(1968)

Italy/Color/93 minutes

Director: Pier Paolo Pasolini

Cast: Terence Stamp, Silvana Mangano, Massimo Cirotti, Anne Wiazeemsky, Laura Betti, Andres José Cruz Soublette.

Genre: Drama—Like many of Pasolini's films, *Teorema* is an exercise in cryptic symbolism whose primary audience is the film scholar.

In Italian with English subtitles.

Plot: Like *Something For Everyone* and *Entertaining Mr. Sloane*, *Teorema* is about a handsome stranger who seduces an entire household only to leave them destroyed.

Terence Stamp plays the stranger who mysteriously appears one day and proceeds to seduce the mother, father, son, daughter and maid. They are each helpless to fend off his magnetic charm and unable to forget him once he has left. Their lives have been transformed and each goes mad after he departs.

While the two other films mentioned are played, at least partially for laughs, this one plays it straight and lacks the charm of its central character. Add to this almost no dialogue from beginning to end, and you're left with an experience nearly as bleak as the film itself.

MPAA Rating: Not rated—Contains male nudity from behind and suggested gay sex.

Awards: The 1968 winner of the Venice Film Festival *Grand Prix* award.

Companion Films: See "Hustlers" in the "Companion Films Index."

THIS BOY'S LIFE ★★★★★
(1993)
US/Color/115 minutes
Director: Michael Caton-Jones

Cast: Leonardo DiCaprio *(Toby Wolff)*, Robert De Niro *(Dwight Hansen)*, Ellen Barkin *(Caroline Wolff)*, Jonah Blechman *(Arthur Gayle)*.

Genre: Drama—Based on the autobiographical 1989 book of the same name by Tobias Wolff.

Plot: Robert De Niro, Leonardo DiCaprio and Jonah Blechman all turn in Academy-Award-caliber performances in this coming-of-age memoir.

DiCaprio plays Toby, a teenager who endures the psychological and physical abuse of Dwight, his insecure stepfather. De Niro's chilling portrayal is one of his finest performances ever. This stepfather from hell makes Toby's life a living hell.

In stark contrast to Dwight's out-of-control macho man's-man character, is Toby's gay friend Arthur (Blechman)—the real hero of the film in many ways. When they first meet, Toby attacks the effeminate young man and calls him a "homo." He may be a homo, but he manages to beat an apology out of Toby and leave him humiliated in front of his friends.

When Dwight learns of the fight he believes that Toby has beaten "Miss" Arthur Gayle and is delighted. He's only sorry that Toby didn't put the boy in the hospital or out of his misery all together.

The boys later become good friends. Both of them are being raised by mothers without real fathers, so they can relate to one another. They both feel like outsiders—aliens, in this alien town named Concrete.

During one very intimate scene, the boys are singing and playing piano side by side, when Arthur leans over and kisses Toby on the cheek. Toby is stunned but doesn't know how to react.

The issue is left ambiguous and never fully resolved. Their friendship continues and Arthur eventually makes it possible for Toby to get a scholarship and leave Concrete and his abusive stepfather.

Set in the late 1950s, the film is handsomely photographed and beautifully captures this long-ago time and place. But it's the performances—DiCaprio's range and surprising depth, and newcomer Blechman's sensitive and on-the-mark small role—that steal the film and make this a hauntingly memorable experience.

MPAA Rating: R—Presumably for child abuse theme.

Companion Films: See "Neighbors, Roommates and Best Friends" in the "Companion Films Index."

THIS SPECIAL FRIENDSHIP ★★★★

(1964)

France/B&W/99 minutes

Director: Jean Dellanoy

Cast: Didier Haudepin (*Alexandre*), Francis Lacombrade (*George*), Michel Boquet (*Priest*).

Genre: Drama—Based on Roger Peyrefitte's 1945 novel. In French with English subtitles.

Plot: Set in a Jesuit school for boys, the repressive attitudes of the Catholic church and deceitful actions of a homosexual priest are contrasted with the natural affection and innocent love shared between two youths.

Francis Lacombrade plays George, a 16-year-old boy who falls in love with Alexandre (Haudepin) a 12-year-old classmate in a lower grade. As they are counseled daily against impure affections and sinful behavior, the two

boys are forced to share their intimacies in secret.

Eventually their relationship is discovered, and the younger boy is driven to suicide, following a lie told him by the priest. Though a number of films dealing with this topic have been made since, none have told it more powerfully nor more sensitively than this early film.

MPAA Rating: Not rated

Companion Films: See "Boys Schools" and "Religion" in the "Companion Films Index."

THUNDERBOLT AND LIGHTFOOT ★★

(1974)

US/Color/114 minutes

Director: Michael Cimino

Cast: Clint Eastwood (*Thunderbolt*), Jeff Bridges (*Lightfoot*), George Kennedy (*Red*), Geoffrey Lewis (*Goody*), Catherine Bach (*Melody*), Gary Busey (*Curly*), Roy Jenson (*Dunlop*), Vic Tayback (*Mario*), Dub Taylor (*Station attendant*).

Genre: Comedy—Cimino made his feature directorial debut with this comedy-drama about a group of bungling buddies who plan a safe-cracking heist.

Plot: Jeff Bridges plays Lightfoot, a car thief on the run. He literally runs into Thunderbolt (Eastwood), a fellow thief on the run, and they reluctantly become partners in crime.

A wise-cracking, irreverent young man, Lightfoot provokes all the guys with his sophomoric sexual double entendres. In one scene he enrages Red (Kennedy), a humorless fellow thief by pretending to kiss him. In another homophobic scene, a young man, for no apparent

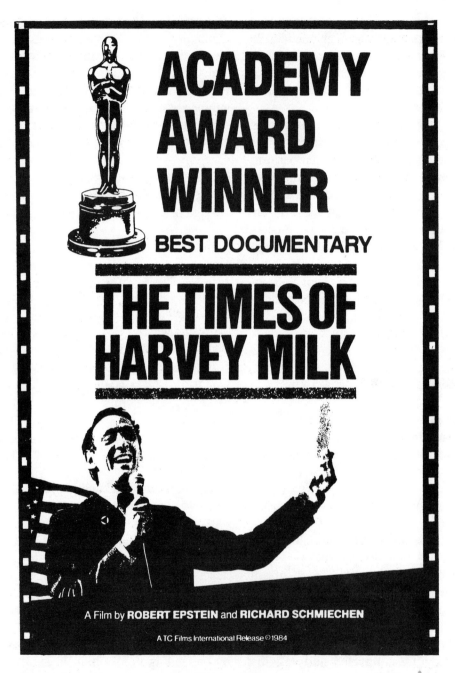

Director Robert Epstein and producer Richard Schmiechen were the first to accept Oscars in 1985 for a film with a gay theme made by openly gay filmmakers.

reason, jokes about a guy he knew who took his dick out of his pants and put it in another guy's hand. The shocked lad apparently just stood there holding it, having a difficult time deciding what to do with it. Be forewarned that the level of humor never rises any higher than this.

Bridges received an Oscar nomination for dressing up in female drag to rob a bank—now that's original. Catching a glimpse of himself in the mirror in a long blonde wig and a tight dress, he pouts his lips and says, "Oh you sexy bitch, I'd even go with you myself."

No one in this film is openly gay, but all the men spend an inordinate amount of time attempting to mask their fear of it. Inbetween, there's a thin veneer of a story about a group of thieves who plan the perfect safe-cracking heist, only to have all of their plans undone by double-crossing buddy, Red. In the end, Thunderbolt and Lightfoot escape and find their own treasure, but before they can enjoy it, Lightfoot dies of internal injuries received from the double-crossing Red.

This homophobic, predictable buddy film is nevertheless worth watching for two very captivating early performances by Eastwood and Bridges.

Quotes:

"Oh man, I'm dizzy."

—*Bridges*

"What do I want? I want your ass."

"Now flattery's not going to get you anywhere."

—*Kennedy and Bridges*

"You know, I don't think of us as criminals. I feel proud of myself."

—*Bridges*

MPAA Rating: R—Strictly for language.

Awards: Jeff Bridges received an Academy Award nomination for *Best Supporting Actor.*

Companion Films: See "Closet Cases" and "Homophobia" in the "Companion Films Index."

TIMES OF HARVEY MILK, THE ★★★★★
(1984)

US/Color/92 minutes

Filmmakers: Robert Epstein and Richard Schmiechen

Narrator: Harvey Fierstein

Genre: Documentary

Plot: Using film clips, photos and interviews, the filmmakers paint a powerful portrait of the life and times of controversial and openly gay San Francisco city supervisor Harvey Milk.

Milk, along with Mayor George Moscone, was assassinated in 1976 by a disgruntled former supervisor, Dan White. White was sentenced and received only four years for his crime, thus sparking the famous San Francisco riots.

Milk embodied the gay liberation movement and symbolized the new gay power and visibility worldwide. The filmmakers have captured this unprecedented historical time in a powerful, fascinating and moving tribute.

MPAA Rating: Not rated.

Awards: Winner of the 1985 *Best Documentary Feature* Academy Award. In addition the film won multiple Emmys, a Peabody and the New York Film Critics *Circle Award.*

Postscript: Richard Schmiechen died from complications of AIDS on April 7, 1993, at age 45 in Los Angeles.

Companion Films: See *Changing Our Minds: The Story Of Dr. Evelyn Hooker,* also by Schmiechen.

Also see "Biographies" and "Documentaries" in the "Companion Films Index."

TO BE OR NOT TO BE ★★★

(1983)
US/Color/108minutes
Director: Alan Johnson
Cast: Mel Brooks *(Frederick Bronski)*, Anne Bancroft *(Anna Bronski)*, James Haake *(Sasha)*, Tim Matheson *(Andre)*, Charles Durning *(Col. Erhard)*, Jose Ferrer *(Soledski)*.
Genre: Comedy—A remake of the Jack Benny-Carole Lombard classic.
Plot: Played for laughs, of course, Mel Brooks and Anne Bancroft play famous husband-and-wife actors Frederick and Anna Bronski, starring in a musical titled *Naughty Nazis*. The year is 1939, and Hitler is about to attack Poland.

Going underground, the Bronski's are forced to hide out in the apartment of Anna's flamboyant gay dresser Sasha (Haake). Sasha is eventually identified by the SS as a homosexual and forced to wear a pink triangle. Jokingly he complains to Anna, "I hate it. It clashes with everything." Later she asks him where he's going, and he replies, "Don't wait up, I have a late date with another triangle." But the humor soon enough turns to terror when the SS come to arrest him and send him to the camps.

To escape the soldiers who have come to the theatre for him, Sasha dresses in female drag and joins the chorus line on stage, providing a wonderful sight gag. But when his wig falls off, he's arrested and taken away in tears. The Bronski's manage to free their friend, however, who in turn becomes a hero who helps others escape.

In the final scene, the acting troupe is ordered to play a command performance for Hitler and the SS army. They cleverly use the occassion to make their escape to England. Walking a tragicomic tightrope, the film manages to be humorous and heartwarming at the same time.
Quotes:
" Would you like to see my bomber?"
—*Matheson*
"I've always felt that true love should never stand in the way of a good time."
—*Bancroft*
"Let's face it sweetheart, without Jews, fags and gypsies, there *is* no theater."
—*Brooks*
MPAA Rating: PG
Trivia: Director Alan Johnson choreographed the now famous scene from *The Producers*, "Springtime For Hitler."
Companion Films: See "Fascists and Nazis" in the "Companion Films Index."

TOGETHER ALONE ★★★

(1992)
US/B&W/87 minutes
Director: P.J. Castellaneta
Cast: Todd Stites *(Bryan)*, Terry Curry *(Brian)*.
Genre: Drama—Highly stylized, low-budget black-and-white, gay-themed drama about unsafe sex, AIDS and sexual identity.
Plot: Terry Curry plays Brian, a gay man who has spent the night with a stranger. Todd Stites plays the other man, a married bisexual, also named Bryan. In the heat of the moment, they neglect to practice safe sex. The next morning the realization of the possible consequences sinks in and they begin to discuss what they have done.

The entire film, in fact, is a real-time conversation that takes place, for the most part, in a single room. But because of the terrific performances and imaginative camerawork, the story avoids being claustrophobic or static and remains compelling.

It is for these reasons that it won numerous festival awards, both locally and abroad.

MPAA Rating: Not rated.

Companion Films: See "AIDS" in the "Companion Films Index."

TOO MUCH SUN ★

(1991)

US/Color/110 minutes

Director: Robert Downey

Cast: Robert Downey, Jr. *(Reed Richmond)*, Eric Idle *(Sonny Rivers)*, Ralph Macchio *(Frank Della Rocca, Jr.)*, Andrea Martin *(Bitsy Rivers)*, Jim Haynie *(Father Seamus Kelly)*, Laura Ernst *(Susan)*, Jennifer Rubin *(Gracia)*, Leo Rossi *(George)*, Howard Duff *(Old Man Rivers)*.

Genre: Comedy

Plot: In this sophomoric and insulting comedy, Howard Duff plays Old Man Rivers, a dying millionaire. His minister, a greedy Father Kelly (Haynie), discovers that both Rivers' son, Sonny (Idle), and daughter, Bitsy (Martin), are gay, however, and persuades O.M., who is on his deathbed, to leave his fortune to the church. That is, unless the son or daughter naturally conceives a child within a year.

In the race to conceive, the flamboyant Sonny attempts to have sex with numerous women with no success. All the while Bitsy is off in search of the child (Macchio) she had out of wedlock years ago. All the characters are played for laughs, but somehow the humor falls short in this mindless farce. The only good line in the film is when Sonny explains when he introduces his father to his lover that, "It's not like losing a son—it's like gaining another son."

MPAA Rating: R—For language and subject matter.

Companion Films: See "Sissies" in the "Companion Films Index."

TOOTSIE ★★★★★

(1982)

US/Color/119 minutes

Director: Sydney Pollack

Cast: Dustin Hoffman *(Michael Dorsey/Dorothy Michaels)*, Jessica Lange *(Julie)*, Teri Garr *(Sandy)*, Dabney Coleman *(Ron)*, Charles Durning *(Les)*, Sydney Pollack *(George/agent)*, Bill Murray *(Jeff)*, George Gaynes *(John Van Horn)*, Geena Davis *(April)*, Doris Belack *(Rita)*, Ellen Foley *(Jacqui)*, Estelle Getty *(Middle-aged woman)*.

Genre: Comedy—About a desperate, out-of-work New York actor who resorts to dressing in disguise as a woman to land a job.

Plot: Dustin Hoffman plays Michael Dorsey, a struggling actor/waiter who learns from his agent that nobody in New York or Hollywood wants to work with him because of his reputation as being difficult. "No one will hire you," shouts his agent George (Pollack). "Oh yeah," replies Michael. To prove his agent wrong he auditions for the role of hospital administrator Emily Kimberly on a popular daytime soap—and gets it.

Getting it is the easy part, however. Keeping it and keeping his friends and co-workers

Dustin Hoffman starred in *Tootsie*, one of the most successful and critically acclaimed films of 1982.

from discovering his secret proves to be the real challenge—and all the fun. When Michael's alter ego, Dorothy, becomes a media sensation, "her" contract is renewed for another year. Unfortunately, Michael has fallen for his co-star, Julie (Lange) and wants to end the charade. In the meantime, Julie's father Les (Durning) has fallen in love with and proposes to Dorothy. This is just the beginning, however, as things get increasingly complicated and clever from here. Julie decides that Dorothy is a lesbian while his friend Sandy (Garr) asks him if he is gay.

Finally, when the show is forced to go live, Michael sees this as his opportunity to reveal his true identity as a man, in a very believable—if melodramatic—climax. Intelligently written and finely acted, the film is full of wit, charm and double entendres. This is the way movies used to be made—with an added twist.

Quotes:
"You're just the wrong height."
"I can be taller."
"No, you don't understand, we're looking for someone shorter."
"Oh, look. I don't have to be this tall. I'm wearing lifts. I can be shorter."
"Really, we're looking for somebody different."
"I can be different."
"We're looking for somebody else, okay?"
　　—Casting director and Hoffman
"Pardon me, but is my acting interfering with your talking?
　　—Hoffman
"Shame on you, you macho shit."
　　—Hoffman
"I'd like to make her look a little more attractive. How far can you pull back?"

"How do you feel about Cleveland?"
　　—Belak and a cameraman
"God, I begged you to get some therapy."
　　—Pollack
"They almost didn't hire me because they thought I was too feminine."
　　—Hoffman
"You're psychotic."
"No I'm not. I'm employed."
　　—Pollack and Hoffman
"It works, but don't play hard to get."
　　—Pollack
"I'm telling you, if I didn't have a dress on, I'd kick his arrogant ass in."
　　—Hoffman
"I have a little mustache problem."
"Some men find that attractive."
　　—Hoffman and Lange
"I am Dorothy. Dorothy is me. There's a woman in me."
　　—Hoffman
"You've got to listen to me Michael. There are no other women like you. You're a man."
"Yes, I realize that of course, but I'm also an actress."
　　—Pollack and Hoffman
"I'm just afraid you're going to burn in hell for all of this."
"I don't believe in hell. I believe in unemployment, but I don't believe in hell."
　　—Murray and Hoffman
"Bulls are bulls, and roosters don't try to lay eggs."
　　—Durning
"Honesty in many ways is a relative term."
　　—Hoffman
"Were you ever famous?"
"No."

"Then how can you be a has-been?"
—Hoffman and Gaynes
"Oh, no one would call you stupid to your face."
—Murray
"Aren't we still friends?"
"No, we are not friends. I don't take this shit from friends—only from lovers."
—Hoffman and Garr
"The only reason you're still living is because I didn't kiss you."
—Durning
"I was a better man with you, as a woman, than I ever was with a woman, as a man. Know what I mean? I just gotta learn to do it without the dress."
—Hoffman
"Sex changes everything. I've had relationships before where I know a guy and then have sex with him, and then I bump into him someplace, and he acts like I owe him money!"
—Garr

MPAA Rating: PG—Hoffman and Gaynes exchange a kiss on the lips. Gaynes doesn't realize that Hoffman is really a man.

Awards: *Tootsie* appeared on more critics' top-ten lists than any other film of the year. Jessica Lange won a *Best Supporting Actress* Oscar for her role. She was also nominated for *Best Actress* for *Francis*. *Tootsie* also received nominations for *Cinematography, Film Editing* and for *Best Picture*, losing out to *Gandhi*.

Companion Films: See "Drag Queens" in the "Companion Films Index."

TORCH SONG TRILOGY ★★★★
(1988)
US/Color/117 minutes

Director: Paul Bogart

Cast: Harvey Fierstein *(Arnold)*, Anne Bancroft *(Ma)*, Matthew Broderick *(Alan)*, Brian Kerwin *(Ed)*, Karen Young *(Laurel)*, Eddie Castrodad *(David)*, Ken Page *(Murray)*, Charles Pierce *(Bertha Venation)*, Axel Vera *(Marina Del Rey)*.

Genre: Comedy—Based on the popular Broadway comedy-drama hit by actor-writer Harvey Fierstein about a female impersonator looking for love and respect and unwilling to accept anything less.

Plot: In the film's opening scene, the year is 1952, the place is Brooklyn, New York. Anne Bancroft opens her bedroom closet door to discover her very young son Arnold dressed in drag and applying makeup.

From this moment on, the tone of this warm, campy and moving personal story is set. Fast forward 20 years and Arnold (Fierstein) is now a professional female impersonator living and working in New York.

Like the play, the film is divided into three parts—or the three most important relationships in his life—spanning the decade of the '70s. This was a time before AIDS when the word "tragedy" had an entirely different meaning. The trilogy begins when Arnold meets and falls in love with Ed (Kerwin), a confused bisexual man unable to commit completely to a man. The year is 1971. Eventually Ed leaves Arnold for a woman.

Three years later, Christmas, 1973, Arnold meets, and reluctantly falls in love with Alan (Broderick), an attractive, younger—much younger—man.

Four years later and it's the summer of 1977. Despite their physical differences, they've managed to have a lasting relationship and have

Harvey Fierstein wrote and starred in the hit Broadway play *Torch Song Trilogy* in the early 1980s. He went on to star in the 1988 film version.

even decided to adopt a child together. On the eve of the happy occasion, however, Alan is tragically murdered by gay bashers.

Three years later, spring 1980, Arnold's mother is planning a visit. He has neglected to tell her about his adopted gay son David (Castrodad) who has been living with him for a year. Throughout his life Arnold's mother has never accepted his lifestyle and has insisted over the years that it is just a phase. On this visit, however, Arnold forces the issue in a very powerful scene and demands that his mother accept him or no longer be a part of his life.

As he defends himself and his life, Arnold is a man who has grown to love himself, partly as a result of the love he's received from the three most important men in his life—Ed, Alan and David.

It's rare when a film is as successful as the play from which it's adapted. To its credit, the film not only succeeds, but takes on a life of its own that surpasses the play in many ways.

Quotes:

"I swear I'm aging about as well as a beach-party movie."

—*Fierstein*

"There's nothing I need from anyone except love and respect, and anyone who can't give me those two things has no place in my life."

—*Fierstein*

"How can sleeping with a woman make you proud of yourself if you know you'd rather be with a man?"

—*Fierstein*

"Speak up—I'm a drag queen, not a mind reader."

—*Fierstein*

"Try as I may, I just can't walk in flats."

—*Fierstein*

"The next time you feel you have to say 'I love you' to someone, say it to yourself—and see if you believe it."

—*Fierstein*

"You shove your sex life down my throat like aspirin."

—*Bancroft*

"'Whoops' is when you fall down an elevator shaft. 'Whoops' is when you accidentally douche with Drano. This is not a 'whoops.'"

—*Fierstein*

"David is gay. He came that way."
"Nobody comes that way."

—*Fierstein and Bancroft*

MPAA Rating: R—Contains gay kissing scenes between Broderick and Kerwin, and Broderick and Fierstein.

Trivia:

Estelle Getty (TV's *The Golden Girls*) played the role of Ma on Broadway.

Companion Films:

See "Coming Out," "Drag Queens" and "Men and Boys" in the "Companion Films Index."

Two, I do not kill people, okay?"
—*Eleniak*

MPAA Rating: R—Contains violence, profanity and female nudity.

Companion Films:
See "Drag Queens" in the "Companion Films Index."

UNDER SIEGE ★★★

(1992)
US/Color/102 minutes
Director: Andrew Davis
Cast: Steven Seagal *(Casey Ryback)*, Tommy Lee Jones *(William Strannix)*, Gary Busey *(Commander Krill)*, Erika Eleniak *(Jordan)*.
Genre: Action
Plot: In the 1990s, even bone-crunching he-men action heroes like Steven Seagal find themselves exchanging witty gay repartee. In this ultra-violent actioner, Seagal single-handedly takes on a group of terrorists who have hijacked a naval destroyer loaded with nuclear weapons.

In one scene, a group of shipmates teases him about his uniform. "Hey, where's your whites?" asks one. "Poor boy, doesn't have a dress uniform," yells another. "Nah," replies Seagal, "I've got the dress. I forgot the pumps."

Gary Busey, Seagal's nemesis, on the other hand goes all the way. Dressing in drag as a "Miss July" pinup, he plays it strictly for laughs, just before he pulls out a gun and kills an officer. The film is full of insulting gay jokes and unoriginal humor that continues to be recycled even today.

Quotes:
"I have two rules. One, I do not date musicians.

URINAL ★★

(1988)
Canada/Color/100 minutes
Director: John Greyson
Cast: Pauline Carey, Paul Bettis, Lance Eng.
Genre: Drama—A low-budget, original, offbeat first feature.
Plot: Like *My Dinner With Andre*, *Urinal* is simply a film about people engaged in a literate conversation. In this film, however, the conversation is about historical homosexual repression by the police. The group's primary focus is public restrooms. The conversations are juxtaposed with lectures and interviews.

It also differs in that the individuals having the conversation are all dead gay artists, including Japanese writer Yukio Mishima, Russian filmmaker Sergei Eisenstein and American poet Langston Hughes. The fictional Dorian Gray makes a cameo as an undercover gay cop.

At times amusing, this highly original documentary-style film won't appeal to everyone.

MPAA Rating: Not rated.

Companion Films:
See "Cops" in the "Companion Films Index."

VERY NATURAL THING, A ★★★

(1973)
US/Color/85 minutes
Director: Christopher Larkin
Cast: Robert Joel *(David)*, Curt Gareth *(Mark)*, Bo White *(Jason)*.
Genre: Drama—A low-budget independent feature and the first film to present gay liberation as a theme. Originally titled *For As Long As Possible.*
Plot: A ground-breaking film in many ways, it was nevertheless criticized by gay and nongay critics alike for being a melodramatic love story that simply mirrored clichéd heterosexual love stories.

In the first half of the film, David (Joel), a New York City teacher, begins a monogamous relationship with Mark (Gareth), an insurance salesman. Desperately trying to create a straight, idealized "marriage," they find it incompatible with who they really are, and forcing it eventually leads to their breakup.

Left confused and alone, David goes to the other extreme and becomes sexually promiscuous. Still searching for an identity, he meets Jason (White), a photographer, at a New York City gay-pride rally. Jason helps him define a whole new relationship with a whole new set of rules and ideals.

Having found happiness, the two run naked into the surf in the film's final frame.

Review: Film reviewer Judith Crist described the film this way, "If the gay lib movement wants its own mediocre movie preachment— here it is."
MPAA Rating: Not rated—Contains male nudity.
Companion Films: See "Unhappy Homosexuals" in the "Companion Films Index."

VIA APPIA ★★

(1992)
Germany/B&W/90 minutes
Director: Jochen Hick
Cast: Peter Senner *(Frank)*, Guilherme de Padua *(Jose)*, Yves Jansen *(The director)*, Margarita Schmidt *(Lucia)*, Jose Carlos Berenguer *(Sergio)*, Gustavo Motta *(Ulieno)*, Luiz Kleber *(Mario)*.
Genre: Drama—A low-budget, cinema verite-style, film-within-a-film format. (Via Appia is the gay district of Rio de Janeiro.)
Plot: Peter Senner plays Frank, a former airline attendant who has been diagnosed with AIDS. Desperate to confront the man who intentionally infected him, he returns to the scene of the crime—taking along a film crew to document his search.

(Having spent the night with a man named Mario (Kleber), Frank woke to find a message left behind: "Welcome to the AIDS Club.")

In his attempt to locate Mario, he searches the gay bathhouses, discos, hotels and parks. Even with a solid premise, this slow-moving and dark film is hampered by its technical limitations.
MPAA Rating: Not rated—Contains numerous scenes of full-frontal male nudity.

Companion Films: See "AIDS" in the "Companion Films Index."

VICTIM ★★★★
(1961)
UK/B&W/100 minutes
Director: Basil Dearden
Cast: Dirk Bogarde *(Melville Farr)*, Peter McEnery *(Boyd Barrett)*, Sylvia Sims *(Laura)*, Dennis Price *(Calloway)*, Anthony Nicholls *(Lord Fullbrook)*, Derren Nesbitt *(Sandy)*, Margaret Diamond *(Miss Benham)*, Norman Bird *(Harold Doe)*, Donald Churchill *(Eddie)*, John Barrie *(Det. Inspector Harris)*, Charles Lloyd Pack *(Henry)*, Nigel Stock *(Phip)*, Frank Pettit *(Barman)*, Dawn Beret, Alan Howard.
Genre: Thriller—Considered a ground-breaking film at the time for its sensitive handling of homosexuality and hate crimes. While the film is a bit melodramatic, it's just as pertinent and poignant today.
Plot: Dirk Bogarde plays Mel Farr, a courageous bisexual barrister, who sacrifices his marriage and career to entrap the blackmailers responsible for the suicide of his former lover Boyd Barrett (McEnery). At the same time, the film puts the entire British system on trial for encouraging blackmail and homophobia by making homosexuality a criminal act.

As Farr's investigation leads him to the blackmailers, he discovers that Barrett wasn't the only homosexual being blackmailed. It seems that an entire group of gay friends is being squeezed. When they learn what Barrett plans to do, they turn on him out of fear of being exposed themselves.

Variety praised the film and proclaimed,

"The homosexuals involved are not caricatures but are shown as varying human beings. There are a philanthropist peer, an actor, an aging barber, a hearty car salesman from a good family, a photographer, a bookseller and a factory clerk."

This very tight plot is full of twists and turns, all leading to a surprising climax. Not only is one of the blackmailers gay himself (Nesbitt), but one of the gay men being blackmailed (Stock) has given the blackmailers names of all of his homosexual friends in lieu of payment. The mastermind behind the blackmailing, while a bit clichéd, is a perfect symbol for society's hatred of homosexuality and tolerance of hate.

In the final scene, Sandy (Nesbitt), the gay blackmailer, attempts to describe his partner, "You really are a bit odd aren't you? Oh, I don't know, a cross between an avenging angel and a peeping Tom."
Quotes:
"Well, it used to be witches. At least they don't burn you."
　—*Howard*
"But Mr. Garr is married sir."
"Those are famous last words."
　—*Cairney and Barrie*
"If the law punished every abnormality we'd be kept very busy."
　—*Barrie*
"Fear is the oxygen of blackmail."
　—*Bogarde*
"Nature played me a dirty trick."
　—*Pack*
"Perhaps for him it was love. He died for it to protect me."
　—*Bogarde*
"Do you ever wonder about a law that makes

Alex Karras comes out of the closet to James Garner in *Victor/Victoria* (1982).

us all victims of any cheap thug that finds out about our natural instincts?"

   —Mandrake

"They disgust me. I felt physically ill. They're everywhere. The police do nothing. Someone's got to make them pay for their filthy blasphemy."

   —Diamond

"Is that how you feel about it?"

"I'm a policeman, sir. I don't have feelings."

   —Bogarde and Barrie

"Why can't he stick with his own sort."

   —Beret

"You'll never forgive me, will you?"

"It's not your fault you haven't got enough brains to understand."

   —Beret and Howard

MPAA Rating: Not rated.

Companion Films: See "Murderers" in the "Companion Films Index."

VICTOR/VICTORIA ★★★★

(1982)

US/Color/133 minutes

Director: Blake Edwards

Cast: Julie Andrews (*Victor/Victoria*), Robert

Preston (*Toddy*), James Garner (*King*), Lesley Ann Warren (*Norma*), Alex Karras (*Squash*), John Rhys-Davies (*Cassell*).

Genre: Comedy—A madcap comedy about a down-on-her-luck woman who's forced to play a man impersonating a woman. Based on a 1933 film titled *Viktor/Viktoria*.

Plot: This inspired film opens in Paris, 1934. Victoria (Andrews) is an out-of-work singer willing to do anything for food. She has also been kicked out of her living quarters and is in need of a place to stay. As luck would have it, she crosses paths with Toddy (Preston), a gay cabaret singer and promoter. Toddy is experiencing a bit of bad luck himself, what with boyfriend problems and having been fired from his job that very day.

Before long, the two are sharing his flat and he has come up with a plan to land them both on easy street—if they don't end up in jail. Toddy manages to promote Victoria as Victor, a famous female impersonator. They also pretend to be male lovers. The scam is a smashing success with only one hitch. Victor meets straight businessman King (Garner) and, much to his surprise, they fall in love. To the film's credit it's full of many moments like this when male and female sexuality become confused in very humorous and often unsettling situations. From here on out, Toddy and Victoria spend much of their energy trying to keep the charade intact. At the same time, King and others are spending theirs trying to unmask what they believe is a fraud.

Playing King's blonde bombshell girlfriend Norma, Leslie Ann Warren nearly steals the film with her outrageously funny performance. While Alex Karras, who plays King's bodyguard Squash, offers up one of the film's most touching and surprising moments. Squash, having walked in on King and Victor in bed together, with tears in his eyes, comes out of the closet and confesses to his boss that he too is gay. He doesn't know that Victor is really a woman, which makes the scene all the more amusing. To add to the farce, Squash falls for Toddy and the two end up in bed together.

In the end, the charade unravels because of love. Victoria chooses to forsake her career for the man she loves. A traditional happy ending with a twist makes this a charming, fast-paced, must-see sexual romp.

Quotes:
"I'll sleep with you for a meatball."
    —*Andrews*
"You get your money's worth!"
"I'd say we both get my money's worth."
    —*Toddy's boyfriend and Preston*
"Thank you, thank you, you're most kind. In fact, you're every kind."
    —*Preston*
"It is a moron who gives advice to a horse's ass."
    —*The waiter*
"I'm hooorny!"
    —*Warren*
"There's nothing more inconvenient than an old queen with a head cold."
    —*Preston*
"Kill him but mustn't kiss him."
    —*Preston*
"Pretending to be a man has its disadvantages."
    —*Andrews*
"You look better in Richard's clothes than he does. But then he looks better out of them."
    —*Preston*

"You're kidding. You really are queer. But you're so attractive."

—Warren

"If you think I'm worried about everyone thinking I'm a fag, you're right."

—Garner

MPAA Rating: R—For language and sexual situations.

Awards: Academy Award winner for *Best Original Song Score/Adaptation.* Also received nominations for *Best Actress* (Julie Andrews), *Best Supporting Actress* (Leslie Ann Warren), *Best Screenplay, Best Art Direction* and *Best Costume Design.*

Companion Films: See "Drag Queens" in the "Companion Films Index."

VOICES FROM THE FRONT ★★★

(1992)

US/Color/87 minutes

Filmmakers: Robyn Hutt, Sandra Elgear and David Meieran.

Genre: Documentary—The battle in this powerful documentary is between people af-flicted with AIDS and an inhuman and seemingly uncaring bureaucracy.

Plot: The focus of this admittedly one-sided film is on the AIDS activist movement in America (the ACT-UP group especially) and how they are forcing the government into action. The enemy of these activists is red tape, politics, ignorance, foot-dragging, hospital mistreatment of AIDS patients—and an assortment of other heart-wrenching horrors perpetrated and perpetuated by a system that is out-of-touch with the needs of its people.

In one of 12 interviews, writer Vito Russo, who wrote the seminal work on homosexuality in the movies, *The Celluloid Closet,* states that to conquer AIDS means "changing the system." Russo died of the disease before the film's completion.

While tackling a difficult and painful topic, the filmmakers have managed to capture the spirit of this move-ment with humor, warmth and humanity.

MPAA Rating: Not rated.

Companion Films: See "AIDS" in the "Companion Films Index."

W

WE THINK THE WORLD OF YOU ★★
(1988)
UK/Color/100 minutes
Director: Colin Gregg
Cast: Alan Bates *(Frank)*, Gary Oldman *(Johnny)*, Frances Barber *(Megan)*, Liz Smith *(Millie)*, Max Wall *(Tom)*, Ryan Batt *(Dickie)*, Kerry Wise *(Rita)*.
Genre: Comedy—An offbeat, quirky film about a man's desperate search for love and affection.
Plot: Set in London in the 1950s, Alan Bates plays Frank, a stable, middle-aged gay man in love with Johnny (Oldman), a confused, unstable bisexual. Johnny is unhappily married and has three children. Johnny tries to recapture the love of his youth by buying Evie—a dog like the one he loved and lost as a child. A poor lad, Johnny steals the money to buy the dog and is arrested. The irony is that he is put in jail for a year and unable to be with the dog.

Frank and Johnny's wife, Megan (Barber), are jealous rivals, and she keeps him from visiting Johnny in prison. Johnny's mother, however, is fond of Frank and keeps him abreast of Johnny's well-being. But before long, Frank has fallen out with Millie (Smith) and her husband Tom (Wall) over their mistreatment of Johnny's dog.

The running joke is that Johnny, his wife and his parents continually say they think the world of everyone else, but in fact are ill-equipped to demonstrate their love or affection for each other—or even for the dog.

Lonely and frustrated, Frank finds his only affection and friendship in Evie, the dog. Johnny finally relents and lets Frank buy the dog. But after a year of mistreatment by the family, the dog is just as dysfunctional as the other members of the family and proceeds to turn Frank's life upside-down.

In essence this is the simple story of a gay man trapped in a destructive relationship with a dog—a situation not all that removed from the experience of many.
MPAA Rating: PG
Companion Films: See "Bisexuals" and "Prisoners" in the "Companion Films Index."

WE WERE ONE MAN ★★★
(1981)
France/Color/118 minutes
Director: Philippe Vallois
Cast: Serge Avedikian *(Guy)*, Piotr Stanislas *(Rolf)*, Catherine Albin *(Jenine)*.
Genre: Drama—A love story between a French peasant boy and a German soldier set in 1943 during the war. In French with English subtitles.
Plot: Serge Avedikian plays Guy, an innocent peasant who nurses Rolf (Stanislas), a young German soldier, back to health after he has been injured in a battle. When Rolf has recovered, he makes plans to rejoin his platoon, but Guy pleads with him to stay. Reluctantly Rolf stays on and the two develop a very special friendship. They bathe together, hunt together, talk about their lives, compete in strength contests and mostly fight—like two lovers.

Guy even offers to let Rolf sleep with his

Gary Oldman and Alan Bates are an odd couple in *We Think The World Of You* (1988). Bates eventually leaves Oldman for his dog.

girlfriend Jenine (Albin), but he isn't interested. One night they get drunk, dance together and have a very sensuous food fight. Having to relieve themselves, they pull out their penises and fill up a few drinking glasses. At this point they also compare sizes. One thing leads to another and Rolf tries to kiss Guy, who pulls away.

This becomes the turning point in their relationship. Rolf, feeling rejected himself, rejects Guy in turn. Guy, who's an escapee from a mental institution reacts violently. When they make up, Rolf confesses his love for Guy. Afraid of losing him, Guy decides to sleep with his friend and they make passionate love. Jealous of their relationship, Jenine turns Rolf in to the authorities and he's taken away. Obsessed with Rolf and unable to let him go from the beginning, Guy manages to hold onto the man he loves in a surprising—and tragic—ending to an idyllic love story.

Appealing performances and original characterizations make this a memorable story.

Quotes:

"Nothing is easy. Life is a battle. There is no room for weaklings."

—Stanislas

"I want you to stay here forever with me. Kiss

226

me as if I was a woman."
—*Stanislas*
MPAA Rating: Not rated—Contains numerous scenes of Avedikian and Stanislas in full-frontal nudity, gay sex and gay kissing scenes. Sex and nudity are presented very casually and naturally.
Companion Films: See "Coming Out" and "Murderers" in the "Companion Films Index."

WHAT HAVE I DONE TO DESERVE THIS? ★★

(1984)
Spain/Color/100 minutes
Director: Pedro Almodovar
Cast: Carmen Maura (*The Mother*).
Genre: Comedy—The usual Almodovar off-the-wall, bizarre black humor. In Spanish with English subtitles.
Plot: This simple story is about the ultimate dysfunctional family. The only member of this odd group who appears to be well-adjusted is the youngest son Miguel, who's gay.

Maura plays a poor woman who works as a maid to put food on the table. To escape her drudge of a life, she sniffs glue and pops No-Doz. Her oldest son is a drug pusher; her younger son is gay. Her mother-in-law is an eccentric woman who hoards her money. Her husband is a cab driver and an insensitive oaf. One of her neighbors is a prostitute, and the other is a child with telekinetic powers. One day she's had enough, so she murders her husband with a ham bone. This sets in motion a series of events that set her free from her dreary life and offers up an opportunity to begin again.

In one scene, Maura asks her son Miguel if he's been sleeping with his friend's father again.

In another, more outrageous moment, an obviously gay dentist finds himself taken with the young man and convinces the mother—which doesn't take much—to let him "adopt" the boy. In return, Miguel will receive all the oral treatment he needs.

In the end, Miguel returns to his mother stating that he's too young to be tied down to one man. With his help, it looks as if it might be possible to make a new start and get on with her life.
MPAA Rating: Not rated—Contains nudity and profanity. In the opening scene, a man is seen in full-frontal nudity standing in a public shower. He's joined by Maura, who's fully clothed, and they proceed to have sexual intercourse.
Companion Films: See "Men and Boys" and "Murderers" in the "Companion Films Index."

WHEN THE PARTY'S OVER ★★

(1992)
US/Color/115 minutes
Director: Matthew Irmas
Cast: Rae Dawn Chong (*M.J.*), Elizabeth Berridge (*Frankie*), Sandra Bullock (*Amanda*), Fisher Stevens (*Alexander*), Brian McNamara (*Taylor*), Kris Kamm (*Banks*).
Genre: Drama
Plot: Set in Los Angeles, *When The Party's Over* is a modern-day drama about a group of roommates struggling with their identities. It also explores the paths they will each take when it's time to grow up and move on.

The story culminates during a New Year's Eve party held by the friends—three very different women and a struggling gay actor (Kris Kamm). Roommate M.J. (Rae Dawn

Chong) provides the friction that ignites the spirits and emotions of this group through her manipulations. The group interactions and melodrama take over and keep the plot moving in all directions from there.

This is a film aimed at a younger audience who will appreciate this group of characters' coming-of-age struggles.

MPAA Rating: Not rated.

Companion Films: See "Neighbors, Roommates and Best Friends" in the "Companion Films Index."

WHERE THE DAY TAKES YOU ★★★
(1992)
US/Color/92 minutes
Director: Marc Rocco
Cast: Dermot Mulroney *(King)*, Lara Flynn Boyle *(Heather)*, Balthazar Getty *(Little J)*, Sean Astin *(Greg)*, James LeGros *(Crasher)*, Ricki Lake *(Brenda)*, Kyle MacLachlan *(Ted)*, Peter Dobson *(Tommy Ray)*, Stephen Tobolowsky *(Charles)*, Will Smith *(Manny)*, Adam Baldwin *(Officer Black)*, Laura San Giacomo *(Interviewer)*.
Genre: Drama—An all-star cast of up-and-comers fills out this tragic drama about the life of street kids in Hollywood, California. This is a beautifully photographed film about a very ugly and down-beat topic.
Plot: Dermot Mulroney plays King, a 21-year-old leader of a group of homeless runaways and throw-aways who have banded together to survive on the streets. They survive by stealing, selling drugs and through prostitution. Their means of survival, however, is eventually the very thing that tears this "family" apart.

In the opening scene, King is being released from jail. Hooking back up with the street kids the first question they ask him is, "Sucked any cocks." He replies, "Just your dad's." Homosexuality and male prostitution are revealed to be just another necessary evil in this film—another way to survive on the streets.

Getty, as Little J, stands apart in the film as a young, confused boy forced into hustling. In a couple of scenes Little J hooks up with Charles (Tobolowsky), a wealthy, neurotic gay man who gets off just listening to young boys talk about sex. In a scene where the man wants only to caress J's face, the act repulses J as much as if he were being humiliated and defiled. This is a very potent scene. In the next scene J's taking target practice on beer bottles with his new gun. He spits out the word "faggot" as he aims and shoots.

In desperation, however, he returns to Charles who takes him in for a few days. But when he discovers J's gun he insists that he leave. J blows up, but spares the man's life as he lies pleading on the floor. J is the most volatile and edgy of the group, and eventually triggers a tragic end.

MPAA Rating: R—For language, violence and drug use. A realistic look at the gritty side of life. Award-winning-caliber performances and topnotch technical credits make this a noteworthy film.

Trivia: Christian Slater appears in an uncredited cameo.

Companion Films: For other films with Dermot Mulroney see *Longtime Companion* (1989) (you won't recognize him).

Also see "Homophobia" and "Men and Boys" in the "Companion Films Index."

WHERE'S POPPA? ★★

(1970)
US/Color/87 minutes
Director: Carl Reiner
Cast: George Segal *(Gordon)*, Ron Leibman *(Sidney)*, Ruth Gordon *(Mother)*, Rob Reiner *(Roger)*, Trish Van Devere *(Louise)*.
Genre: Comedy
Plot: George Segal plays Gordon, a middle-aged man living with his mother. On his father's deathbed he made a promise not to put his senile mother (Gordon) into a rest home.

Set in New York City, Gordon calls on his brother, Sidney (Leibman), to help him take care of his mother who is single-handedly ruining his social life.

Sidney lives on the opposite side of Central Park and uses it as a shortcut to his brother's. Unfortunately, he's mugged each time he enters. The first time he's mugged he is stripped of his clothing and forced to run through the city naked. The next time he is "forced" by a gang to rape a woman passing by. The woman turns out to be an undercover male vice cop in drag.

The joke, in very bad taste, is on the gang, however. Following the rape, the arresting officer sends Sidney a dozen long stem roses with a card thanking him for a wonderful evening. He also asks for his phone number. Sidney is flattered and asks his brother if he should give it to him.

This film has aged about as well as Gordon's mother and moves at a slower pace.
Quotes:
"Gordon, if poppa comes home and catches you dressed like that he's going to be very disappointed."
—Gordon
"Where is the arresting officer?"
"I don't know. He was all shook up. He had never been raped before."
—Segal and Leibman
"You almost scared me to death."
"*Almost* doesn't count."
—Segal and Gordon
MPAA Rating: R—Contains male nudity from behind.
Companion Films: See "Rape" in the "Companion Films Index."

WOMEN IN LOVE ★★★★

(1969)
UK/Color/129 minutes
Director: Ken Russell
Cast: Glenda Jackson *(Gudron)*, Alan Bates *(Rupert)*, Oliver Reed *(Jerold)*, Jennie Linden *(Ursula)*, Eleanor Bron.
Genre: Drama—Based on the D.H. Lawrence classic, this is a tale of sexual repression and expression between a man and a woman, and between a man and another man—very controversial for its time.
Plot: A sensuous, sumptuous film set mostly in the English countryside, the story centers on Jerold (Reed), a wealthy young man, and his friend Rupert (Bates). Rupert is in love with life's sensual pleasures and unable to be fulfilled only by a woman. He craves the emotional, spiritual and physical love of another man—Jerold. Jerold, however, is unable or unwilling to return his friend's feelings completely—though during a nude wrestling scene both men appear to reach a sexual climax together.

To do what's expected of them, the men romance Gudron and Ursula (Jackson and Linden), a pair of sisters from working-class homes. The women fall in love with the men, but their love isn't returned in equal measures. The contrasts between what women need in a relationship and what men need are repeatedly exposed.

When Jerold's sister drowns in the lake it becomes a metaphor for a woman's love of a man. Her new husband is also drowned trying to save her, leaving Jerold to claim, "She killed him." In a sense this is a story about how the demanding, jealous, possessive love of a woman can be deadly, while male love is less demanding, but just as dangerous in its own way.

In the end, unable to be fulfilled in his relationship with a woman and unable to allow himself to be fulfilled in a relationship with a man, Jerold kills himself in a quiet and dramatic scene. Standing over his body Bates cries, "He should have loved me. I offered it." "You can't have two kinds of love," reasons Ursula. "You can't have it because it's impossible." "I don't believe that," replies Bates.

While death plays a big role in this story, it is sensuality and sexual expression that take center stage. Sensuality extends to almost everything in the film. One of the most sexually suggestive scenes revolves around the eating of a fig. This is a scene reminiscent of another seductively eaten meal in *Tom Jones*, starring Albert Finney. Bates proclaims to his surprised friends, while dining, "Like a prostitute the burstin' fig makes a show of her secret." There are many delicious secrets to be found in *Women In Love*.

Quotes:
"I would like to die from our kind of life and be born again."
　　—Bates
"I just reached the conclusion that nothing matters in the world except the right person to take the edge off."
"Meaning a woman of course."
"Failing that, an amusing man."
　　—Bates and Reed
"You can't do much in a stuffed shirt."
"Very well then. Let's strip and do it properly."
　　—Bates and Reed
"You like to be affected don't you?"
　　—Reed's mother
"You always think you can force the flowers to come out."
　　—Linden
"Aren't I enough for you?"
"You are enough as far as a woman."
　　—Linden and Bates

Awards: Jackson won the 1970 *Best Actress* Academy Award for her role. Ken Russell also received a nomination for *Best Director*.

MPAA Rating: R—Contains a legendary nude wrestling scene between Bates and Reed containing full-frontal nudity as well as other scenes of casual male and female nudity throughout.

Companion Films: See "Bisexuals" and "Closet Cases" in the "Companion Films Index."

WONDERLAND ★★

(1989)
UK/Color/103 minutes
Director: Philip Saville
Cast: Emile Charles (*Eddie*), Tony Forsyth (*Michael*), Robert Stephens (*Vincent Barbari*), Clare Higgins (*Eve*), Robbie Coltrane (*Annabelle*), Carsten Norgaard (*Dolphin man*).
Genre: Thriller—Formerly titled *The Fruit Machine*.
Plot: Emile Charles and Tony Forsyth play gay

teenage friends Eddie and Michael. Eddie is a sweet and innocent boy with an unusual love for dolphins. Michael is an attractive hustler, who knows his way around the streets. Together they help one another survive on the streets.

Set in Liverpool, the two friends manage to escape and are forced into hiding after witnessing a gangland-style murder at a local gay nightclub.

Taken in and given a place to stay by a wealthy older gay man in the seaside town of Brighton, the boys feel safe and come to enjoy their new situation. But before long, the killers catch up with them and their new life is shattered.

MPAA Rating: R

Companion Films: See "Men and Boys" in the "Companion Films Index."

WORD IS OUT: STORIES OF SOME OF OUR LIVES ★★★★★

(1977)

US/Color/130 minutes

Filmmakers: Peter Adair, Lucy Massie Phoenix, Rob Epstein, Veronica Selver, Nancy Adair, Andrew Brown.

Genre: Documentary—Originally titled *Who Are We?*

Plot: A landmark film, this was the first major film to explore American gay culture and history from a gay perspective.

More than 200 videotaped interviews were edited down to 26 open, honest, revealing, humorous, and heartwarming conversations with gay men and lesbians. These brave men and women represent a cross-section of America. Ranging in age from 18 to 77, from prom queen to poet, the diversity of occupation, race, background and class is impressive. The only thing these individuals all have in common is their shared sexual identity.

The result is a powerful testament to the gay experience and a breakthrough oral and visual history.

This is a must-see film for all gay men and lesbians, old and young.

MPAA Rating: Not rated.

Companion Films: See "Documentaries" in the "Companion Films Index."

WORLD ACCORDING TO GARP, THE

★★★★

(1982)

US/Color/136 minutes

Director: George Roy Hill

Cast: Robin Williams *(Garp)*, Mary Beth Hurt *(Helen Holm)*, Glenn Close *(Jenny Fields)*, John Lithgow *(Roberta)*, Hume Cronyn *(Mr. Fields)*, Jessica Tandy *(Mrs. Fields)*, Swoosie Kurtz *(Hooker)*, Amanda Plummer *(Ellen James)*.

Genre: Drama—Based on the bestseller by John Irving. This is a quirky tale about a boy and his mother and their fateful lives.

Plot: Set in 1944, the story follows the life of Garp (Williams) from beginning to end. Glenn Close plays Garp's mother, Nurse Jenny Fields, a strong, independent woman who wants a baby, but not a husband. In unorthodox fashion for the time, she becomes pregnant and gives birth to a son, whom she names Garp.

On the surface, this is a story about an obsessed woman and her son. On another level, this is a story about castration and the destructive nature of sex. Sex equals death in this quirky, humorous tale.

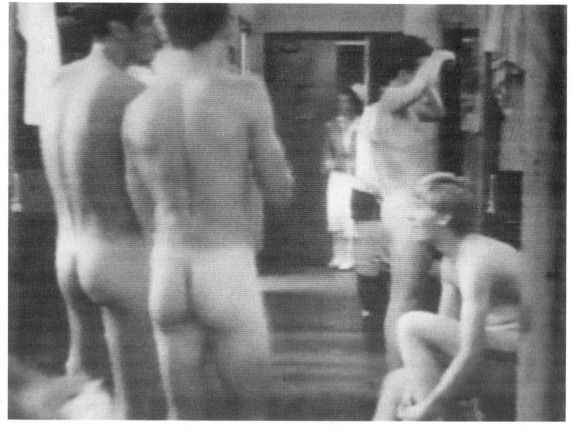

Another locker room scene. This from *The World According To Garp* (1982).

From little boys getting their penises caught in their zippers to big boys having their penises cut off—or worse, bitten off—this is a story about women who castrate men. But it is also a story about older men who cut out the tongues of little girls and younger men who destroy the lives of older women. Men and women are enemies in this tale and the only normal person seems to be Roberta (Lithgow), a former tight end with the Philadelphia Eagles who underwent an operation to become a woman. "Every-one here has something missing," she says, explaining to Garp the retreat his mother has created to help women who have been damaged by men.

Innocent and joyful, Garp rebels against the sexual extremism he witnesses around him and tries to live a normal life, but his life, too, is shattered in the end by the war between men and women.

Quotes:

"I love kids. I didn't know I loved them so

much until I became a woman. If I'd known, I would have had some when I was a man."
   —*Lithgow*
"Don't you dare say 'sperm' in this house."
   —*Cronyn*
"I didn't need a ring, mother. I needed his sperm."
   —*Close*
"Eighteen. Is there any word in the English language as sexy as that?"
   —*Williams*
"I am a helpless romantic in a male chauvinist world."
   —*Lithgow*
"I had mine removed surgically under general anesthesia, but to have it bitten off in a Buick—it's a nightmare."
   —*Lithgow*
"Okay wrestlers, we have a big meet tomorrow so no beating the meat tonight."
   —*The coach*
"You know why Santa Claus can't father a child? Because he comes down the chimney."
   —*The coach*
"Is that the latest fashion?"

"No, mom. It's the oldest profession."
   —*Close and Williams*
"I wish I was a girl. If I was a girl I'd take off all my clothes and look at myself for hours in the mirror."
   —*A young boy*
"Is that his name? Sounds like a flavor in a gay ice cream parlor. Strawberry Swirl, Chocolate Mocha Madness, Michael Milton."
   —*Williams*

Awards: In her film debut, Glenn Close was nominated for a *Best Supporting Actress* Academy Award for her role as Jenny. John Lithgow was nominated for *Best Supporting Actor*. *Tootsie* and *Victor/Victoria* were nominated the same year for numerous Academy Awards, including a nomination for *Tootsie* for *Best Picture*.

MPAA Rating: R—For nudity (another nude shower scene featuring numerous male bottoms from behind), profanity, sexual situations and violence.

Companion Films:
See "Drag Queens" in the "Companion Films Index."

XYZ

YEAR OF LIVING DANGEROUSLY, THE
★★★
(1982)
US/Color/115 minutes
Director: Peter Weir
Cast: Mel Gibson *(Guy Hamilton)*, Linda Hunt *(Billy Kwan)*, Sigourney Weaver, Michael Murphy *(Pete Curtis)*, Bill Kerr *(Col. Henderson)*, Noel Ferrier *(Wally O'Sullivan)*.
Genre: Drama
Plot: Mel Gibson plays Guy Hamilton, an Australian journalist who is sent to Jakarta, Indonesia, in 1965 to cover the political unrest of the time. What he discovers is danger, jealousy, friendship and romance.

Linda Hunt, in an Academy-Award-winning performance, plays Billy Kwan, a sensitive, caring man who's eventually killed trying to make a difference in the lives of the people of Jakarta. His sensitivity, however, does not extend to a fellow journalist (Noel Ferrier) who happens to be gay. In a scene in which the journalist discusses how the country's ruler uses his people, Billy responds violently, "You're right, he does use his people as objects of pleasure. But then so do you, only you do it with boys!" This in fact is a story about how everyone uses everyone else to get what they want.
Quotes:
"Is that pornography or is that art?"

"If it's in focus, it's pornography. If it's out-of-focus, it's art."
　　—Murphy and Hunt
Awards: Linda Hunt won a *Best Supporting Actress* Academy Award for her performance as a man.
MPAA Rating: R—Contains violence, profanity and full-frontal male nudity.
Companion Films: See "Men and Boys" in the "Companion Films Index."

YOU ARE NOT ALONE ★★★★
(1980)
Denmark/Color/90 minutes
Directors: Lasse Nielsen and Ernst Johansen
Cast: Anders Agenso, Peter Bjerg.
Genre: Drama—A sweet and charming coming-of-age love story set in a Danish boys' school. In Danish with English subtitles.
Plot: In this touching tale of budding adolescent sexuality, hypocrisy and repression are the lessons to be learned from the adults in charge. The topic the boys are most interested in, however, is sex.

Bo is a sensitive 15-year-old. While most of the boys have their eyes on the local girls, Bo is taken with the stern headmaster's son, Kim. Kim is equally infatuated with the older boy, and before long, their innocent crush turns into a romantic and sexual relationship. This is no ordinary adolescent love affair. This one comes with everything—a secret hideaway, a swimming hole and back scrubbing in the showers.

Ignored and abused by adults, these maturing boys are forced to turn to one another for emotional support. When a particularly rebellious boy is expelled from the school to serve as an example to the others, his classmates refuse to let him be the lone scapegoat and band together to demand that he be reinstated.

In the end, they've learned the most important lesson of all—to an adolescent boy—that they are not alone in their feelings and desires.

MPAA Rating: Not rated—Contains full-frontal male nudity, gay sexuality and gay kissing scenes involving Bo and Kim.

Companion Films: See "Boys Schools" and "Coming Out" in the "Companion Films Index."

YOUNG SOUL REBELS ★★

(1991)

UK/Color/105 minutes

Director: Isaac Julien

Cast: Valentine Nonyela (Chris), Mo Sesay (Caz), Dorian Healy (Ken), Frances Barber (Ann), Jason Durr (Billibud), Gary McDonald (Davis), Ray Shell (Jeff), Sophie Okonedo (Tracy), Danielle Scillitoe (Trish), Debra Gillett (Jill), Shyro Chung.

Genre: Drama—An energetic and musically charged indy pic.

Plot: British cult-feature director, Isaac Julien brings to the screen an offbeat psychosexual drama set in London in the summer of 1977.

The plot centers around two black pirate-radio disc jockeys, Chris (Nonyela) and Caz (Sesay). Chris is obsessed with bringing soul music into the mainstream. Taking on the establishment, though, is an uphill but often humorous battle.

When a mutual gay friend (Shyro Chung) is murdered while cruising a London park, their lives are dramatically changed. The film switches directions and becomes more of a murder mystery. Chris is arrested for the murder, but it's Caz's new boyfriend who appears to be the true killer.

Though uneven, this energetic film contains many worthwhile moments.

MPAA Rating: Not rated—Contains explicit gay sex scenes and male nudity.

Companion Films: See "Murderers" in the "Companion Films Index."

ZORRO, THE GAY BLADE ★

(1981)

US/Color/93 minutes

Director: Peter Medak

Cast: George Hamilton (Don Diego Vega and Ramon "Bunny" Wigglesworth), Ron Leibman (Esteban), Lauren Hutton (Charlotte), Brenda Vaccaro (Florinda).

Genre: Comedy

Plot: George Hamilton plays Don Diego, a self-centered ladies' man who learns of his father's secret identity after his death. His father was none other than the legendary Zorro, and he passes on his destiny and secret identity to his son.

Hamilton also plays his twin brother Ramon, now known as Bunny Wigglesworth. Bunny returns home after 20 years at sea with the British Navy. It seems that his father, fearing he wasn't masculine enough, sent him off to sea to make a man out of him (so much for that theory).

Don Diego is temporarily laid up following an accident, so Bunny steps in to fulfill his duties as Zorro. Bunny, however, wouldn't be caught dead in basic black and decides to make a statement with his costume. From plum purple to banana yellow, his "fruity"-colored outfits with frilly hats draw attention.

Robbing from the rich to give to the poor, Zorro incurs the wrath of Esteban (Leibman), the loud-mouthed tax collector, who eventually captures Don Diego, the real Zorro. But before Zorro can be executed, Bunny saves the day—in gold lamé.

This is a silly, sophomoric farce with a few memorable moments.

Quotes:

"Are you aware that your husband is responsible for making thousands of people miserable?"
"Really? And I thought he was just irritating me."
—*Hutton and Vaccaro*

"Do you agree, sir, that I have a point?"
"Indeed, it must be difficult to find a hat that fits it properly."
—*Leibman and Hamilton*

"They say the Navy makes men. Well, I'm living proof. They made me."
—*Hamilton*

"Walk for you? Why you've seen me walk before."
"Yes, but you always do it with such manliness. I never tire of watching you."
—*Hamilton and Leibman*

"How do you defend yourself?"
"Well, actually I'm not all that bad with a whip."
—*Hamilton and Hamilton*

"Remember, my people, there is no shame in being poor ... only [in] dressing poorly."
—*Hamilton*

"If only I could have one night in your booties."
—*Hamilton*

MPAA Rating: PG
Companion Films: See "Heroes" and "Sissies" in the "Companion Films Index."

ADDITIONAL FILMS

In an effort to be the most complete guide possible, this section includes additional films featuring gay themes or characters. Many contain only minor gay characters or scenes, but are nevertheless worth noting.

ABUSE ★★★
(1983) Director: Arthur J. Bressan, Jr.
Larry Porter plays a gay film student who falls in love with an abused young boy, played by Raphael Sbarge.

ACCATTONE ★★
(1961) Director: Pier Paolo Pasolini
This director's first feature centers on a young pimp who wants to leave the street life, but is torn between conflicting desires.

AIRPLANE! ★★★
(1980) Director: Jim Abrahams, David Zucker and Jerry Zucker
Peter Graves stars in this spoof full of gay jokes, sight gags and one-liners.

ALEXANDRIA ... WHY? ★★★
(1978) Director: Youssef Chahine
An autobiographical tale about a love affair between an Arab and an English soldier.

ANDERS ALS DIE ANDEREN ★★★
(1919) Director: Richard Oswald
Conrad Veidt plays Paul Korner, a promiscuous violinist who is sent to prison for participating in homosexual acts.

ANDERSON TAPES, THE ★★★
(1971) Director: Sidney Lumet
Martin Balsam plays an antique dealer and aging queen, not to mention, a thief. The role is played for laughs.

ANDY WARHOL'S FRANKENSTEIN ★★
(1974) Director: Paul Morrissey
Udo Kier plays the mad doctor who creates the perfect man. But there's a hitch—his perfect man isn't attracted to women!

ARMY OF LOVERS, OR REVOLT OF THE PERVERTS ★★★★
(1978) Director: Rosa von Praunheim
A personal view of the gay movement in America and the extremes to which it is forced to go to attain equal rights.

BEETHOVEN'S NEPHEW ★★★
(1985) Director: Paul Morrissey
In this French/German film, Ludwig Von

Beethoven is tormented by his obsessive love for his handsome young nephew.

BEN-HUR ★★★★

(1959) Director: William Wyler
Charlton Heston plays Ben-Hur. Stephen Boyd plays Messala, his lifelong friend and only true love—at least according to many critics.

BEVERLY HILLS COP ★★★★

(1984) Director: Martin Brest
Eddie Murphy does an offensive imitation of a "faggoty" stereotype. Bronson Pinchot plays a less offensive gay character.

BIRD ON A WIRE ★★★

(1990) Director: John Badham
Mel Gibson pretends to be a swishy, gay hair-dresser and uses it as a getaway disguise—now that's certainly original.

BLACK LIZARD ★★★

(1968) Director: Kinji Fukasako
Female impersonator Akihiri Maruyama plays the evil, campy vamp and jewel thief Black Lizard. Yukio Mishima makes a cameo appearance.

BLACULA ★★

(1972) Director: William Crain

Stephen Boyd and Charlton Heston in a revealing scene from *Ben-Hur* (1959).

A black Dracula takes a liking to a white "faggot" in this variation on a theme.

BLIND TRUST ★★
(1987) Director: Yves Simoneau
A Canadian thriller that finds the hero to be a gay guard who attempts to thwart an armed robbery.

BLOODY MAMA ★★
(1970) Director: Roger Corman
Shelley Winters plays Ma Barker. Bruce Dern plays her homosexual son. He also just happens to be a murderer.

BODY OF EVIDENCE ★
(1993) Director: Uli Edel
Madonna explains to a jury that she left her former lover (Frank Langella) because he was in bed with another man and she couldn't compete.

BOLERO ★★
(1981) Director: Claude Lelouche
James Caan plays a father and his suicidal gay son, Jason, in a dual role.

BOOM! ★★
(1968) Director: Joseph Losey
Noel Coward plays the Witch of Capri, a "screaming queen" to rival all others.

BOSTON STRANGLER, THE ★★★
(1968) Director: Richard Fleischer
Hurd Hatfield plays Terence Huntley, a wealthy, gay murder suspect.

BRAIN DONORS ★★★
(1992) Director: Dennis Dugan
A wacky, slapstick send-up of the Marx Brothers' films with numerous gay jokes and one-liners.

Also stars George De La Pena (*Nijinsky*).

BREAD AND CHOCOLATE ★★★
(1973) Director: Franco Brusati
Straight men dress in drag and put on a show to relieve their boredom. One of the transvestites is a little too convincing.

BRINGING UP BABY ★★★★
(1938) Director: Howard Hawks
Caught wearing a frilly nightgown, Cary Grant utters the famous words, "I've just gone gay—all of a sudden."

BROADWAY MELODY, THE ★★
(1929) Director: Harry Beaumont
A Broadway producer threatens to fire his prissy costume designer for giggling once too often.

BUDDIES ★★★
(1985) Director: Arthur J. Bressan, Jr
The first independent feature to depict an AIDS love story.

BUMPING INTO BROADWAY ★★
(1919) Director: Hal Roach
Gus Leonard plays Ma Simpson, a stern boarding-house landlady.

BURNING SECRET ★★★
(1988) Director: Andrew Birkin
A homoerotic, coming-of-age tale of a young boy who is befriended by a baron in 1919.

BURROUGHS ★★★★
(1983) Director: Howard Brockner
The charmed life and work of infamous New York writer William S. Burroughs.

BUSTING ★★
(1974) Director: Peter Hyams.
Elliott Gould and Robert Blake play vice cops who take pleasure in busting members of the homosexual low-life.

CANTERBURY TALES ★
(1972) Director: Pier Paolo Pasolini
Set in England and based on Chaucer's classic tales, the film takes a disturbing look at sexuality in the Middle Ages.

CAPRICE ★★★
(1967) Director: Frank Tashlin
My Favorite Martian and transvestite-psycho killer Ray Walston is done in by Doris Day.

CHARLEY'S AUNT ★★
(1941) Director: Richard Day
Jack Benny impersonates Dona Lucia, his wealthy aunt from Brazil, in this Victorian farce. Edmund Gwenn plays his admirer.

CHRISTINE JORGENSEN STORY, THE ★★★
(1970) Director: Irving Rapper
John Hansen plays George/Christine in this bio pic. In one scene, while still a man, he is forced to fend off a rapist.

CLINIC, THE ★★
(1981) Director: David Stevens
A day-in-the-life comedy set in an Australian VD clinic, and featuring numerous gay characters.

COLEGAS ★★★
(1982) Director: Eloy de la Iglesia
In this Spanish drama, Jose and Antonio are life-long teenage "pals" who are forced into hustling to raise money to help Antonio's sister.

COONSKIN ★★
(1975) Director: Ralph Bakshi
Animated feature includes a sadomasochistic black transvestite named Snowflake.

CORRUPT ★★
(1983) Director: Roberto Faenza
Harvey Keitel plays a NYC police officer who becomes involved in a sadomasochistic relationship with Johnny Lydon, a punk, aka Johnny Rotten.

DAMNED IN THE USA ★★★
(1992) Filmmaker: Paul Yule
Anticensorship documentary takes on fundamentalists and antipornography conservatives Sen. Jesse Helms, Donald Wildmon and others.

DANZON ★★★
(1992) Director: Maria Novaro
Tito Vasconcelos plays a colorful transvestite night-club owner in this Spanish film.

DAY FOR NIGHT ★★★
(1973) Director: Francois Truffaut
Jean-Pierre Aumont plays Alexander, an aging actor with a young lover. Alexander is killed in a car crash while returning from the airport with the young man.

DAY OF THE JACKAL, THE ★★★
(1973) Director: Fred Zinnemann
Edward Fox is an assassin who murders a gay man he picks up in a Turkish bathhouse. This is a very brief scene in a very long movie.

DAY OF THE LOCUST, THE ★★★
(1975) Director: John Schlesinger
The late Paul Jabara (*Midnight Cowboy, Honky*

Tonk Freeway) plays a female impersonator who sings one brief number, "Hot Voodoo."

DEATH ON THE BEACH ★
(1988) Director: Enrique Gomez
A repressed homosexual teenager goes on a rampage when his mother tries to set him up on a date with a girl.

DECAMERON, THE ★★
(1970) Director: Pier Paolo Pasolini
A homoerotic adventure set in the 14th century and based on the stories of Boccaccio.

DELIVERANCE ★★★
(1972) Director: John Boorman
A group of buddies on a vacation is terrorized by backwoods mountain men. Ned Beatty is raped.

DER SPRINTER ★★★
(1985) Director: Christoph Boll
Wieland Samolak plays a young track star who goes "straight" to make his mother happy.

DESIRE ★★★★
(1989) Director: Stuart Marshall
This moving documentary chronicles the gay and lesbian movement in Germany during the 1920s and '30s—ending in the concentration camps.

DESPERATE LIVING ★★
(1977) Director: John Waters
Mink Stole stars in this "monsterous fairy tale" as a murderess who finds refuge in a village of perverts ruled by Edith Massey, as Queen Carlotta.

DEVIL'S PLAYGROUND, THE ★★
(1976) Director: Fred Schepsi
Young boys and older men are not always successful at repressing their homosexual desires in an all-boys seminary.

DORIAN GRAY ★
(aka The Secret Of Dorian Gray)
(1970) Director: Massimo Dellamano
An English/Italian update of the classic Oscar Wilde tale of narcissism. The film stars Helmut Berger as Dorian.

DRESSED TO KILL ★★★
(1980) Director: Brian De Palma
Michael Caine plays a doctor who's also a transvestite psychopath—a perfect match in Hollywood.

DRUM ★★
(1976) Director: Steve Carver
John Colicos plays a violent white master who rapes and tortures black slaves. One of his victims is played by former heavyweight boxer Ken Norton.

EAT THE RICH ★★
(1987) Director: Peter Richardson
Transsexual Lanah Pellay plays Alex, a waiter who has been fired from his job in an upper-class restaurant and is bent on revenge in this English comedy.

EIGER SANCTION, THE ★★
(1975) Director: Clint Eastwood
Jack Cassidy plays a doomed, stereotypical sissy with a dog named Faggot.

EMPTY BED, AN ★★★
(1986) Director: Mark Gasper
John Wylie plays an elderly man facing the loneliness of old age because he never was able to

commit to a relationship.

ENTER THE DRAGON ★★★
(1973) Director: Robert Clouse
No one escapes the kung fu master, especially not the gay character.

EROTIKUS: HISTORY OF THE GAY MOVIE ★★★
(1975) Director: L. Brooks
A documentary history of erotic gay cinema from the early days until the '70s. Narrated by porno director Fred Halsted.

EVIL UNDER THE SUN ★★★
(1982) Director: Guy Hamilton
Roddy McDowell plays Rex Brewster, a bitchy, gay gossip columnist in this Agatha Christie murder mystery.

EXODUS ★★★
(1960) Director: Otto Preminger
Sal Mineo received a Best Supporting Actor Academy Award nomination for his portrayal of a rape victim.

FACE TO FACE ★★★
(1976) Director: Ingmar Bergman
Liv Ulmann's doctor is one of those characters rare in the movies—a happy, well-adjusted homosexual.

FALLING DOWN ★★★
(1993) Director: Joel Schumacher
"Alternative lifestyle, my ass," screams Frederic Forrest—a demented, homophobic, fag-bashing skinhead—at two gay customers.

FEARLESS VAMPIRE KILLERS, THE ★★
(1967) Director: Roman Polanski
Subtitled, "Pardon me, but your teeth are in my neck." Iain Quarrier plays Herbert, an effeminate, gay vam-pire who falls for Polanski.

FEMALE TROUBLE ★★★
(1974) Director: John Waters
Divine is pure camp as Dawn Davenport, an abused child who grows up to be an abused woman.

FISHER KING, THE ★★★
(1991) Director: Terry Gilliam
Michael Jeter almost steals the movie when he delivers a singing telegram in drag—a very memorable scene.

FLESH ★★
(1969) Director: Paul Morrissey
An Andy Warhol, soft-porn, underground-art film, starring Joe Dallesandro—as a gay hustler, of course.

FLESH AND THE DEVIL ★★★
(1927) Director: Clarence Brown
Lars Hanson and John Gilbert play army buddies who are separated by a woman—Greta Garbo. When she tragically drowns, they are happily reunited.

FLESH GORDON ★★
(1974) Director: Howard Ziehm
The good guy in this one is a gay man and he has a good time with the straight Flesh Gordon—as a reward for his good deeds.

Cary Grant dons female drag once again in *I Was A Male War Bride* (1949).

FORBIDDEN PASSION ★★★
(1980)
Michael Gambon plays Oscar Wilde in this BBC film about the life and times of the infamous homosexual playwright.

FOREVER MARY ★★
(1990) Director: Marco Risi
Mario, a transvestite prostitute, falls in love with his reform-school teacher played by Michele Placido in this hard-boiled Italian drama.

FREEBIE AND THE BEAN ★★
(1974) Director: Richard Rush

James Caan corners and kills a murderous transvestite with an attitude (played by Christopher Morley).

FREEDOM PARADISE ★★★
(1989) Director: Sergei Bodrov
Volodya Kozyrev plays Sasha, a 13-year-old boy who escapes from reform school and embarks on a search for his father. Along the way he loses his innocence.

FUN DOWN THERE ★★
(1989) Director: Roger Stigliano
A homely, awkward young man comes of age, so

to speak, when he comes out in NYC.

FUNNY LADY ★★★

(1975) Director: Herbert Ross

Roddy McDowell plays Bobby, the pansy chorus boy. James Caan plays Billy Rose, an insecure man who uses Bobby as a doormat.

GARBO TALKS ★★★

(1984) Director: Sidney Lumet

Harvey Fierstein, playing a lonely gay man vacationing on New York's Fire Island, doesn't get lucky with Ron Silver.

GENESIS CHILDREN, THE ★★

(1972) Director: Anthony Aikman

This homoerotic tale stars Peter Glawson as the leader of a group of young American boys who shed their inhibitions—and their clothing—on a vacation in Italy.

GLENGARRY GLEN ROSS ★★★

(1992) Director: James Foley

To call a man a "faggot," "fairy," or "cocksucker" is still considered the ultimate insult. This film elevates humiliation to an art form.

HAIRSPRAY ★★★

(1988) Director: John Waters

In his final role, Divine plays Ricki Lake's mother in this 1950s sendup.

HAPPY BIRTHDAY GEMINI ★★★

(1980) Director: Richard Benner

Based on the hit Broadway play, Robert Biharo plays a father who comes to accept his son's (Allen Rosenberg) homosexuality.

HE'S MY GIRL ★

(1987) Director: Gabrielle Beaumont

A low-budget, gender-bender farce. A boy needs a date in order to win a contest. He talks his best friend into dressing in drag and pulling off the charade.

HIDDEN PLEASURES ★★★

(Los Placeres Ocultos)

(1977) Director: Eloy de la Iglesia

Spain's first openly gay film about a closeted banker who tragically falls in love with a young student.

HONKY TONK FREEWAY ★

(1981) Director: John Schlesinger

A jeep full of gay men provide comic relief in this otherwise sophomoric comedy.

I WAS A MALE WAR BRIDE ★★★

(1949) Director: Howard Hawks

Cary Grant is seen once again in drag. This time he uses it to get the girl.

IN A GLASS CAGE ★★

(1986) Director: Agustin Villaronga

A violent horror film about a Nazi doctor and child molestor who's tormented by a young man bent on revenge. Filmed in Spanish with English subtitles.

INCIDENT, THE ★★★

(1967) Director: Larry Peerce

Martin Sheen and Tony Musante play hoodlums who terrorize an insecure gay man, played by Robert Fields, on the subway.

IRENE ★★★

(1926) Director: Alfred E. Green

George K. Arthur plays Madame Lucy, a bitchy dressmaker and the queen bee of the fashion world.

IRRECONCILABLE DIFFERENCES ★★
(1984) Director: Charles Shyer
Stuart Pankin plays Shelley Long's effeminate gay personal secretary. A very brief role played for comic relief.

IT'S LOVE I'M AFTER ★★★
(1937) Director: Archie Mayo
Eric Blore as Diggs, the quintessential sissy, who is in love with his straight boss, played by Leslie Howard.

JERKER ★★★
(1991) Director: Hugh Harrison
Erotic telephone sex between two men eventually turns into a relationship.

JOY OF SEX, THE ★
(1984) Director: Martha Coolidge
Teenage T&A exploitation rip-off comedy. A girl drives her former boyfriend into the arms of a man in this insulting, one-gay-joke film.

Franklin Pangborn *(It's Love I'm After),* who played the quintessential sissy in countless films, is pictured here in a frilly nightgown in *The Crazy Nut.*

George Sanders plays the Warlock, a female impersonator in *The Kremlin Letter* (1969).

JUST IMAGINE ★★
(1930) Director: David Butler
An early science-fiction film set in the 1980s on Mars. Visiting Earthlings call the male inhabitants "queens."

JUSTINE ★★★
(1969) Director: George Cukor
Cliff Gorman plays the vicious queen who meets with an unfashionable death.

KREMLIN LETTER, THE ★★
(1970) Director: John Huston

George Sanders plays an old queen who doubles as a spy. His counterpart is a black lesbian spy.

L-SHAPED ROOM, THE ★★
(1962) Director: Bryan Forbes
Brock Peters plays Johnny, a frustrated gay man in love with a straight man, played by Tom Bell.

LA CAGE AUX FOLLES II ★★
(1981) Director: Edouard Molinaro
Ugo Tognazzi and Michel Serrault are reunited in this sequel that doesn't live up to its predecessor.

LA CAGE AUX FOLLES III: THE WEDDING ★

(1986) Director: Georges Lautner

Ugo Tognazzi and Michel Serrault are once again reunited in this sequel proving that sometimes you can get too much of a good thing.

LA DOLCE VITA ★★★★

(1960) Director: Federico Fellini

A transvestite predicts a homosexual world in the future.

LA TRUITE ★★★

(The Trout)

(1982) Director: Joseph Losey

Isabelle Huppert is a scheming woman who wants all she can get out of life. Her gay husband helps her get it. In French with English subtitles.

LAST MARRIED COUPLE IN AMERICA, THE ★★

(1980) Director: Gilbert Cates

Everyone gets divorced in this sexual farce, including the gay couple, Donald and Reggie, played by Stewart Moss and Colby Chester.

LAST OF ENGLAND, THE ★★★

(1988) Director: Derek Jarman

Using homoerotic images and artful vignettes, Jarman creates a personal vision of man's demise.

LAST OF SHEILA, THE ★★

(1973) Director: Herbert Ross

Richard Benjamin plays the homosexual with a secret. Written by Anthony Perkins and Stephen Sondheim.

LAUGHING POLICEMAN, THE ★★

(1973) Director: Thomas Rickman

Bruce Dern plays a homophobic cop stationed in San Francisco's gay district.

LEAVING NORMAL ★★★

(1992) Director: Edward Zwick

Christine Lahti and Meg Tilly joke about the possibility of a boy growing up to be gay because of the way his mother has decorated his room. The funniest scene in the film.

LEFT HANDED GUN, THE ★★★

(1958) Director: Arthur Penn

Many critics claimed that Paul Newman's Billy the Kid was a bit light in the saddle. Also stars Hurd Hatfield. Screenplay by Gore Vidal.

LESSONS AT THE END OF SPRING ★★★

(1989) Director: Oleg Kavun

A gritty, realistic tale of a 13-year-old boy's loss of innocence while held captive in a depraved Russian prison.

LION IN WINTER, THE ★★★

(1968) Director: Anthony Harvey

"Richard the Lion-Hearted" has a thing for the king of France.

LIQUID SKY ★

(1983) Director: Slava Tsukerman

Anne Carlisle plays the dual roles of the androgynous Jimmy, "The most beautiful boy in the world," and Margaret, the sadomasochistic punk who "kills with her cunt."

LITTLE BIG MAN ★★★

(1970) Director: Arthur Penn

Robert Littlestar plays Littlehorse, a gay American Indian. The film stars Dustin Hoffman.

LONELY KILLERS, THE ★★
(1972) Director: Boris Szulzinger
Dominique Rollin and Roland Maden are vicious gay killers.

LOOKING FOR LANGSTON ★★★
(1988) Director: Isaac Julien
Director Julien goes in search of the real black poet Langston Hughes in this short, stylized film.

LOT IN SODOM ★★
(1933) Directors: James Watson and Melville Webber
An avant-garde film featuring a roving band of homosexual Sodomites.

LOVE BITES ★★
(1988) Director: Marvin Jones
Kevin Glover and Christopher Ladd star in this comic variation on the Dracula love-story theme.

LOVE MEETINGS ★★
(1964) Director: Pier Paolo Pasolini
A rarely seen documentary focusing on young Italian men and their attitudes toward sex and love.

LOVE POTION #9 ★★★
(1992) Director: Dale Launer
A shy young man goes to a gypsy (Anne Bancroft) for a love potion. She fears that he may be a homosexual after looking at his palm's love line.

LOVED ONE, THE ★★
(1965) Director: Tony Richardson
Rod Steiger plays mortuary cosmetologist Mr. Joyboy. A mama's boy, his character is a flamboyant closet case that will make you squirm.

LUDWIG ★★
(1972) Director: Luchino Visconti
Helmut Berger plays gay King Ludwig, who sleeps with the stable boy in this film biography.

LUST IN THE DUST ★★
(1985) Director: Paul Bartel.
The late female impersonator, Divine, playing Rosie Valdez, bares his considerable buttocks not once, but twice, in this sophomoric spoof of the spaghetti western.

MALA NOCHE★★★
(1986) Director: Gus Van Sant
The director's first feature involves a grocery store owner (Tim Streeter) who makes the mistake of falling in love with a young boy.

MALCOLM X ★★★
(1992) Director: Spike Lee
Malcolm is sent to jail for robbing a wealthy gay man of his jewelry and other possessions.

MAN LIKE EVA, A ★★
(1985) Director: Radu Gabrea
Eva Mattes plays the late filmmaker Rainer Werner Fassbinder.

MANDINGO ★★
(1975) Director: Richard Fleischer
Lily-white masters are sexually attracted to their black slaves.

MANNEQUIN ★★★
(1987) Director: Michael Gottlieb
Meshach Taylor steals the film as Hollywood Montrose, a screaming (literally) queen and window dresser who drives a pink Cadillac with license plates reading "Bad Girl."

MEATBALLS II ★
(1984) Director: Ken Weiderhorn
The only bright spot in this film is Felix Foxglove, the limp-wristed, lisping, military camp lieutenant, played with restraint by John Laroquette.

MEN IN LOVE ★★★
(1990) Director: Marc Huestis
An independent feature about a man embarking on a journey that helps him come to terms with the the AIDS death of his lover.

MIKE'S MURDER ★
(1984) Director: James Bridges
Mark Keyloun plays Mike, a street hustler and bisexual, who, before being murdered, lives for some time with a gay black sugardaddy, played by Paul Winfield.

MISS FATTY IN CONEY ISLAND ★★★
(1917) Director: Fatty Arbuckle
Fatty Arbuckle is wooed by Al St. John, an unsuspecting suitor.

MISS FATTY'S SEASIDE LOVERS ★★★
(1915) Director: Fatty Arbuckle
Arbuckle plays a little rich girl on a family outing to the beach.

MISS O'GYNIE ET LES HOMMES-FLEURS ★★★
(1974) Director: Sammy Pavel
The relationship between two gay men is disrupted by a woman.

MO' MONEY ★★
(1992) Director: Peter Macdonald
Damon Wayans masquerades as a flamboyant gay customer in a jewelry store as part of a credit-card scam during a shopping spree.

MONDO TRASHO ★★
(1970) Director: John Waters
The director's first feature film introducing the divinely sexy, camp-female impersonator, Divine.

MORNING AFTER, THE ★★★
(1986) Director: Sidney Lumet
Jane Fonda's flaming gay friends are used as comic relief in this murder mystery.

MULTIPLE MANIACS ★
(1971) Director: John Waters
A black-and-white remake of sorts of the horror film *Two Thousand Maniacs*. Divine helps trash Christianity and other well-established institutions.

MYRA BRECKINRIDGE ★
(1970) Director: Michael Sarne
Based on Gore Vidal's best-selling novel, Raquel Welch plays Myra, a transexual who rapes Rusty (Roger Herren), an all-American boy and turns him gay!

NIGHT SHIFT ★★
(1982) Director: Ron Howard
Henry Winkler tells Michael Keaton that he has sunk as low as he can go, until he spots a homosexual jail mate and realizes he could be worse off.

NIGHTHAWKS ★★★
(1978) Directors: Ron Peck and Paul Hallam
Ken Robertson plays Jim, a gay school teacher who cruises the bars and is unable to have a lasting relationship.

NORMAN IS THAT YOU? ★★★
(1976) Director: George Schlatter
Dennis Dugan and Michael Warren play an interracial gay couple in this sophomoric comedy.

ODE TO BILLY JOE ★★★
(1976) Director: Max Baer
Robby Benson plays Billy Joe McAllister, a repressed young man who kills himself after having an affair with a man.

ONE FLEW OVER THE CUCKOO'S NEST ★★★★
(1975) Director: Milos Forman
Two of the mental patients are gay. The film won the *Best Picture* Oscar.

ONLY WHEN I LAUGH ★★★
(1981) Director: Glenn Jordan
James Coco plays Jimmy Perino, Marsha Mason's gay best friend, who says, "Next to sex, dishing with the girls is the best thing I know."

ONLY YESTERDAY ★★★
(1933) Director: John Stahl
The quintessential sissy, Franklin Pangborn plays a stereotypical flamboyant interior decorator with an equally prissy friend, played by Barry Norton.

P.J. ★★
(1968) Director: John Guillermins
A private eye, played by George Peppard, takes on Sheldon Kwell (Severn Darden), a murderous queen, and his friends at the Gay Caballero bar.

PASSED AWAY ★★★
(1992) Director: Charlie Peters
Tim Curry plays a ballet dancer, while William Petersen plays a homophobic father who is afraid that his son is gay just because he wears an earring.

PAWNBROKER, THE ★★★★
(1965) Director: Sidney Lumet
Set in the Harlem ghetto, Brock Peters plays a gay pimp.

PEPI, LUCI, BOM AND THE OTHER GIRLS ★★
(1980) Director: Pedro Almodovar
This is the director's first feature film. It contains his trademark bizarre characters, homoerotic sexuality and violence.

PETULIA ★★★
(1968) Director: Richard Lester
Richard Chamberlain plays a confused married man and closet case.

PICTURE OF DORIAN GRAY, THE ★★★★
(1945) Director: Albert Lewin
Hurd Hatfield and George Sanders star in Oscar Wilde's classic tale of narcissism.

PINK FLAMINGOS ★★★
(1972) Director: John Waters
In this ultimate cult midnight movie, the director and the star, Divine, became infamous as "The filthiest people alive."

POLYESTER ★★★
(1981) Director: John Waters
Francine Fishpay (Divine) and Todd Tomorrow (Tab Hunter) embark on a tragic—and smelly—love affair.

PORTRAIT OF JASON ★★
(1967) Director: Shirley Clarke

Jason Holiday is a young, black gay hustler who shares his story in this straightforward documentary.

POSITIVE ★★★
(1990) Directors: Rosa von Praunheim and Phil Zwickler
Part two of an AIDS documentary trilogy focusing on New York City's gay community.

PRIVATE SCHOOL ★
(1983) Director: Noel Black
Matthew Modine, Jonathan Prince and Michael Zorek dress in drag to slip into an all-girls' dormitory.

QUEEN, THE ★★★
(1968) Director: Frank Simon.
A documentary backstage look at the 1967 Miss All-American Camp Beauty Pageant and drag show.

RADIO DAYS ★★★
(1987) Director: Woody Allen
Dianne Wiest comforts her date, Robert Joy, when a sentimental song reminds him of his male lover who has departed.

ROAD WARRIOR, THE ★★★
(1981) Director: George Miller
The film's bad guys are a roving gang of musclebound leather boys on motorcycles called the Humunguns. When the blond male lover of one of the men is killed by Mel Gibson, the war is on.

ROBBY ★★
(1968) Director: Ralph C. Bluemke
A homoerotic tale of a young white boy who becomes a castaway on an island. The only other inhabitant is a young black boy whom he befriends.

ROMAN SPRING OF MRS. STONE, THE ★★
(1961) Director: Jose Quintero
Lotte Lenya plays a pimp who procures wealthy clients, both men and women, for her stable of beautiful young men. Warren Beatty plays Paolo, a hustler with a very bad Italian accent.

ROMANTIC ENGLISH WOMAN, THE ★★★
(1975) Director: Joseph Losey
Michael Caine and Glenda Jackson are novelists who invite Helmut Berger to share their bed—for inspiration.

RUN OF THE HOUSE ★★
(1992) Director: James M. Felter
When a family man and cab driver (Harry A. Winter) falls for a drag queen (Craig Alan Edwards), his simple life gets complicated.

RUSTLER'S RHAPSODY ★
(1985) Director: Hugh Wilson
Andy Griffith plays a gay gunslinger in this homophobic spoof of the Old West.

S.O.B. ★★
(1981) Director: Blake Edwards
Blake Edwards asks the provocative question, "Is Batman a transvestite?" Robert Vaughn dons sexy red female lingerie.

SACRED PASSION ★★
(1989) Director: Emerald D.H. Starr
Transcendental tantric sex on a tropical island is the focus of this film narrated by poet Gavin Geoffrey Dillard.

An ad for the 1975 film *Saturday Night At The Baths,* which is rarely seen today.

SALOME ★★★
(1922) Director: Alla Nazimova
An outrageous tribute to Oscar Wild featuring two homosexual Syrian soldiers.

SAND AND BLOOD ★★
(1987) Director: Jeanne LaBrune
An older doctor befriends a young matador and each helps the other confront hidden secrets in this homoerotic and violent tale.

SATURDAY NIGHT AT THE BATHS ★★
(1975) Director: David Buckley
The promotional tag line read, "She might forgive him if he were with another woman. Could she go one step further?"

SATURDAY NIGHT FEVER ★★★★
(1977) Director: John Badham
Teenage homophobes tease a gay young man on the street. John Travolta is the only boy secure enough not to go along.

SEPARATE PEACE, A ★★★
(1972) Director: Larry Peerce
A homoerotic coming-of-age tale about two 16-year-old prep-school students based on the John Knowles classic.

SEX IN BONDAGE ★★
(Geschlecht In Fesseln)
(1928) Director: William Dieterle
Blackmail, suicide and homosexuality in prison are presented. This film set the stage for many similar films to follow.

SHAMPOO ★★★
(1975) Director: Hal Ashby
Jack Warden is a homophobe who believes that all hairdressers are gay, including the straight, womanizing stud played by Warren Beatty.

SHE DONE HIM WRONG ★★★
(1933) Director: Lowell Sherman
Two male prisoners are referred to as the "Cherry Sisters" by Mae West in this campy classic.

SIGN OF THE CROSS, THE ★★★
(1932) Director: Cecil B. DeMille
Charles Laughton and his half-naked slave boy drove the censors crazy.

SILENCE=DEATH ★★★
(1990) Directors: Rosa von Praunheim and Phil Zwickler
A documentary look at the New York City artistic community's response to and reflections on the AIDS crisis.

SILENT PIONEERS ★★★★
(1985) Director: Lucy Winer
Documentary focusing on gay seniors and their recollections of the early days before gay liberation.

SLAP SHOT ★★
(1977) Director: George Roy Hill
Paul Newman and Michael Ontkean star in this sexist, homophobic film about insecure hockey players who will stop at nothing to prove they are "real men".

SLAVES OF NEW YORK ★★
(1989) Director: James Ivory
Three black queens lipsync to the Supremes on the street and no one notices. Other odd but entertaining gay characters as well.

SOILERS, THE ★★★

(1923)
A swishy gay cowboy blows Stan Laurel a kiss, exclaiming, "My hero," after Stan wins a bar fight in this comic sendup of the western.

SPIES LIKE US ★★

(1985) Director: John Landis
Everyone pairs off for sex in this Chevy Chase, Dan Aykroyd comedy—including the two gay characters.

SPIKE OF BENSONHURST ★★

(1988) Director: Paul Morrissey
"I don't have to take no orders from no dyke and her slut girlfriend," says young boxer and bigot Sasha Mitchell to his mother and her lover.

SPIT-BALL SADIE ★★★

(1915) Director: Harold Lloyd
Harold Lloyd dresses in drag to play ball on an all-woman baseball team.

ST. ELMO'S FIRE ★★

(1985) Director: Joel Schumacher
Matthew Laurence plays the stereotypical interior decorator and Demi Moore's neighbor.

STAR! ★★★

(1968) Director: Robert Wise
Daniel Massey plays Noel Coward, the legendary Gertrude Lawrence's (Julie Andrews) lifelong friend, in this lengthy musical biography.

STAY TUNED ★★

(1992) Director: Peter Hyams
John Ritter dresses in drag and two French peasants ask, "How come he dresses like a woman?" "I do that sometimes," answers the other.

STEPHEN KING'S SLEEPWALKERS ★★

(1992) Director: Mick Garris
When a slimy gay teacher tries to blackmail an attractive new student (Brian Krause) into having sex, it turns out to be his last trick.

STORYVILLE ★★

(1992) Director: Mark Frost
Bernard Zette plays Tom Plunkett, a tastefully dressed transvestite who saves James Spader's reputation and career.

TAMARIND SEED, THE ★★★

(1974) Director: Blake Edwards
Dan O'Herlihy plays Fergus Stephenson, a double agent with a double life. He's a married man and closeted homosexual.

TELL ME THAT YOU LOVE ME, JUNIE MOON ★★

(1970) Director: Otto Preminger
Robert Moore plays Warren, a crippled gay stereotype raised by a flaming queen played by Leonard Frey.

TENDERNESS OF THE WOLVES ★★

(1973) Director: Ulli Lommel
The film is based on a true story about the infamous Fritz Haarman, a child molester who murdered young boys.

THAT CERTAIN SUMMER ★★★★

(1973) Director: Lamont Johnson
A groundbreaking made-for-television movie featuring a love affair between Hal Holbrook and Martin Sheen.

THEATRE OF BLOOD ★★★

(1973) Director: Douglas Hickox

Vincent Price plays a Shakespearian actor who makes homosexual theater critic Robert Morley eat his words.

THIRD SEX, THE ★★

(1959) Director: Frank Winterstein
Another homosexual young man is cured by the love of a good woman.

TO FORGET VENICE ★★

(1979) Director: Franco Brusati
Two gay men and two lesbians recall their past and the moment they realized they were gay.

TONY ROME ★★

(1967) Director: Gordon Douglas
Private eye Frank Sinatra crosses paths with a gay junkie (Lloyd Bochner) in the gay underground.

TOO OUTRAGEOUS! ★★★

(1987) Director: Richard Benner
The sequel to *Outrageous*, again starring the talented female impersonator, Craig Russell. The film manages to capture much of the energy of the original.

TRIPLE ECHO ★★

(1972) Director: Michael Apted
Brian Deacon is a soldier who dresses in drag to be close to Glenda Jackson, the woman he has fallen for. When Oliver Reed, in turn, falls for the soldier, sparks fly.

UN CHANT D'AMOUR ★★

(1947) Director: Gene Genet
Homoerotic love within the confines of a sado-masochistic hell of prison life is brought to life in this early avant-garde film.

VALLEY OF THE DOLLS ★★★

(1967) Director: Mark Robson
Alex Davion plays Ted Casablanca, an effeminate designer—what else?

VIEW FROM A BRIDGE ★★★

(1962) Director: Sidney Lumet
In order to win over Jean Sorel's girlfriend, Raf Vallone accuses the young man of being a homosexual.

VIRUS KNOWS NO MORALS, A ★★

(1985) Director: Rosa von Praunheim
An irreverent and provocative black comedy about the politics of AIDS.

VISION QUEST ★★★

(1985) Director: Harold Becker
"He grabbed my wad," cries hotel waiter Matthew Modine to a friend after he is accosted in the hotel room of a gay guest.

WARRIOR'S HUSBAND, THE ★★★

(1933) Director: Walter Lang
Ernest Truex plays Sapiens, the effeminate pansy and brunt of a number of gay jokes.

WHERE THE HOT WIND BLOWS ★★

(1958) Director: Jules Dassin
Marcello Mastroianni plays a less-than-virile gay character in this Italian melodrama about manhood.

WHOEVER SAYS THE TRUTH SHALL DIE ★★★

(1985) Director: Philo Bregstein
This Italian documentary explores the life—and violent death in 1975—of gay filmmaker Pier Paolo Pasolini.

Charlie Chaplin was one of the first actors to sustain an entire film in full female drag—sans mustache—in the 1915 film *A Woman*.

WOMAN, A ★★★
(1915) Director: Charlie Chaplin
Chaplin plays a very convincing society woman without the trademark mustache.

WORST BOY IN THE WORLD, THE ★★
(1989) Director: Enrique Gomez
Raul Buefil plays Pepe, a macho gang leader by day and a coy, sexy transvestite by night.

YANKEE DOODLE IN BERLIN ★★★
(1919) Director: Richard Jones
Real-life female impersonator Bothwell Browne plays aviator and leading lady, Bob White.

Z ★★
(1969) Director: Constantine Costa-Gavras
Another gay fascist who is also a killer.

ZENTROPA ★★
(1992) Director: Lars Von Trier
Once he has discovered that his sister is a Nazi, Udo Kier is murdered and becomes just "one less faggot" who needs to be killed in the concentration camps.

COMPANION FILMS INDEX

The following films are grouped by themes. It should come as no surprise that the two largest groups are "Drag Queens" and "Murderers and Victims."

AIDS
As Is
Buddies
Chain Of Desire
Citizen Cohn
Common Threads: Stories From The Quilt
Early Frost, An
Living End, The
Longtime Companion
Men In Love
Parting Glances
Positive
Silence=Death
Silverlake Life: The View From Here
Together Alone
Via Appia
Virus Knows No Morals, A
Voices From The Front

BIOGRAPHIES
Alexandria ... Why?
Bigger Splash, A
Burroughs
Caligula
Caravaggio
Citizen Cohn

Daddy And The Muscle Academy
Edward II
Hours And Times, The
JFK
Looking For Langston
Man Like Eva, A
Mishima: A Life In Four Chapters
Music Lovers, The
Nijinsky
Paul Cadmus: Enfant Terrible At 80
Prick Up Your Ears
Sebastiane
Silverlake Life: The View From Here
Times Of Harvey Milk, The
Whoever Says The Truth Shall Die

BISEXUALS
Cabaret
California Suite
Different Story, A
Edward II
Entertaining Mr. Sloane
Ernesto
Everlasting Secret Family, The
Fourth Man, The
Menage

Mike's Murder
Miss O'Gynie Et Les Hommes-Fleurs
Romantic Englishwoman, The
Scenes From The Class Struggle In Beverly Hills
Something For Everyone
Sunday Bloody Sunday
We Think The World Of You
Women In Love

BLACKMAIL

Advise And Consent
Best Man, The
El Diputado
Victim
View From A Bridge

BOYS SCHOOLS

Another Country
Best Way, The
Devil's Playground, The
If...
Maurice
Separate Peace, A
This Special Friendship
You Are Not Alone

CLOSET CASES

Advise And Consent
Ben-Hur
Best Way, The
Blue Velvet
Boys In The Band, The
Boys Next Door, The
Citizen Cohn
Deathtrap
Der Sprinter
Detective, The
Dorian Gray

Dresser, The
Everlasting Secret Family, The
Flesh And The Devil
Gilda
Hidden Pleasures
Last Of Shiela, The
Leather Boys, The
Looking For Mr. Goodbar
Loved One, The
Maurice
Midnight Cowboy
Miller's Crossing
Music Lovers, The
Naked Civil Servant, The
Ode To Billy Joe
Petulia
Reflections In A Golden Eye
Rope
Scarecrow
Sergeant, The
Servant, The
Strange One, The
Strangers On A Train
Suddenly, Last Summer
Swoon
Tamarind Seed, The
We Were One Man
Women In Love

COMING OUT

Andy Warhol's Frankenstein
Body Of Evidence
Consenting Adult
El Diputado
Ernesto
Friends Forever
Fun Down There
Genesis Children, The

I Was A Male War Bride
Kremlin Letter, The
La Cage Aux Folles
La Cage Aux Folles II
La Cage Aux Folles III: The Wedding
La Dolce Vita
Ladybugs
Liquid Sky
Lust In The Dust
Menage
Miss Fatty In Coney Island
Miss Fatty's Seaside Lovers
Naked Civil Servant, The
National Lampoon's Loaded Weapon 1
Outrageous!
Paris Is Burning
Pink Flamingos
Pixote
Police Academy
Polyester
Private Resort
Private School
Privates On Parade
Producers, The
Psycho
Queen, The
Resident Alien
Ritz, The
Rocky Horror Picture Show, The
Rose, The
Run Of The House, The
S.O.B.
Salome's Last Dance
Slaves Of New York
Some Like It Hot
Some Of My Best Friends Are …
Spit-Ball Sadie
Stay Tuned

Storyville
Too Outrageous!
Tootsie
Torch Song Trilogy
Under Siege
Victor/Victoria
Woman, A
World According To Garp, The
Worst Boy In Town, The
Yankee Doodle In Berlin

FASCISTS AND NAZIS

Cabaret
Conformist, The
Damned, The
El Diputado
Europa, Europa
Falling Down
In A Glass Cage
Salo: 120 Day Of Sodom
Special Day, A
To Be Or Not To Be
Z
Zentropa

HEROES
(AND HAPPY HOMOSEXUALS)

Face To Face
Flesh Gordon
Revenge Of The Nerds
Single White Female
Zorro, The Gay Blade

HOMOPHOBIA

Damned In The USA
Falling Down
Glengarry Glen Ross
I Want What I Want

MILITARY MEN

Biloxi Blues
Privates On Parade
Reflections In A Golden Eye
Salome
Sergeant, The
Strange One, The
Streamers

MURDERERS (AND VICTIMS)

American Gigolo
Anderson Tapes, The
Apartment Zero
Blacula
Bloody Mama
Boston Strangler, The
Boys Next Door, The
Caprice
Choirboys, The
Compulsion
Consequence, The
Cruising
Day Of The Jackal, The
Death On The Beach
Deathtrap
Detective, The
Diamonds Are Forever
Dressed To Kill
El Diputado
Entertaining Mr. Sloane
Fan, The
Fourth Man, The
JFK
Justine
L'Elegant Criminal
L'Homme Blesse
Law Of Desire
Living End, The

Looking For Mr. Goodbar
Miller's Crossing
Prick Up Your Ears
Psycho
Querelle
Rope
Silence Of The Lambs, The
Stephen King's Sleepwalkers
Strangers On A Train
Streamers
Suddenly, Last Summer
Swoon
Victim
We Were One Man
What Have I Done To Deserve This?
Young Soul Rebels

NEIGHBORS, ROOMMATES AND BEST FRIENDS

Adam's Rib
Camille
Can't Stop The Music
Darling
Frankie & Johnnie
Only When I Laugh
Prince Of Tides, The
Protocol
Queens Logic
Single White Female
Taste Of Honey, A
"10"
This Boy's Life
When The Party's Over

ONLY THE LONELY

After Hours
Death In Venice
Empty Bed, An

Fame
Hotel New Hampshire, The
Jerker
L-Shaped Room
Midnight Cowboy
Next Stop, Greenwich Village
Queens Logic
Radio Days
Sebastiane
Special Day, A
Staircase

PRISONERS
(AND REFORM SCHOOL)

Anders Als Die Anderen
Forbidden Passion
Forever Mary
Fortune And Men's Eyes
Freedom Paradise
Improper Conduct
Kiss Of The Spider Woman
Lessons At The End Of Spring
Midnight Express
Night Shift
Pixote
Poison
Scarecrow
Sex In Bondage (Gerschlecht In Fesseln)
She Done Him Wrong
Short Eyes
Un Chant d'Amour
We Think The World Of You

RAPE

Christine Jorgensen Story, The
Conformist, The
Deliverance
Drum
Exodus

Fortune And Men's Eyes
Mandingo
Midnight Cowboy
Myra Breckenridge
Prince Of Tides, The
Scarecrow
Short Eyes
Spetters
Where's Poppa?

RELIGION

Canterbury Tales, The
Damned In The USA
Decameron, The
Devil's Playground, The
Mass Appeal
This Special Friendship

ROMANS

Caligula
Fellini Satyricon
Salome
Salome's Last Dance
Sebastiane
Sign Of The Cross, The
Spartacus

S&M

Coonskin
Corrupt
Cruising
Daddy And The Muscle Academy
In A Glass Cage
L'Homme Blesse
Noir Et Blanc
Querelle
Road Warrior, The
Salo: 120 Days Of Sodom
Servant, The

SISSIES
(AND OTHER STEREOTYPES)

Airplane
Anderson Tapes, The
Bedazzled
Beverly Hills Cop
Bird On A Wire
Blazing Saddles
Boom!
Boys In The Band, The
Brain Donors
Broadway Melody, The
Can't Stop The Music
Car Wash
Choirboys, The
Clinic, The
Cruising
Diamonds Are Forever
Eiger Sanction, The
Enter The Dragon
Funny Lady
Honky Tonk Freeway
Irene
Irreconcilable Differences
It's Love I'm After
JFK
Just Imagine
Little Big Man
Lot In Sodom
Magic Christian, The
Malcolm X
Meatballs II
Mo' Money
Morning After, The
Norman Is That You?
One Flew Over The Cuckoo's Nest
Only Yesterday
Producers, The

Revenge Of The Nerds
Ritz, The
Sleeper
Soilers, The
Spies Like Us
St. Elmo's Fire
Tea And Sympathy
Tell Me That You Love Me, Junie Moon
Too Much Sun
Valley Of The Dolls
Warrior's Husband, The
Zorro, The Gay Blade

UNHAPPY HOMOSEXUALS

Bolero
Bloodbrothers
Boys In The Band, The
Butley
Chorus Line
Dear Boys
Dresser, The
Drifting
Fox And His Friends
I'll Love You Forever...Tonight
Last Married Couple In America, The
Music Lovers, The
My Own Private Idaho
Next Stop, Greenwich Village
Some Of My Best Friends Are …
Taxi Zum Klo
Very Natural Thing, A
Women In Love

VAMPIRES

Blacula
Fearless Vampire Killers, The
Love Bites
Once Bitten

ALPHABETICAL FILM INDEX

RATING INDEX

GENRE INDEX

DOCUMENTARY

DRAMA

MAIL-ORDER VIDEO SOURCES

The following list of mail-order video sources sell and/or rent many of the hard-to-find films featured in this guidebook. This is not intended to be a recommendation or an endorsement of any of the companies listed, but is provided simply as a resource.

Beta Library
836224 Promenade Station
Richardson, TX 75083
214/233-4552
Fax 214/233-6329
Beta Library specializes in Beta-format videos. Mail-order sales only. Small line, some gay-related films.

Captain Bijou
PO Box 87,
Toney, AL 35773
205/852-0198
Specializes in B-movies, foreign, cult, obscure and gay-related. Mail-order sales only.

Critics' Choice Video
PO Box 549,
Elk Grove Village,
 IL 60009-0549
800/367-7765
Fax 708/437-7298
Carries a small selection of gay-related films.

Discount Video Tapes, Inc.
PO Box 7122
Burbank, CA 91510
818/843-3366
Toll-free fax 800/253-9612
Specializes in rare and unusual, foreign, documentary and silent films with a small selection of gay-related films. Mail-order sales and rentals.

Eddie Brandt's Saturday Matinee
6310 Colfax Avenue
N. Hollywood, CA 91606
818/506-4242 or
818/506-7722
Specializes in searching for rare videos. Mail-order sales only.

Evergreen Video Society
228 W. Houston Street
New York, NY 10014
212/691-7362
Specializes in foreign films. Mail-order sales and rentals.

Facets Video
1517 W. Fullerton Avenue
Chicago, IL 60614
800/331-6197
312/281-9075
Fax 312/929-5437
Carries a large selection of hard-to-find gay-related videos for rent by mail and for sale.

Home Film Festival
PO Box 2032
Scranton, PA 18501
800/258-3456
Fax 717/344-3810
Carries a moderate selection of gay-related videos. Many are of the very hard-to-find variety. Sales and rentals by mail.

Insider Video Club
PO Box 93399
Hollywood, CA 90093
800/634-2242, 213/661-8330
Specializes in gay-related videos.

Loonic Video
2022 Taraval Street, #6427
San Francisco, CA 94116
415/526-5681
Specializing in the obscure, the campy and the silents. Mail-order sales only.

Marshall Discount Video Service
PO Box 328
Trenton, MI 48183
313/671-5483
Specializes in independent and foreign films, with over 50,000 titles. Mail-order sales only.

Movies Unlimited
6736 Castor Avenue
Philadelphia, PA 19149
800/523-0823 or
215/722-8398
Fax 215/725-3683
Carries over 25,000 videos, huge catalog, large selection of gay-related films. Short on the more obscure and hard-to-find gay videos. Sales only.

Phoenix Distributors
6253 Hollywood Blvd., #818
Hollywood, CA 90028
800/356-4386, 213/469-0553
Fax 213/469-7041
Carries a small line of non-hardcore gay-related films. Sales only.

Video By Mail
PO Box 1515
Whitney, TX 76692-1515
800/245-4996
Fax 817/694-4865
An excellent collection of gay-related films. Specializes in foreign, cult and independent videos. Mail-order sales and rentals.

Video Dimensions
530 W. 23rd Street
New York, NY 10011
212/929-6135
Specializes in experimental, avant-garde, schlock and exploitation tapes. Mail-order sales only.

Video Library
7157 Germantown Avenue
Philadelphia, PA 19119
800/669-7157 or
215/248-1514
Specializing in out-of-print videos and cult movies. Offers a search service. Good selection of gay-related films. Mail-order sales and rentals.

Video Yesteryear
Box C
Sandy Hook, CT 06482
800/243-0987 or
203/426-2574
Fax 203/797-0819
Carries a large collection of foreign and silent films. Sales only.

Water Bearer Films
205 West End Avenue
Suite 24H
New York, NY 10023
800/551-8304
Specializes in gay-related videos.

FILM FESTIVALS

The following is a list of the three major gay film festivals in the U.S. The mainstream film festivals are also open to the public and often premiere many of the best gay films. Gay film festivals are listed in order of opening dates.

Los Angeles International Gay & Lesbian Film & Video Festival

Gay & Lesbian Media Coalition
8228 Sunset Blvd., Suite 308
West Hollywood, CA 90046
Opens first week in July. Also sponsors a smaller, winter festival held in mid-March.

New York Lesbian and Gay Film Festival

The New Festival, Inc.
80 Eighth Avenue
New York, NY 10011
Opens the first week in June.

San Francisco International Lesbian & Gay Film Festival

Frameline
PO Box 14792
San Francisco, CA 94114
Opens mid-June.

Other national and international festivals of interest:

Palm Springs Film Festival

401 S. Pavilion Way
Box 1786
Palm Springs, CA 92263
Opens in January.

Sundance Film Festival

c/o Sundance Institute
Box 16450
Salt Lake City, Utah 84116
Opens in late January.

Berlin Film Festival

Budapester Str. 50, D-1000
West Berlin 30,
West Germany
Opens in early February.

USA Film Festival

2917 Swiss Avenue
Dallas, TX 75204
Opens in April.

San Francisco Film Festival

San Francisco Film Society
1650 Fillmore St.

San Francisco, CA 94115
Opens early May.

Seattle International Film Festival

c/o Egyptian Theatre
801 E. Pine Street
Seattle, WA 98122
Opens in May.

Los Angeles International Film Festival

American Film Institute
2021 North Western Avenue
Los Angeles, CA 90027
Opens in June.

Melbourne Film Festival

G.P.O. Box 2760 Ee
Melbourne,
Victoria 3001, Australia
Opens in mid-June.

Montreal Film Festival

1455 Rue de Maisonneuve
Ouest,
Montreal, Quebec H3G 1M8,

Canada
Opens in late August.

Telluride Film Festival
c/o National Film Preserve
53 S. Main Street
Box B1156
Hanover, NH 03755
Opens in late August.

Toronto Film Festival
69 Yorkville, Suite 205
Toronto, Ontario, M5R 1B8,
Canada

Opens in early September.

Venice Film Festival
C.A. Giustinian
San Marco, 30124
Venice, Italy
Opens in early September.

New York Film Festival
The Film Society of
Lincoln Center
70 Lincoln Center Plaza
New York, NY 10023-6595
Opens in mid-September.

**Denver International
Film Festival**
Denver International
Film Society
999 18th Street
Suite 1820
Denver, CO 80202
Opens in mid-October.

London Film Festival
National Film Theater
South Bank,
London SE1, England
Opens in November.

INDEX

ABOUT THE AUTHOR

S teve Stewart, author of *Positive Image: A Portrait of Gay America* (published by William Morrow in 1984) and coauthor of the *Film Annual* (published by Companion Publications), began writing about gay issues and about movies in general in the early '70s. It took nearly two decades before he was inspired to combine the two interests. The result is *Gay Hollywood*, the first comprehensive video guide of its kind.

While writing *Positive Image*, he had the privilege of meeting and getting to know Vito Russo, Harvey Fierstein, Quentin Crisp, Christopher Isherwood, Allan Carr and others involved in producing the films reviewed in this volume. Each person was an inspiration.

A native of Southern California, Stewart lived and worked in Hollywood for most of the '70s and '80s. He now resides in and writes from Orange County, California.